THOMAS À KEMPIS

HIS AGE AND BOOK

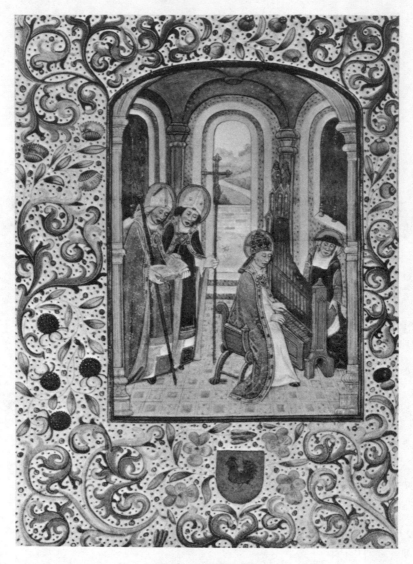

MUSICA ECCLESIASTICA

"CAUSE THE MUSICIANS PLAY ME THAT SAD NOTE
I NAM'D MY KNELL, WHILST I SIT MEDITATING
ON THAT CELESTIAL HARMONY I GO TO"

(*King Henry VIII, Act iv, Sc. ii*)

ILLUMINATED FRONTISPIECE OF THE TREATISE CALLED "MUSICA ECCLESIASTICA" FROM THE
ROYAL MANUSCRIPT 7 B VIII IN THE BRITISH MUSEUM.   THIS MS. CONSISTS OF THE FIRST THREE
BOOKS OF THE TREATISE "DE IMITATIONE CHRISTI," AND BELONGS TO THE THIRD QUARTER
OF THE FIFTEENTH CENTURY.

THOMAS À KEMPIS

HIS AGE AND BOOK

BY

J. E. G. DE MONTMORENCY, B.A., LL.B.

WITH TWENTY-TWO ILLUSTRATIONS

KENNIKAT PRESS
Port Washington, N. Y./London

THOMAS A KEMPIS

First published in 1906
Reissued in 1970 by Kennikat Press
Library of Congress Catalog Card No: 73-103183
SBN 8046-0820-2

Manufactured by Taylor Publishing Company   Dallas, Texas

TO

THE MEMORY OF

MY FATHER

JAMES LODGE DE MONTMORENCY

TABLE OF CONTENTS

LIST OF ILLUSTRATIONS

(These illustrations are all reproductions from fifteenth century manuscripts or printed books.)

INTRODUCTION

DESPITE the vast literature that has gathered round the treatise *de Imitatione Christi*, no apology should be needed for the appearance at the present time of a volume dealing with that work, and with the age in which it was written. The perpetual fascination of the former theme is undeniable, while the wave of mysticism that is now moving across Europe, England, and America, makes the study of the not dissimilar phenomenon that troubled the minds and consciences of men in the fourteenth and fifteenth centuries both monitory and profitable. We hear much to-day concerning the weakening of faith in God, Freedom, and Immortality, and there can be no doubt that the outlook of the western world upon the fundamental dogmas of religion has greatly changed in the last thirty years. The outlook tends to become an inlook, and the movement from one position of spiritual equilibrium to another necessarily involves the dislocation that accompanies any radical change. It is with a sense of despair and a certainty of loss, that many who have grown up in the older school see this tendency in religious thought. To some it seems almost irreligious to

b

seek, with the mystic, the Kingdom of Heaven in
the soul rather than in the firmament and to find
the voice of God not in the earthquake or the fiery
universe, but in the whispers of conscience. Yet
there is nothing surprising in such a tendency.
The mediæval mystics deliberately adopted it in
answer to the spiritual discontents and social
miseries, to the faithlessness and unhappiness, of
their day. The *Imitation of Christ* was, and is,
the apology for this position of introspection—an
apology that has appealed to men with a force
otherwise unknown in profane literature.

An attempt has been made in the following pages
first of all to place before the reader the group of
European movements and events that was responsible for the school of spiritual thought of which
Thomas à Kempis is the most notable representative; secondly, to trace in outline the various
forces—religious, philosophical, and literary—that
came to a focus in à Kempis, and so brought to
life the treatise *de Imitatione Christi*; lastly, to
analyse that treatise in considerable detail so as to
exhibit the body of doctrine that its author drew
from the material that he had gathered together—
a body of doctrine that repels completely the charges
brought against the mysticism of Haemmerlein by
Dean Milman and Thackeray. These writers appear entirely to have missed the author's point

of view, and to have confounded the Outer with the Inner life, despite the very clear and sensible distinction that à Kempis makes between these two broad aspects of man's complex personality.

It has been a laborious task to describe even briefly the historical environment, the structure and the content of the *Imitation*. Many volumes would be required for anything like an exhaustive discussion of the Age and Book of Thomas à Kempis. It seems, however, not possible to explain the extraordinary literary history of the *Imitation*, or to estimate its influence in the future, without some such discussion, though it is impracticable in any limited space to clear up the innumerable questions that arise as soon as a student attempts to deal with the complex age in which à Kempis lived, with the literary texture of his deathless work, and the mystical doctrines with which that work abounds.

It has been assumed, in writing these words, that Thomas Haemmerlein of Kempen is the author of the treatise *de Imitatione Christi*. That is my definite opinion after a very careful consideration of this literary problem, and in the following pages there are set out some of the reasons that have enabled me to make up my mind on that ancient question. The doubt as to the authorship of the *Imitation* has probably aroused more acute controversy than any other problem in pure literature.

The bitterness of the controversialists has been in inverse proportion to the sweetness of the book. Nor has this intensity of feeling altogether passed away. This is more particularly the case with respect to what is known as the Gersen claim. I have never seen any evidence that, on examination, presented even a *prima facie* case for the authorship of a person named John Gersen, Abbot of Vercelli, who is supposed to have flourished in the first half of the thirteenth century. If a thirteenth century manuscript of the *Imitation* can be produced, the cases for John le Charlier de Gerson and Thomas à Kempis would disappear. But this fact would not enthrone the mysterious Abbot. The quotation from St Bonaventura in the fiftieth chapter of the third book would tell as heavily against Gersen as against St Bernard. This fact has to be met, and never has been met, by the Benedictine Order in their curious support of the Abbot discovered for them by Constantine Cajétan in the seventeenth century. But there is no thirteenth century manuscript of the *Imitation*. Manuscripts of this treatise abound throughout Europe, but not a single one that has been examined by competent authorities has been placed earlier than the early fifteenth century, and it must be remembered that the margin of error in dating a mediæval manuscript does not exceed forty years. The " Codex Aronensis " printed by the Benedictine Constantine Cajétan at Rome, in the year 1616, attributes the work to the Abbot John Gersen. Cajétan fruitlessly endeavoured to identify this name as an Abbot of Vercelli. There is no evidence that there was ever an Abbot of Vercelli bearing that name. The Aronensis manuscript is undoubtedly a fifteenth century document. The difficulties of establishing the Gersen authorship are indeed overwhelming. We have first to establish the fact that there was an Abbot of Vercelli bearing that name; then we have to show that the existing fifteenth century manuscripts are transcripts from a lost thirteenth century original; then we have to expunge from the manuscripts all later references, such as the quotation from Bonaventura; finally, having proved the existence of the Abbot of Vercelli and the thirteenth century origin of the work, we have the hopeless task of connecting the abbot and the work. This series of improbabilities destroys the Gersen theory. Gersen, or Gersem, or Gerseem can be nothing but variants of Gerson. The British Museum manuscripts are very strong evidence of this.

The claims of Gerson and Walter Hilton to the authorship are discussed at length in the following pages. The work was certainly attributed to each of them in the first half of the fifteenth century, and in the absence of Thomas à Kempis, the claims of either of them would be strong enough to secure the prize. Certainly the claim in Hilton's case is remarkable enough, for there is nothing in his prose style to exclude him from consideration. This cannot be said with respect to Gerson. I have certainly not cleared up finally the problem that I set out to solve—the explanation of the fact that the treatise, *Musica Ecclesiastica* (consisting of the first three books of the *Imitation*) was for centuries attributed to Walter Hilton, a canon of the same Order as that to which à Kempis belonged. The flaw in Hilton's case and, for the matter of that, in Gerson's case also, is that the student is compelled to lay undue stress on the value of the fact that Gerson's or Hilton's name is in quite early times attached to the work. There was neither copyright nor conscience in these matters during the Middle Ages, and the giving of an author's name is no guarantee at all of authorship. The exact problem that troubles us in the case of the *Imitation* occurs in the case of innumerable treatises of the fourteenth and fifteenth centuries. These are dead, and it does not much matter who wrote them, but we are necessarily concerned with the authorship of the one work that has survived.

Mr Samuel Kettlewell's writings on the *Authorship of the Imitation* and the *Brothers of Common Life* have, of course, been of great assistance to me, and it has been with much diffidence that I have ventured here and there to question his statements or extend his material. His confiding style, real learning, and admirable earnestness disarm all criticism, and I shall be gratified if this volume may be considered in some small measure to supplement his patient labours.

Especial attention may be drawn to one feature of this book. I have reprinted in the first appendix Gerson's little treatise *de Meditatione Cordis*. This work was as popular in the Middle Ages as the *Imitation* itself. It has never been printed as a single work, but probably appeared in print before the *Imitation*, as it was issued under Gerson's name with other tracts of his from Cologne by Ulrich Zel between 1467 and 1472. Manuscripts of the treatise are very rare. I doubt if there is one in England. It was apparently one of a series of tracts of the same type, such as Gerson's *de Simplificatione Cordis*, *de Perfectione Cordis*, and others. Internal evidence indicates that it was a late work, written probably after the Council of Constance, and proves beyond doubt that it was from Gerson's pen. The *editio princeps* differs very considerably from the series of editions between 1485 and 1526, and the series between 1570 and 1575, when it appeared as a supplement to successive editions of the *Imitation*. The text here presented is to some extent composite, the intention being to secure a text as free as possible from the errors and obscurities of early copyists and printers. The Cologne edition of 1467-72 has been in one or two places used to clear up difficulties, but the text is chiefly founded upon that of Milan (1488); another of 1492 without printed place of origin (possibly Ulm); that of Nuremberg (1494); and another of about 1496, issued either at Leipsic or Magdeburg (British Museum, I. A. 10,955). The work is, of course, of real interest as showing the fundamental difference between the style of Gerson and that of the author of the *Imitation*, but it also possesses much intrinsic value. It is from the pen of the last, and certainly not the least of the great Schoolmen ; it was written when the classical Renaissance was actually in sight ; it may be called the last literary work of the Old Age, and it has all the learning and all the humour that distinguished the work of Walter Map two centuries before. The work proves conclusively that Gerson was not, as some critics have thought, the dry remainder biscuit of a dead age, but was in fact the living link between the learning of the Middle Ages and the learning of the Renaissance. The greatest figure of his age, he was, of necessity, associated with its greatest book, and perhaps no finer tribute has been offered to the genius of the humble monk who penned the work than this inevitable association.

It has been a matter of anxious care to secure

contemporary illustrations for the book. The early printed editions have supplied the curious woodcuts here reproduced. The frontispiece is a peculiarly interesting illumination, for it is not only an admirable example of a lost art, but it shows the meaning that the term *Musica Ecclesiastica* conveyed to the mediæval mind. The pages reproduced from manuscripts in London, Oxford, Cambridge, Dublin, and Brussels will, I think, be of particular interest to Colonial, American, and Continental students who are unable to visit the libraries from which these pages are drawn. A definite purpose is served by these reproductions. If we had but an exact reproduction of one page of the unique manuscript of Asser's *Life of King Alfred*, burnt in the great Cottonian fire of October 23rd, 1731, a literary problem of the first magnitude would not have arisen. I have reproduced here eleven pages from various English and Irish manuscripts of the *Imitation*, and the fact that these are brought together from scattered sources will enable scholars to test for themselves with some degree of accuracy the views that I have ventured to express on the authorship question.

A book of this type necessarily owes a great deal to others beside the author. I have to thank various members of the ever-courteous and learned staff at the British Museum Library, and especially of Mr J. A. Herbert of the Department of Manuscripts, for assistance and advice in the ceaseless difficulties that arise in any discussion of problems dealing with manuscripts and early printed books. My acknowledgments are due to His Grace the Archbishop of Canterbury for kindly allowing the reproduction of pages from the Lambeth manuscripts, and I have especially to thank Mr Kershaw, the librarian, for enabling me to identify beyond much doubt the handwriting of Archbishop Sancroft in the attribution, written on MS. 475, of the *Imitation* to Walter Hilton. I have to thank Mr Falconer Madan for valuable information as to the Bodleian manuscripts, and, in particular, for drawing my attention to the interesting Dutch MS. (Marshall, 124). My acknowledgments are also due to the authorities of the various libraries mentioned in the text for their readiness in permitting the reproduction of pages of manuscripts in their possession. The late Dr Shuckburgh and Mr F. W. Head, of Emmanuel College, Cambridge ; and Mr de Burgh, of Trinity College, Dublin, were good enough to give me the most useful information as to the manuscripts in their charge. I have also particularly to thank my publishers for their ready help in the difficult task of securing contemporary illustrations.

J. E. G. DE M.

11 NEW SQUARE, LINCOLN'S INN
August 29th, 1906.

LIST OF MANUSCRIPTS OF THE
IMITATION IN ENGLISH LIBRARIES

(The MSS. marked with an asterisk are entitled *Musica
Ecclesiastica and have only the first three books.)

Place	Reference and reputed Author	Date
1. British Museum.	Royal MSS. C. vii. (*none; part of First Book only*).	*Circa* 1420 (or earlier).
2. British Museum.	Burney MSS. 314 (*Gerson*).	*Circa* 1419 (or earlier).
3. British Museum.	Harley MSS. 3216.	21st Dec. 1454.
4. British Museum.	Additional MSS. 11,437 (*Gerson; first two books only*).	*Circa* 1465.
*5. British Museum.	Royal MSS. 7, B. viii. (*none*).	*Circa* 1470.
6. British Museum.	Harley MSS. 3223 (*Gerson*).	1478.
*7. Lambeth Palace Library.	Codex 475 (*Hilton*).	*Circa* 1450 (or later).
*8. Lambeth Palace Library.	Codex 536 (*none*).	*Circa* 1440 (or earlier).
9. Bodleian Library.	K. D. 37(5) (*none; First Book only*).	*Circa* 1450.
10. Bodleian Library.	Laud Misc. 167(1) (*Gerson or John à Kempis*).	Sixteenth Century.

Place	Reference and reputed Author	Date
11. Bodleian Library.	Marshall 124(6) (*none; lib. ii. cap.* 12 *in Dutch*).	*Circa* 1450.
*12. Bodleian Library.	Laud Misc. 215(1) (*none; Tractatus imperfectus*).	*Circa* 1450.
*13. Bodleian Library.	Bodley 632 (*none*).	*Circa* 1450.
*14. Bodleian Library.	Arch. Seld. Bodley 93 (*none*).	1469.
*15. Magdalen College, Oxford.	Codex xciii. (*none*).	Nov. 29th, 1438.
*(?)16. Emmanuel College, Cambridge.	Codex 77 (*none; Third Book only*).	*Circa* 1450.
*17. Emmanuel College, Cambridge.	Codex 83 (*none*).	*Circa* 1450.
*18. Cambridge University Library.	G.g. 1, 16 (*none; in English*).	*Circa* 1450.
*19. Library of Trinity College, Dublin.	(*None; in English.*)	*Circa* 1450.
*20. Coventry Grammar School MSS.	(*None.*)	*Circa* 1460.
21. Formerly in Sir Thomas Phillipp's Collection.	(*In Greek. Noted by Mr Kettlewell as among the Guildford MSS.*)	Seventeenth Century.

[*Note.*—Four manuscripts entitled *Musica Ecclesiastica* were in the Syon Library in the Fifteenth Century, and in the Sixteenth Century William Bonham and Reiner Wolfius each possessed a manuscript (noted by John Bale) with the same title. These may or may not be identical with some of the MSS. mentioned above. The above list contains five manuscripts not noted by Mr Kettlewell, namely, 8, 9, 11, 16, and 19. Four of the manuscripts are dated, namely, 1438(15), 1454(3), 1469(14), and 1478(6).]

LIST OF SOME OF THE OTHER MANUSCRIPTS CITED

LIST OF PRINTED EDITIONS OF THE IMITATION CITED

Reputed Author	Place	Date
6. Gerson	Louvain.	1485?
7. None (First Book only)	Cologne.	1486?
8. Gerson	Venice.	1486.
9. Thomas à Kempis	Argentine.	1487.
10. None	Ulm.	1487.
11. None	Ulm.	1487.
12. None (in German)	Ulm.	1487.
13. Gerson	Venice.	1488.
14. Gerson	Milan.	1488.
15. Gerson	Augsburg.	1488.
16. Gerson	Paris.	1489.
17. Thomas à Kempis	Louvain.	1489.
18. Thomas à Kempis	Argentine.	1489.
19. Gerson	Paris.	1491.
20. None	Ulm (?).	1492.
21. Thomas à Kempis	Luneborch.	1493.
22. Thomas à Kempis (his collected works)	Nuremberg.	1494.
23. Thomas à Kempis	Leipsic or Magdeburg.	1496?
24. Gerson	Venice.	1496.
25. Gerson	Paris.	1496.
26. Gerson	Florence.	1497.
27. Gerson	Paris.	1498.
28. Thomas à Kempis	Cologne.	1501.
29. Gerson (in English)	London.	1503-4.

ERRATA

p. 5, line 1 : for *Baarlam* read *Barlaam*.
p. 136, line 4 : delete the words *and to Gerard Groote*.

THOMAS À KEMPIS

HIS AGE AND BOOK

THE AGE OF THOMAS À KEMPIS

THE late fourteenth and early fifteenth century in Europe is a period difficult to realise, for it is a period both of preparation and dissolution. Change and decay are visible on every side. Internal forces of disruption challenge observation. External forces, ominous and destructive, compel attention. But change and reconstruction can also be observed. The New Learning is beginning to move almost unnoticed from East to West—a fitful dawn, the precursor of a new day destined to reveal vast continents of knowledge and belief. The New Mysticism too is come, the Religion of the Inner Soul that fain would shuffle off the mortal coil of corrupt and unholy formalism. It is everywhere on a sudden. It is in Sweden, England, France, Germany, Italy. No one is free from its influence. The Pope at Avignon trembles and is afraid. The New Mysticism moves even faster than the New Learning, and thoughtful men begin to find one or other or both of these movements more important than even the Great Schism of the West.

Both are beginning to influence the Universities and even the Great Councils of the Church. Jean le Charlier de Gerson, the most Christian Doctor, last and not the least of the great theologians, carried from Paris to Pisa, from Pisa to Constance, mystical forces of reform sufficient to abash the monstrous triarchy that filled the vicariate of Christ.

Nor did the New Learning and the New Mysticism exhaust the reconstructive and recreative forces of Christendom. Pressure from the East was answered by expansion West and South, and the revelation of new continents. Yet all these forces must have seemed vague and unreal enough to the pessimists and worldlings of that generation. Central Europe was distraught with private war and unchecked lawlessness. The German Emperors received no divine gift of government with the bestowal of their crown at Rome—itself the scene of every vice, the home of every negation of goodness. There was no peace, no sense of rest in any part of Europe, from Ireland to the confines of Asia. England was rent by internal wars and discontent, following on the desolation of the Black Death. That Oriental plague moving West, in the mid-fourteenth century, prepared the way for the hundred years of disaster, desolation, shame, and destruction—the veritable reign of anti-Christ—which preceded, necessitated, but obscured the advent of the new worlds of religion, thought, and exploration. On all sides was the darkness of night. In

Spain were many kingdoms, but the Moor and the Crescent still dominated this part of the extreme West. From the middle of the thirteenth century when the great Subutai with his marvellously handled Mongol armies conquered Poland and Hungary, all Eastern Europe, and even Central Europe, had stood in dread of some new portent in the East. A century later it came.

The Ottoman tide of humanity at last overflowed from Asia Minor into Europe, heedless of raging Constantinople and the Byzantine call to the careless West. The Ottoman Turks under Orchan first obtained a permanent position in Europe by the capture of Gallipoli in 1358—some twenty years before Thomas à Kempis was born. During his childhood they isolated Constantinople from the Christian West, and the fall of that city accompanied by the extinction of the Eastern Empire on May 29th, 1453, was the completion of a long and disastrous struggle. Some reference to the position of the Eastern Empire must be made, for it throws light on the general conception of Christianity that pervaded Europe in the age immediately preceding the Renaissance. The needs of Constantinople, in face of the age-long threat of the Ottoman, were ever being placed before the secure monarchies of Europe. The Emperors pleaded that they ruled a buffer kingdom which alone stood between Europe and the hordes of Asia. Such ground for assistance for the most part fell away in the thirteenth century, when it was seen that Europe was open to the East elsewhere and that the Mongol was even a worse foe than the Ottoman. But if the Emperors could no longer play upon the needs of Europe, her superstition (as Gibbon would say), or her sense of Christian solidarity was open to conviction. The Greek had the *filioque* clause with which to barter in times of need. The dream of the re-union of Christendom, the healing of the schism of the Greek and Latin Churches was ever evoked when the strong arm of the schismatic West was needed to prevent the rising of the Eastern Crescent. Never perhaps before in all the doubtful and unhappy Erastian preoccupations of the Orthodox Church had the precious tenets of Christianity been employed in so scandalous a fashion. At no time did the Greek Church intend re-union, and yet the farce of reconciliation was maintained by servile and ignoble ecclesiastical politicians for more than a whole century in face of the Ottoman peril. So degraded had Christianity become in its Eastern centre that when St Sophia was dedicated to the uses of the Crescent, it certainly suffered no spiritual diminution. There was scarcely a degree of degradation that the Orthodox Church was not prepared to suffer. Its embassies to Rome and Avignon, made in bad faith and happily crowned with discredit and unsuccess, are among the more lamentable incidents of history. Yet they answered an unconscious and glorious purpose. When the learned

Calabrian Baarlam in 1339 was despatched as an ambassador by the younger Andronicus to Benedict XII. with a plea for the union of the Churches, he met Petrarch and set in motion that revival of letters which resulted in the Classical renaissance. But the heedless Pope of Avignon and the careless monarchs of Europe rejected all political advances. Nine years later, Clement VI., magnificent and infamous, received the envoys of Cantacuzene in Avignon, that cheerful Babylon of the West, and after much entertainment sent Bishops with them on their return to Constantinople to discuss meaningless propositions for the re-union of what both parties were pleased to regard as Christendom.

John Palaeologus, a Western both by descent and inclination—for his mother was Anne of Savoy— was alone perhaps in his desire for the union of the Churches. In 1355 he placed the Eastern Church under the control of Innocent VI. ; and fourteen years later, when the whole of the Empire, with the exception of Constantinople, was in the hands of the Ottomans, he himself, journeying by sea, visited Urban V., who had just returned from Avignon to Rome, and admitted the doctrines of the Catholic Church and the double procession of the Holy Ghost. In the same year the German Emperor of the West was also entertained. Urban, says Gibbon, "enjoyed the glory of receiving in the Vatican the two imperial shadows who represented the majesty of Constantine and Charlemagne." Help, however, was not forthcoming, and the Emperor of the East returned to Constantinople by sea after a brief arrest for debt at Venice.

Thirty years later, at the end of the fourteenth century, Constantinople was still isolated from Europe by land when Manuel, the son of John Palaeologus, renewed the attempt to secure the help of the Western princes. It was useless for him to solicit the aid of Rome or Avignon. The Western Church had its own schism to heal. Manuel was magnificently entertained in Paris and not less magnificently in London, but seething Europe had no interest in the affairs of the East, and Manuel returned to find that the danger had passed. The mighty Timour had broken the Ottoman power, and a generation was to die before the attack on Constantinople could be resumed in earnest. During this period there was no talk of re-union. Indeed, until after the Council of Constance, the possibility of re-union would have been remote even had the Greeks been earnest in their Christian professions.

Rome for a century and a half before the conclusion of the Great Schism of the West had ceased to be the residential see of the Vicar of Christ. Before the opening of the fourteenth century the Popes had ceased permanently to reside amid the broils and dangers of the ruinous city. Boniface VIII., in 1303, was settled at Anagni in the French dominions. A breach between the Pope and Philip the Fair resulted in the excommunication of the King and the expulsion of the Pontiff. His successor, Benedict XI., hurled the harmless bolts of the Church from Rome, but Clement V., a nominee of the French Court, abandoned the city and led his Court across the Alps in search of a new Rome. In 1308 the wanderers finally settled at Avignon and acquired its sovereignty. The seventy years of captivity had begun and eight Popes in succession ruled Western Christendom in not unpleasant exile. Clement V. was succeeded by John XXII., Benedict XII., Clement VI., Innocent VI., Urban V., Gregory XI., and Clement VII. Widowed Rome rejoiced to receive Urban V. in 1367, but three years' sojourn was enough, and he returned to die in his beloved Avignon in 1370. His successor, Gregory XI., after seven years by the Rhone, removed the Papal Court once more to Rome, where he died in 1378, and he was succeeded by a Roman Pope, Urban VI. For the moment it seemed as if the widowed and mystic Jerusalem had regained her spouse, but the Cardinals during the summer fled across the Alps and there elected an Anti-Pope, Clement VII.

The Great Schism had begun. The seventy years of captivity had been a fitting prelude to the scenes that were to follow. Petrarch had hardly exaggerated the position when he had declared of Avignon, "veritas ibi dementia est, peccandi licentia magnanimitas et libertas eximia. Stupra, incestus, adulteria, pontificalis lasciviae ludi sunt." In the struggle that followed between the Babylon of the West and the Jerusalem of Italy we see the forces of iniquity struggling with the nerveless efforts of political expediency.   The forces of righteousness in the main stood aside from the struggle, if we except the noble figure of Jean Gerson wrestling in the darkness for the preservation of a Church that had ceased to preserve or even demand the respect of Christendom.

It is desirable to realise in some measure these various forces, for without so doing it is not possible fully to appreciate the most singular position in which the Christian world—to use a comprehensive phrase—has ever found itself.   We must endeavour to realise an invisible Church recognising Christ and Christ alone as its Founder and Head, and working without conscious unity of effort for the regeneration of Christendom like yeast in a measure of meal. We must at the same time realise a formal, visible, and official Church, highly organised, immensely rich, claiming, and in an extraordinary measure exercising, control over the persons, the purses, and the spiritual personalities of men ; a Church with incomparable traditions and possessing unlimited power ; a Church that had emerged weakened but triumphant from three centuries of conflict with the temporal power of Europe.

We have to watch this Church, sated with worldliness and honeycombed with corruption, rapidly losing its spiritual and its temporal power and becoming a private corporation of enormous wealth under the patronage of its eldest daughter the Kingdom of France. We see its managers abandon the great capital that created its organisation and settle in a city of Southern France which forthwith becomes the open *cloaca* of Europe and the *Magna Meretrix* of the Middle Ages. We see the Catholic Church watching in vain for a spiritual awakening. We see Rome sick almost to death of Roman fever and raving with Rienzi as its voice. Further West we see Constantinople in its death throes, false to the last and faithless even to the painted rags that symbolised its Christianity.

The Orthodox Church was beyond recovery. At the most it could hand on an insane tradition of corruption and superstition to the most savage tribes of Eastern and Northern Europe. But the Catholic Church even in the depths of its degradation was great both in its political instincts and its power of recuperation. It had, it had always had, the power of producing both saints and statesmen, and in the hour of its need, while the Church Invisible was slowly permeating Europe with what a writer of the late fourteenth century called the New Faith,[1] it made effort after effort to leave its Slough of Despond. Slothfully, unwilling, it returned to Roma Aeterna, and this was the signal for the huge forces of degradation to join issue with the political

[1] Adam of Usk

party which saw that the only hope for Catholicity lay on the banks of the Tiber.

Nor were the forces only political that undertook this notable effort. The invisible Church turned from its silent labours to precipitate the result. Reluctant Popes saw visions and dreamt dreams. Catherine of Siena and Bridget of Sweden disturbed with relentless minds the peace of Avignon and the sloth of death.

St Bridget was not least among the remarkable revivalists of the fourteenth century and was certainly the sanest of them all. She was born in the year 1304, one of the Royal House of Sweden. At the age of sixteen she married Ulpho, Prince of Nericia, in Sweden. She bore him eight children, and after his death in 1344 she retired from the world and devoted herself to good works and a life of austere contemplation. She founded the great double monastery of Wastein in the Diocese of Lincopen in Sweden, and imposed the Rule of St Augustine.

Her writings are full of interest, and in the beginning of the sixteenth century had some vogue in England. The most practical minded of women, she endeavoured to combine the life of Mary, who represented in her phraseology the life contemplative, with the life of Martha, who represented the life active. Some of her sayings are of value as representing the singularly sane outlook of a prominent mystic of the fourteenth century.

" He that fasteth muste take hede that he be not

overmoch enfebled and made weyke by his un-
resonable fastyng "[1]

" The contemplatyve man maye nat be ydel."

" If he be wery and temptation rise in his prayers
he may labour with his handes some honest and
profitable werke either for him selfe if he have nede
or for other."

" If the contemplatyve man have nat sufficient to
lyve withal but through his labour than may he
make the shorter prayers for his necessary laboure
and that labour shalbe the perfection and encreasyng
of his prayer."

" Also the contemplatyve man must hate his owne
wyl, ofte remembre his dethe, fly curiosytie, al mur-
muringe ane grudgynge, alway remembre the right-
wysenesse of God and take hede of his owne affections."

The following passage may be taken to heart to-
day as deeply as when it was written :—

" The sonne of God speketh to saynt Bryget and
sayth, he that desyreth to visyte the londes of the
infydels ought to have v thinges. The first is that
he discharge his conscience with trewe confessyon
and contrition as though he should forthwith dye.
Seconde that he put awaye al lyghtnesse of maners
and of apparyl nat takynge hede to newe customes
or vanytyes but to such laudable customes as his

---

[1] *Certayne revelacyons of Saint Birgette* (London, 1535 ?, Godfray).
Printed with the translation of *The Imitation* and *The Golden Epistle*
of St Bernard. *The Revelations* were first printed at Lubec in 1492.

auncesters have used before tyme.   Thyrdly that he
have no temporall thynge but for necessyte and to
the honoure of God and yf he knowe any thynge un-
ryghtwysely gotten eyther by hym selfe or by his
auncesters that he restore it whether it be lytel or
great.   Fourthly that he labour to the intent that
the unfaythful men may come to the trewe catholy-
cal faythe not desyrynge theyr goodes ne catel or
any other thynge but to the onely necessitie of the
body.   Fifthly that he have full wyll gladly to
dye for the honoure of God and so to dyspose hym-
selfe in laudable conversation that he maye deserve
to come to a good and a blessed endyng.   Amen."

It may be imagined that a lady possessed with
such ideas filled the Courts of Rome and Avignon
with fear and aversion.   She strove with all her
might to secure the abandonment of Avignon.   The
return of Urban V. in 1367 must have filled her
with joy, while his flight to die in Avignon in 1370
was certainly calculated to point a moral.   Bridget
is said to have foretold the speedy death of the
fugitive Pope.   His successor, Gregory XI., remained at Avignon the prey of superstitious fears,
and when at last he was drawn to Rome by Saint
Catherine of Siena he died within a year, warning
men on his death-bed against visionaries of either
sex.   It would seem legitimate to think that the
experiences of these saints in Avignon and Rome,
would have taught them that it was not the seat of
the Church but its mind—its universal and corrupt-

ing influence—that mattered.   Saint Bridget's faith
in the Church, however, won for her a posthumous
reward.   She died in 1373 at the age of seventy in
Rome, after a prayerful pilgrimage to Jerusalem, and
within a few years an unreformed Church with its
centre at Rome sanctioned, at Basle, her Revelations
and enrolled her, at the Council of Constance, among
the Saints.

Saint Catherine, the daughter of James Benincasa, a
dyer, was born at Siena in 1347.   From childhood she
sought the contemplative life.   On her refusal to marry
at the age of twelve she was deprived of the means of
solitary contemplation, and henceforth, we are told,[1]
the Holy Ghost "taught her to make herself another
solitude in her heart; where amidst all her occupations
she considered herself always as alone with God ; to
whose presence she kept herself no less attentive, than
if she had no exterior employment to distract her."
With regard to this period of her life, she wrote (in her
treatise, *Concerning God's Providence*) "that our Lord
had taught her to build in her soul a private closet,
strongly vaulted with the divine providence, and to
keep herself always close and retired there; he assured
her that by this means she should find peace, and perpetual repose in her soul, which no storm or tribulation could disturb or interrupt."   In 1365 she received
the habit of the third Order of St Dominic and, enter-
ing a nunnery, for three years never spoke to any one
but God and her Confessor.   "Her days and nights

[1] *Lives of the Saints*, vol. iv. p. 330.

were employed in the delightful exercises of contemplation : the fruits whereof were supernatural lights, a most ardent love of God, and zeal for the conversion of sinners." This saint, famous for her life, her visions, and her mystic treatises (such as that on *Consummate Perfection*), ventured in June 1376 into the tainted atmosphere of Avignon and interceded with Gregory XI. on behalf of the city of Florence. That superstitious Pope turned to Catherine of Siena for a solution of his doubts. He had vowed to return to Rome : what was his duty? She replied without knowledge of the vow, " Fulfil what you have promised to God."

It is a curious spectacle, the vision of these holy women moving amidst the corruption of Avignon and Rome. They represented the invisible Church of Christ, and they were moved to intervene in the affairs of the visible Church of Anti-Christ. A sense of wonder fills the mind as we see the Cardinals of Avignon questioning the Saint of Siena on the meaning of the Interior Life, and listening to her revelations as to the sufferings of the Founder of Christianity and as to the revolutions of earthly kingdoms. Little good, one must think, could come of such trafficking between the forces of good and evil. Yet she touched the superstitious heart of corruption, and one cannot forget that Christ Himself argued with the doctors in the Temple. After she left Avignon in September 1376 she wrote more than once to the wavering Pope, urging his return to Rome. He appears to have followed her as far as Genoa for further advice, and at last, in January 1377, in fear of forces visible and invisible, carried his Court to Rome, to die there anathematising all visionaries. Catherine threw herself into the Papal election of 1378 with all the energy of a politician, and until her death, in April 1380, worked actively for Urban VI. and against Clement VII. and the revived Court of Avignon. These women, and other less notable visionaries who took sides in the Great Schism that followed the death of Gregory XI., served no adequate purpose in the regeneration of Christendom by their efforts to bring down from Heaven that pattern of Rome which was evidently laid up in their celestial visions. The visions of a Jeanne d'Arc might bring victory to the temporal arm, but they did nothing to make new the heart of Christendom. More worldly forces were needed to cleanse the sinks of Europe. Womanhood was accounted little in the days of the Great Schism.

Yet it is not altogether just to speak of the famous man who rendered the revival of Roman Catholicism possible as a worldly force. Jean le Charlier de Gerson was without any doubt the most remarkable personality of the age in which the *De Imitatione Christi* was written and the tragedy of the Great Schism enacted. He was born of obscure parentage in the hamlet of Gerson, near the village of Barby, on December 14th, 1363. His mother was a woman

of notable holiness, and Gerson compared her to
Monica, the mother of Augustine. The curé of
the village saw in his devout little choir boy the
seeds of great things and sent him to school at
Réthel. Hence he passed to the College of Rheims
at the age of fourteen, and some years later, provided with what we should call a scholarship, he set
out, cheered by many blessings, on the long walk to
Paris. He entered the Royal College of Navarre,
where the famous Pierre d'Ailly became his friend.
He immediately made his mark both in University
affairs and as a student of the Trivium and Quadrivium. So popular did he become, that he was
elected as the representative of the " Nation " of
France in the College for the purposes of the election
of the Rector. In 1381 he took his degree in Arts
and passed to the study of Theology. About this date
he adopted the name of Gerson as a result of
punishment undergone through the confusion of his
personality with that of a man of a similar birth
name. There was perhaps a certain foreshadowing
of the future in the new name—for Gerson may be
compared with the Hebrew word meaning exile.

In 1387 an apparently fortuitous opportunity gave
Gerson his great chance in life.

One of the startling theological controversies of the
Middle Ages suddenly arose. A monk named Jean
de Montesson propounded the not unreasonable theory
that the mother of Our Lord was conceived in sin, and
that the contrary doctrine was opposed to Holy Writ.

The Theological Faculty of Paris condemned the proposition and directed the monk to retract. He maintained his position, and was denounced to the University who confirmed the judgment of the Faculty, and referred the offender to the Bishop of Paris. The bishop passed sentence forbidding Montesson to continue the offence of promulgating his doctrine. The monk appealed to the Anti-Pope at Avignon. Clement VII. nominated a Commission headed by three Cardinals to consider the question. The University was represented at the hearing by two religious and two secular doctors (including Pierre d'Ailly, Grand-master of Navarre). D'Ailly took Gerson with him to Avignon.

In 1387 the Great Schism of the West had been in progress nine years, and Christendom was divided beyond repair in its allegiance. Gibbon has briefly summed up this question of allegiance during the Schism. "The vanity rather than the interest of the nation determined the Court, and Clergy of France. The states of Savoy, Sicily, Cyprus, Arragon, Castille, Navarre and Scotland were inclined by their example and authority to the obedience of Clement VII., and, after his decease, of Benedict XIII. Rome, and the principal states of Italy, Germany, Portugal, England, the Low Countries, and the kingdoms of the North, adhered to the prior election of Urban VI., who was succeeded by Boniface IX., Innocent VII., and Gregory XII." The schism literally rent the most intimate countries

B

asunder : England and Scotland differed in their
obedience, the Spanish kingdoms and Portugal
owned a different spiritual head.   This was scarcely
the season at which to raise for discussion and decision
a question of such curious moment as that of the
Immaculate Conception, nor was Avignon at this
period exactly the place that could with decency be
chosen for the discussion of such a question.   Moreover, a discussion before Clement and a decision by
Clement could not possibly be accepted by Rome.
It was perhaps this fact that delayed for something
like five centuries the official enunciation of the
doctrine that the Anti-Pope was now called upon to
examine.

D'Ailly spoke first, addressing Clement VII. and
his College of Cardinals.   He was followed by
Gerson, whose keen eloquence and transparent piety
drew forth the personal approval of the schismatic
Pope.   Three days later Clement pronounced in
favour of the University, and Montesson forthwith
fled from Avignon to Arragon, and two years later
was declared contumacious and excommunicated.
It is noticeable that he based his doctrine upon the
words of Holy Writ, and refused to be answered by
any other evidence.   It was a sign of the times.
The Invisible Church with one accord was turning
back from formalism and tradition to Scripture.
The authority of Scripture was not to be over-ridden
by any other authority.   In Montesson's opinion not
only was the doctrine of the Immaculate Conception

not found in, but it was absolutely denied by, Holy Scripture. That being the case, it was impossible for him to yield, though like many others he preserved his loyalty to the Pope of his nation, and fled to one of the few countries that admitted his spiritual sway, and where the penalty of excommunication could run. The decision of Clement was never binding on the faithful. This Apollinarian doctrine was supported by Gerson at the Council of Constance, and was perhaps implied as a doctrine of the Church at the Council of Trent, but it was not until 1854 that it was officially imposed upon the Roman Church by Pius IX. The University of Paris, however, had no doubt on the subject, and expelled the Dominicans from their midst on the ground that Montesson was one of them. In 1403 Gerson secured their return.

In 1387, on his return from Avignon, Gerson took orders, and became, in the words of a contemporary, "a seraph at the altar." His piety now, as always, and his fervent faith, were undeniable. At this time he wrote a famous panegyric on Saint Louis, applying to him the phrase, *servire autem Deo, regnare est*. The style of the tract is noticeable. It is full of recondite allusions to history and ancient authors. It has nothing in common with the style of the *Imitation*.

In 1392 he became a Doctor in Theology. At this date d'Ailly was Chancellor of the University and Confessor to Charles VI., the mad king.

Gerson's progress thenceforward was very rapid, and it is worthy of record that he drew into the religious life of the time many of his numerous brothers and sisters. His intense affection for them and his parents are notable facts in a life that for the most part was absorbed in the mad whirl of a bad age. His active mind saw the evils of the time, and was not overwhelmed by them. He saw the Schism ruining the Catholic Church, he saw the corruption of the great cities, the intolerable conditions of life even in France, that most habitable part of the West, and the general signs of dissolution in the society of Europe. On the other hand he knew well that there was reason for hope. In the way of scholarship what he did not know was not knowledge, and he must have been conscious of the slow revival of classical scholarship, of the wealth of learning introduced from the East by Barlaam the Calabrian in 1339, and by the successive embassies from the Bosphorus. He, too, knew of the hidden but ceaseless religious revival that was moving throughout Europe. He was himself at heart, though not by education, a mystic, a profound contemplative, who looked earnestly for the Kingdom of God. In education and religion he saw the twofold force that would regenerate Christendom. They were the forces that had made his own career possible, that had raised him from obscurity into the doubtful daylight of kings. The education of children seemed to him the primary secret of regeneration, and he spent the years after his fall in the teaching of little children.

His power as an orator was great. He was the founder of the great line of French preachers. His speech was free and merciless, but this did not exclude him from the delivery of sermons to the Court, where by the year 1396 he had secured great influence. It says a good deal for Gerson that when on the elevation of Pierre d'Ailly to the episcopate in 1398, he himself was offered the Chancellorship of the University of Paris, he was able to refuse the posts of Almoner and Confessor to the King which d'Ailly had held with the Chancellorship. This great office should not, he felt, be hampered by personal service to the King.

As Chancellor of Notre Dame he was in a position that had been occupied by one hundred and sixty bishops, thirty-nine cardinals, and six popes—Gregory IX., Adrian V., Boniface VIII., Innocent VI., Gregory XI., and Clement VII.[1] From the year 1227 when Gregory IX., the nephew of Innocent, became Pope the Chancellorship had been a step to the Papal throne. Adrian V. became Pope in 1276; in 1294 Benedict Cajétan ascended the throne as Boniface VII. Innocent VI. (1352), Gregory XI. (1370), and Clement VII. (1378), were in Gerson's own age, and the latter was the reigning Pope of his obedience. Gerson was in a position that might quite possibly lead to the

---

[1] See *Jean Gerson, sa Vie, son temps, ses œuvres*, by A. L. Masson (Lyons, 1894).

throne of Avignon. He threw himself into the work
of the Chancellorship with characteristic energy. He
himself taught in the Cloister School the children
of the poor, declaring that they were the children of
God and the inheritors of the Kingdom of Heaven,
and that it was therefore as great an honour to teach
them as to teach the Dauphin. He went as the
representative of Charles VI. in a deputation of
the University to Benedict XIII., the successor of
Clement VII. In the year 1400 he accepted, in
his desire to see practical clerical work, a cure at
Bruges, which he managed to combine with his work
as Chancellor. It was during this period that he composed several works in French, including *Le Traité
de Mendicité Spirituelle.* He did all he could, by
writing in the vulgar tongue, and by means of
education, to bring the best thought into the lives of
the people. It was in recognition of this fact that
he was called "le Docteur du peuple et le Docteur
des petits enfants." This use of the vernacular was
perhaps Gerson's most important educational work.
His treatise *de scavoir bien mourir* was largely used
in the parish churches. His "L'A B C des simples
gens" was also much in vogue. The introduction
is a short statement of the undenominationalism which
seemed to him sufficient as a working religion for
the people. "Entendez-vous," it runs, "petits
enfants, fils et filles, et aultres gens simples, je vous
escripray en françois cet A B C, qui contient la Patre
nostre, laquelle Dieu fist de sa propre bouche ;

INDEX OF CHAPTERS OF THE FIRST BOOK AND PART OF THE FIRST
CHAPTER OF THE FIRST BOOK OF THE TREATISE CALLED "MUSICA
ECCLESIASTICA:" FROM MS. 536 IN THE LAMBETH PALACE LIBRARY.
THIS MS. CONSISTS OF THE FIRST THREE BOOKS OF THE TREATISE
"DE IMITATIONE CHRISTI" AND BELONGS TO THE FIRST HALF OF
THE FIFTEENTH CENTURY.

l'ave Maria, que l'Ange Gabriel adressa à la Vierge Marie ; et le *Credo* qui fut fait par les Apôtres ; et les X Commandements, et aultres points de notre religion chrétienne, lesquels ont été révélés de Dieu, et montrés au commencement en la claire lumière de grande foy dedans les âmes des saintes personnes, et auxquels on doit croire."

The "other points" are denominational enough, but it is clear that Gerson chiefly laid stress, in the teaching of simple folk, on the simple facts of Bible Christianity. The interesting discussion on the seven virtues, the seven gifts of the spirit, and so forth, is full of mediæval formalism, enlightened with a very human touch, but the heart of the matter is in the elements of Christian fact and truth. The spiritual, educational, and material needs of the age were ever present to the heart, ever stirring the mind of this great Christian doctor. In a far wider sense than Saint Bridget he realised the interaction of the life contemplative and the life active. In every life, he felt, there must be a mingling of prayer and work incapable of disentanglement. With simple people faith and work must both be simple, but must both be in vital union. But the world, he saw, was going very ill at the end of the fourteenth century. Writing from Bruges to Pierre d'Ailly he declared "le corps de la chrétienté est couvert de plaies de la tête aux pieds. Tout se précipite du mal dans le pire, et chacun apporte sa part à la masse d'iniquités." This was written in regard to the superstitions and gross abuses of the parish churches on Feast Days such as the Holy Innocents' Day. That on such a day—the children's day—religion should suffer its supreme eclipse seemed to him significant of the canker at the very base of society. If the world was to be redeemed, redemption must begin with the children. Therefore in his little tract *de Innocentia Puerili* he attacked—as the educationalist of every age must attack—the corruption of childhood by the influence of bad pictures and bad books. If the fountain is poisoned how can the rivers of life be pure? But it was not only impurity but the grossest superstition that tainted the age. Hence he attacked in no measured terms the pseudo science of astrology : "c'est par l'expérience, par les lois divines et morales que la raison humane doit se diriger, et non par des superstitions ridicules." His Platonic mysticism recognised a double manifestation of Divine Power in the natural and the supernatural worlds, but such manifestation was essentially reasonable, and was both spiritually and intellectually degraded by superstition.

But it was not only with his pen that Gerson taught the first principles of that social renaissance of which he was the first expositor in Europe, the spiritual forerunner of Fenélon, Rousseau, and the Revolution. He was an eloquent preacher. At a Provincial Council at Rheims he attracted great attention, while his famous sermon at Notre Dame on *The Passion of our Lord Jesus Christ* was preached to an immense congregation. He had become the

man of the hour, and when, after the death of the
Duke of Burgundy in 1404, a civil war between the
Burgundian and the Orleanist parties combined with
the plague to ruin the whole land, the people turned
for help to the eloquent Chancellor of Paris. His
influence at Court and his power of brilliant and
fearless speech were used unstintingly on behalf of
the people. He fiercely attacked the Orleanist party,
and in his great sermon of October 7th, 1405,
preached before the King, his family, and the noble
families of France, he set out in terrible detail the
miseries of the land.

A summary of the sermon will give some idea of
the state of France at the opening of the fifteenth
century. The opening passage is striking enough :
"Vivat Rex! Vivat Rex! Vivat Rex! Vive le Roy!
Vive le Roy! Vive le Roy! Vive corporellement,
vive moralement et politiquement! Vive spiritu-
ellement et pardurablement!" He prays for good
counsellors for the King, good education for the
King's son. The troops must be properly paid in
order to prevent them pillaging the people : "Se ils
ne payent, ils pilleront et roberont sur les povres
gens très oultrageusement." Then follows the vivid
passage in which the Chancellor describes the results
of the cruel taxation of the people. "Las! Un
povre homme aura-t-il payé son imposition sa taille,
sa gabelle, son fouage, son quatriesme, les esprons du
roy, la saincture de la reyne, les truages, les chaucées,
les passages, peu lui demeure ; puis viendra encore

une taille qui sera créée, et sergents de venir et de engager pots et pouilles. Le povre homme n'aura pain à manger, sinon par adventure, aucun peu de seigle ou d'orge. Sa povre femme gerra, et auront quatre ou six petits enfants au fouyer, ou au four qui, par adventure, sera chauld, lesquels demanderont du pain, criant à la rage de faim. La povre mère si n'aura que bouter ès-dents un peu de pain ou il y ait du sel." To increase the misery of this awful but common picture, we see the brutal unpaid soldiery adding infamy to woe. These were the simple annals of the poor. How can the King, cries the preacher, with a flash of the deadly irony for which he was famous, "how can the King, seeing such servitude, call himself Francorum Rex—the King of the Free." Up the ages we hear the cry of Rousseau, Man is born free, and lo! everywhere he is in chains. Gerson is almost brutally frank. He describes the peasant as "pillé par princes ou par gens d'armes." He adds emphatically, "Toy, Prince, tu ne fais pas tilz maux, il est vrai, mais tu les souffres." The receiver is worse than the thief. Children, men, beasts, are all dying of hunger: "Dieu, par sa grâce, y vueille mettre remède par le moyen de vous, très nobles et excellents seigneurs, à fin que le roy vive de sa vie civile et politique : *Vivat rex !*"

We may well believe that this great sermon did more than make a great sensation at the time. It permeated through the country in manuscript form.

The earliest extant manuscript is one of 1406, which belonged to the King's niece, Marie, the daughter of the Duc de Berri. It was not forgotten. It was printed in the year 1500, and again in 1561 and 1588. In it we see the statement of the case of the people as it was to be presented by the direct forerunners of the Great Revolution. At the time this bold intervention in social questions merely added to Gerson's already great reputation and strengthened the University of Paris. The Duke of Orleans complained in vain.

The problem of the hour was, however, the Great Schism. Upon its solution seemed to depend the future of Europe. The University of Paris played an important part in the movement that led to the restoration of Catholicity. At first it disliked the idea of recognising the Anti-Pope Clement VII., but it was divided on the subject, the various "nations" following the views of the nationalities they nominally represented. When Pietro Thomacelli succeeded Urban VI. at Rome as Boniface IX. in 1389, the University proposed that the Schism should be ended either by a General Council or a compromise, or the retirement of both popes. The majority of the cardinals favoured the last proposal, and Clement VII. seems to have died of chagrin in 1394 on learning this decision. The Schism might now well have ended, but the cardinals at Avignon suddenly changed their policy and elected as their choice, Pope Benedict XIII. To deal with the new situation the King called together an ecclesiastical assembly or council at Paris in 1395.

This body recommended the retirement of both popes, but Benedict absolutely refused to resign despite the prayers of the University and of the King's envoys that he would not tear the seamless garment of Christ. A second assembly of 1398 recommended the withdrawal of obedience with the cessation of supplies, and the troops of the King actually besieged the Pope, whose cardinals had fled, in Avignon. At this moment the Duke of Orleans intervened on behalf of the Lord of Avignon, and the party of reform were compelled to yield. Gerson heading a deputation from the University to the inflexible Benedict in 1403, appealed for reunion, that Jerusalem might no longer be widowed and desolate. He had with great regret recognised Benedict, and little was gained by the recognition. Boniface IX. died at Rome in 1404, and the Roman cardinals proposed that Benedict should resign and end the schism. This was refused, and they thereupon elected Cosmo Meliorati as Innocent VII. The new pope took an oath to do all that was possible, even to the renunciation of the See, to restore peace. He died of old age in November 1406, and was succeeded by the Venetian, Ange Corrario, as Gregory XII. Gerson approached both popes in order to secure reunion, but the efforts were fruitless, and he continued to labour tirelessly both with pen and voice to create a new public opinion on the whole question of Church Government and Church Reform. In January 1408 Charles VI. of France declared that if re-union were not established before Ascension day and a sole pope elected, his kingdom would cease to be neutral. Benedict at once excommunicated the King, and placed the kingdom under an interdict. He was a really strong pope, and had the Church been united in his time would have gone far as a reformer. The University replied by excommunicating the Pope as a heretic and a schismatic, whom none need obey. A third Gallic Council was called, and a position of neutrality was adopted until the assembly of a General Council. The other nations agreed, and it was decided to call a General Council of the Church at Pisa.

At this moment France was in a furious uproar. The Duke of Orleans was assassinated by the orders of John the Fearless, Duke of Burgundy, on November 23, 1407, but such was the hatred in which the King's brother was held that practically all Paris sided with Duke John, and the Orleans family were forced in 1409, after his triumphant return from Flanders, to come to some terms with him. But Gerson, though the enemy of the Duke of Orleans, found it impossible to justify the murder, and denounced the crime in unmeasured terms. He attacked the University supporters of the Duke of Burgundy, led by Doctor Jean Petit, with all his power, and became at once the head in Paris of the Orleanist party—henceforth known as the

Armagnacs in consequence of the marriage of the young Duke of Orleans with the daughter of the Count of Armagnac. That was the position in France when the Council of Pisa was opened in the Cathedral on Lady Day 1409. It was an immense Assembly, and included doctors in theology from all parts of Europe. The rival popes, Gregory XII. and Benedict XIII., were summoned, and in their absence were declared contumacious, and the vacancy of the Holy See was announced. Gerson, who was the deputy of the Church of France, argued here, as later (thereby drawing on himself the wrath of the Vatican, still muttering even to-day), that a General Council could depose and was superior to the pope. The cardinals forthwith on adopting this argument entered into conclave and elected the Cardinal of Milan, Pietro Filargo of Candia, a Franciscan and a doctor of Paris. He chose the name of Alexander V. At the request of the Council, Gerson harangued the new pope. He called upon him to restore the kingdom to Israel in all her former splendour. Alexander agreed to the propositions put forward by the Council, and announced that another Council would be called together in 1412 to consider the Reformation of the Church.

The only result that the Council of Pisa produced was an addition to the number of popes, and a further rent in the seamless garment which in the jargon of the time signified the Catholic Church. Indeed the

Church was about to face the crowning scandal of the Middle Ages. The pontificate of Alexander was brief. He had settled at Bologna, but called to Rome by the fickle inhabitants of the restless city he at once set out on his journey. He died while crossing the Apennines on May 3, 1410, after a pontificate of ten months and fifteen days. The election of his successor illustrates with an unspeakable force the utter ungodliness of the Roman Church at the time. As a matter of policy it was desirable to end the schism. Yet it was not the seamless garment of Christ that was in danger, but the wealth-getting capacity of the Western Church. The talk of peace and reunion—except in the mouths of a few men like Gerson—was sheer hypocrisy. Although this is almost obvious to the unprejudiced student of history, it would be difficult absolutely to bring home the charge of hypocrisy to the official Church were it not for the action of the conclave of cardinals who met at Rome to elect a successor to Alexander V.

The man they chose was Baldassarre Cossa, Cardinal of Bologna, who ascended the pontifical throne under the divine name of John—John XXIII. He was, says Gibbon, the most profligate of mankind. His crimes, his loathsome offences against every law of God and man, were notorious in his own day *before* his election. He was a jovial monster, the details of whose iniquities have been made the subject of original research by a German specialist. There

was no particular reason why he should have been
elected, except that he represented the current taste
in wickedness of the Roman cardinals.   It is painful
to find that modern Roman Catholic writers dealing
with this period, such polished and sympathetic
writers as M. A. L. Masson (to whose life of Gerson
all students must be indebted), should not only accept
without comment the fact of the election of Pope
John XXIII., but should actually complain of the
action of the Civil power in detaining him in prison
after his deposition.   The position of modern Roman
Catholicism is not strengthened by refusing to recognise that Anti-Christ was reigning in Rome in the
year 1410.   Nothing perhaps is more astonishing
in the remarkable history of the mediæval papacy
than the acceptance of John by the Reform party.
A strain of weakness, a yielding to expediency runs
through the character of Gerson, and the fact that
he not only placed himself within the obedience of
the new Pope, but actually accepted at his hands
the appointment of Pénitencier de l'Eglise de Paris
is perhaps the chief stain upon a great character.

His position was, however, singularly difficult.
John secured the recognition of the University
of Paris, and the anti-Gerson party led by Jean
Petit in the University was very strong.   It is
probable that if Gerson had refused to accept John
as the legitimate successor of the man appointed by
the general Council of Pisa, his position as Chancellor would have become intolerable.   It was bad

enough in any event in the interval between the
Councils of Pisa and Constance. The sons of the
late Duke of Orleans were endeavouring to avenge
their father's murder. The whole country was
ravaged by the conflicting forces of the Armagnacs
and the Burgundians. Paris was sacked by the
white-hooded Cabochiens or Burgundians on April
28th, 1413. They were led by Caboche and Jean
Petit. Gerson himself escaped with difficulty, and
watched from the towers of Notre Dame the destruction of his house and his beloved books. In
the following September the Armagnacs carried the
capital by assault, and after a desperate conflict
peace was restored. Gerson, at the price of considerable self-respect, retained his ascendency in the
University, and preached a sermon of reconciliation
at Saint Martin des Champs. Pope John would not
have been abashed had ecclesiastical Europe shrunk
from him, but he had to face no such difficulty.
Having won the University of Paris, and Gerson, he
had won all. He was elected at Bologna, but passed
on to Rome, where he made fourteen cardinals,
including three members of the University.

It was not long before the forces of evil as represented by John came into active conflict with the re-
forming forces, which in one shape or another formed
or gave political strength to the Invisible Church.
Central Europe was seething with discontent. The
connection between Bohemia and England due to
the marriage of Anne, the daughter of King Wences-

c

las, to Richard II. of England, had led to the importation into Bohemia, and thence to Germany, of Wiclivism. Social and religious discontent went hand in hand. A vile and corrupt Church and a brigand baronage were faced by an incensed peasantry and by a deep religious movement long stirring and now roused to active life by the passionate preaching of John Hus. Within a month of the election of John XXIII., the official Church had begun its attack on the real forces of reform—not on the reformers of Pisa, not on mediating reformers like Gerson, but on the men who, as far as could be seen, represented the great under-current of holiness and faith, which men like the official Pope recognised as the real danger to Established Catholicism. In June 1410, Wiclif's works were burnt at Prague, and in the following March, Pope John XXIII. in solemn form excommunicated John Hus. It was a dramatic moment in the history of Christianity. Hus replied that he would only obey the Pope in so far as his commands were in accordance with those of Christ. The excommunication was renewed and the city of Prague laid under an interdict. The issue was boldly joined and the combat between Christ and Anti-Christ in terms begun. It remained to be seen what the official Church, as distinct from the official Pope, would do. Would Gerson, one of the greatest influences in the Church, a keen reformer and a theologian of the first rank, support a policy deliberately aimed at suppressing all that remained of spiritual Christianity in Europe?

A General Council had been promised for 1412, and John had the effrontery to call it at Rome. It met early in 1413. It was very sparsely attended. Rome offered few attractions to the followers of Gregory XII. now living under the protection of Ladislaus of Naples or to those of Benedict XIII. Moreover, John's reputation had not improved. The scandal of his life, though it scarcely shocked the cardinals, was not attractive to the bishops of Christendom. The only act carried was a Bull against the writings of Wiclif. Having thus pledged the Church to the policy of suppressing reform, John adjourned the sittings of the Council, the resumption to take place at Constance on All Saints' Day, 1414. In fact it met two days later. It was the scene of Gerson's greatest triumphs. For the moment he had secured his position in Paris, and his journey to Constance was one of singular interest to himself, for he passed through Rheims, where he received almost royal honours, and revisited his old home. The Council's first business was to consider the disunion of official Christendom. John XXIII. was supported by France, Poland, England, Hungary, Portugal, the kingdoms of the North, and parts of Italy and Germany. Practically the whole of what is now Protestant Europe supported this sinister representative of Roman Catholicism. Benedict XIII., now resident at Peniscola, was supported by Castile, Arragon, Navarre, Scotland,

Corsica, and Sardinia, and by the Counts of Foix and Armagnac. Gregory XII. was the nominee of part of the kingdom of Naples, Romagna, part of Germany, Bavaria, the Palatinate of the Rhine, Brunswick, Luxembourg, Hesse, Trèves, a part of the electorates of Mayence and Cologne, and the territorial bishops of Worms, Spires, and Verdun. The seamless garment of the Church was indeed rent, and wondering Europe, distraught with every misery, believed that the age of Anti-Christ had come.

The work before the Council was immense, and indeed dangerous, but Sigismund guaranteed the safety of the delegates who poured in from all quarters. Gerson, as the representative of the University of Paris and ambassador of the King of France, is said to have led to Constance no less than two hundred doctors of Paris. A hundred thousand observers are reported to have flocked to the town, including eighteen thousand ecclesiastics. The Council had three main subjects to discuss : errors against the faith, the re-establishment of ecclesiastical discipline, and the extinction of the Schism. John, who had called, or induced the Emperor Sigismund to call, the Council, was present at the first sitting in order to have his election confirmed. He evidently feared no rebuke ; he was above both the moral and the civil law of Europe. He claimed to preside. An accident prevented this final blow to the moral authority of the Church. The representatives of Benedict and Gregory refused to take part in the proceedings if this were allowed, and as their presence was necessary in order to heal the Schism,, John was pressed to abdicate. He agreed, and the worthy Pierre d'Ailly declared that this act showed grandeur of soul. Such an utterance by a man of the undoubted personal goodness of d'Ailly seems incomprehensible. The truth was that all things were to be sacrificed to a policy of expediency that would secure once more a United Church. If Saint Gregory could have recourse to expediency, could lavish letters of almost fulsome adulation on the murderer of the Emperor Maurice, surely an ex-Chancellor of the University of Paris could praise the spiritual grandeur of the most profligate of mankind.

But John was under no misapprehension. He understood the formulæ of the Middle Ages and, having put off the sheltering crown, fled for his life to Schaffouse, where he placed himself under the protection of the Emperor Frederick of Austria. He was the third anti-Pope, and it was the business of the distressed Council to supply the Church with an official representative. Gerson once more convinced the not reluctant assembly of the Church that a General Council is superior to a Pope, and at the twelfth session, on May 25th, 1415, John XXIII. was deposed. It is perhaps not altogether a matter for surprise that he accepted the decision of the Council and agreed not to entertain the idea of re-election even if he were invited! The fact was that he was at this date in the hands of the Emperor

Sigismund, and the secular arm looked with dis-
favour on offences and on a career that Gibbon
has deftly summed up in a mordant and unpleasant
epigram. For three years the ex-Pope was detained
in prison by Sigismund, a fact which fills M.
Masson with indignation. To those faithful persons
who believe that the efforts of Gerson, d'Ailly, and
the moderate reformers of Constance had a
cleansing effect on the Church, may be com-
mended the last stage of John's career. With
this stage Gibbon fortunately was not familiar.
His comment would have been justified, and one
more bitter gibe against Christianity would have
been recorded. Indeed it was difficult for an
historian of the eighteenth century, dealing only
with the history of Christianity in Rome, to realise
that any good thing could come out of Nazareth.

Cossa returned to Rome after his release
from prison. He was familiar with the city
long before his adventure as a pontiff. The
bitterest days of the Schism were among his
pleasantest recollections. He was in Rome when
Adam of Usk, the English clerical fugitive from
justice, arrived there in 1402. He was then
Cardinal-Deacon of the title of St Eustace, and
received the wanderer kindly, was kissed by
him on foot, hand, and cheek, and passed him on
to Cosimo dei Migliorati, who afterwards became
Innocent VII. This was the ripest period of
Roman simony, the period, as Adam says, when

" everything was bought and sold, so that benefices were given not for desert, but to the highest bidder." Cossa must have been present at the great scene of September 29th, 1404, when an embassy of the kings of the Avignon obedience came to Rome and waited upon Boniface IX. —a man gorged with simony—to endeavour to bring him into the way of re-union. Boniface shrieked at the embassy: " Thy lord is false, schismatic, and very anti-Christ"; to which Pierre de Rabat, Bishop of St Pons de Tomières, in the province of Narbonne, replied with warmth : " My lord is holy, just, true, catholic; and he sits upon the true seat of St Peter "; and added with bitter meaning, " nor is he simoniac."

Benedict XIII., the Lord of Avignon, was indeed almost the only respectable papal figure of that age. He had some conception of the dignity of the episcopal office. Rabat's reply appears to have smitten Boniface ; Adam of Usk, at any rate, attributes his death two days later to the interview and the punishment of God. He was succeeded by Cossa's friend, Cosimo dei Migliorati, the nominal Cardinal of Bologna. It is at this date that Adam tells his story of the Roman wolves: " Being lodged near the Palace of St Peter, I watched the habits of the wolves and dogs, often rising at night to this end. For, while the watch-dogs barked in the gateways of their masters' houses, the wolves carried off the smaller dogs from the midst of the larger ones, and

although, when thus seized, the dogs, hoping to
be defended by their larger companions, howled
the more, yet the latter never stirred from their
posts, though their barking waxed louder. And
so I pondered on the same sort of league which
we know doth exist in our parts between the great
men of the country and the exiles of the woods."
The English priest might have added that when
he rose to watch the wolves of the Campagna
fighting the dogs of Rome in the streets of the
Eternal City, he was observing in brief the history
of feudal and ecclesiastical Europe.

Rome at the opening of the fourteenth century
was corrupt beyond imagination. The story of
the false prophet calling himself Elias who came
to Rome at that date baffles belief. It is told by
Adam of Usk as a somewhat ordinary affair. It
is therefore not altogether surprising that a man
like Baldassarre Cossa should have attained the
popedom, even though the appointment took place
in pursuance of the reformatory measures of the
Council of Pisa. What, however, does seem surprising, is that the new Pope, the nominee of the
Council of Constance, should have treated with
contempt the reformatory measures of the Council.
John XXIII. had been deposed, Gregory XII.
had agreed on terms to retire, and only the
hardy and respectable Benedict XIII. stood out.
Legal proceedings had been taken against him,
and at the thirty-seventh session of the Council

he had been deposed, and the faithful released from their obedience. It is true that the brave old Pope of Avignon stood out against the sentence till his death in 1423, but the Council having done all that was possible to heal the Schism, on 11th November 1417 appointed a Roman of famous birth, Otto Colonna (Martin V.), as Pope.

One of the first acts of the new head of the Church, the leader of Roman society, was to recall Baldassarre Cossa to Rome, to rescue him from the tyranny of the secular arm, and give this putative poisoner of Pope Alexander V. his proper place in the College of Cardinals. He received him, we are told, with manifestations of honour and gratitude and made him the doyen of the Sacred College. Cossa was gratified by this tardy recognition of his merits and became the faithful subject of the Conciliar Pope, dying at last in the sulphurous odour of sanctity and amidst the benedictions of the Church which he had ruled. This was one fruit of the Council of Constance, a tangible proof that a party of moderate reformers cannot afford to enter into compromises with the fundamental evils of their time. The Schism was not even ended. It was destined to become visible once more before the revival of Rome as the city of the Renaissance.

The Council of Constance touched the problems of the day from other points of view than that of its disastrous settlement of the Great Schism of the West. It dealt elaborately with questions of discipline and

questions of faith, and in the lengthy debates on these
questions which were now stirring all Christendom,
Gerson played a brilliant and leading part. The
conservatism of his views was in remarkable contrast
to the views of earlier years. But he had come to
the conclusion that the social peace of Europe
depended upon the re-establishment of the Catholic
faith and the Catholic discipline. He carried all
before him. Mr Neville Figgis, writing upon
" Politics at the Council of Constance," [1] declares
that he was "great indeed . . . great in his influence and his activity, greater perhaps in his
learning and devotion, greatest of all in the possession of a sense of humour, which leads him to
omit many arguments on account of his 'brevitatis
amor.'" His sympathy must in many ways have
been with John Hus, who appealed against his excommunication by Pope John XXIII. to the Council.
" He was not prepared to submit unconditionally to
the authority of the pope, for Christ, he contended,
is the real head of the Church, the pope only His
representative, and His commands are supreme.
A pope in mortal sin has no authority, is indeed
Anti-Christ, and from Anti-Christ he was entitled
to appeal to Christ. By what right have you
deposed John XXIII., demanded the bold prisoner,
if the power of the Pope is absolute?" [2] Such a

[1] *Transactions of the Royal Historical Society* (1899), vol. xiii.
(N.S.) pp. 108-9.
[2] Mackinnon's *History of Modern Liberty*, vol. i. pp. 160-1.

declaration must have made Gerson wince. He could scarcely share his friend d'Ailly's high opinion of the Pope. He was actually at the moment engaged on his work dealing with the distinction between true and false visions, in which he lays stress upon the free and voluntary power of God. Yet Gerson could not afford, it was not expedient, to rank himself on the side of even such a mild heretic as Hus, and with all the learning of Paris he overwhelmed the noble Bohemian and was consenting unto his death.

Yet not even the dire pressure of expediency and the dangerous gift of compelling eloquence could altogether blind the eyes of the great Chancellor to the dangers of his policy. The forces of iniquity were strongly represented at the Council of Constance. It was their business to destroy not only Wiclivism, not only Hussism, but all the purifying forces of Christianity, and even conservative reformers like Gerson himself. The dreamer of dreams, the seer of visions, the honest sower of good seed, were all alike abhorrent. Christ Himself they would have persecuted as they persecuted those who followed Him. This hatred of all that was good must have been the motive that inspired the attack upon the Brothers of Common Life, one of whom at that very time was writing the purest devotional treatise, not only of that, but of any age. Matthew Grabon led the attack. He asserted that a community could only be lawful if approved by the Holy See. The whole matter was referred for Gerson's decision, and for once he resisted the temptations of expediency. He rejected the doctrine that such a Brotherhood required the sanction of a Pope who was possibly, and in fact usually, immersed in mortal sin. The proposition touched the very ground of the convictions that had ruled all his earlier life. The Brothers of Common Life held the two chief doctrines of his faith, that purity of life and the education of children were the twin saviours of society. The work of the Brotherhood as a purifying and teaching community was now famous through the West, and the attack was in itself an outrage. Gerson therefore upheld in this matter his position as an educationalist and a contemplative.

In one other matter he faced the evil advisers of the Council. He deliberately attacked the doctrines of Doctor Jean Petit, the member of his own University who had attempted to justify the murder of the Duke of Orleans. Petit was now dead, and though his views were formally condemned, the matter was carried no further. The Duke of Burgundy was too formidable a person for even a General Council to attack. From that moment, however, Gerson was a marked man. Despite all his diplomacy and eloquence, men recognised that his heart was with the movement of reform and that he was in spirit, if not in action, a member of the Invisible Church. Such a man was abhorrent to Burgundians and Vaticanists alike. There was no doubt as to the party he would follow if Christianity

in the Apostolic sense ever again became a power
in Europe. For the moment, however, he was
covered by the safe conduct granted to the
Members of the Council, and up to the last shone
as the leader of the Assembly. At the forty-
fifth and last session held on April 22nd, 1418,
Cardinal Zabarella, Archbishop of Florence, addressed Gerson officially as "Superexcellens Doctor
Christianitatis," and thenceforth he was known to
Christendom as the Most Christian Doctor. From
this almost theatrical blaze of glory, he stepped
straightway into darkness and exile. His attack on
the Burgundians and probably his want of sympathy
with the Roman cardinals had made his position not
only politically impossible but absolutely dangerous.

With his two faithful secretaries he fled, on
the breaking up of the Council, from monastery to
monastery, pursued by the fear of assassination.
In Bavaria he learnt that Paris had been ravaged
by insurrection and massacre. Return was obviously
impossible. He eventually reached Rathembourg in
the Tyrol, and from there he retired on the invitation
of the Duke of Austria to the safe Benedictine abbey
of Moelck. There he wrote his *Theological Consolations*. In 1419 the murder of the Duke of Burgundy
rendered a return to France possible. But all
ambition seems to have passed from the great Chancellor's heart. He returned, but not to throw himself
into the passionate intrigues of Paris, or into the
whirl of events that followed the stricken field of

Agincourt, when patriotism was made subservient to the conflicts of revolutionary parties and a typical visionary of the fifteenth century, in the person of Jeanne d'Arc, became the saviour of society. The world no longer appealed to him. It had been too much with him. Its choicest fruits had proved but dust and ashes. His triumphs at Constance had been unprofitable. The evil spirit had been expelled from the Church, the Church itself had been swept and garnished. But the expelled spirit, now united with its spiritual leaders in corruption, had returned to Rome, and the last state of that Church was worse than the first. Well might Gerson put aside the world. It had rewarded him in its accustomed fashion. He had left France and his own people in almost regal guise. He returned to France to throw himself in his brother's arms and to declare that he was a mere suppliant for the mercy of God. He came to Lyons, to the monastery of the Celestines, of which his brother John was the first prior, and there he lived for four years, engaged in prayer and contemplation and in the writing of devout works.

It has been suggested that he wrote *The Imitation* partly at the Abbey of Moelck and partly or mostly at Lyons. I can see no evidence to support this view. When at Moelck the bitterness of the reaction after the glorious ending of the Council of Constance was with him, and we know in fact that his *Consolations of Theology* were written there and largely consisted of a reasoned attack on his old enemy long dead, Jean Petit. This was not the spirit of the *Imitation,* not the atmosphere in which the *Imitation* could have been written. Men do not beat dead dogs with one hand and write down with the other the painful aspirations of the purified soul. It is true that when Gerson had settled in Lyons about the year 1420, his mental and spiritual view of life was in harmony with the outlook of parts at any rate of the *Imitation.* But at that date I have no doubt whatever that the *Imitation* was already written. I have elsewhere discussed the date of composition of the little treatises that form this work, and it seems to me impossible to suppose that they were completed later than the year 1420. I think 1410 is more nearly the date. If this is so, it is clear that Gerson could not have been the author. It is moreover certain that the *Imitation* was complete in 1425, and it appears to me improbable in the highest degree that this elaborate and highly finished work was written between 1420 and 1425 by a man prematurely old, filled with disappointment and sorrow and divorced by every consideration of human nature from the supreme structural artificiality of the *Imitation.* The work was built up phrase by phrase. It is a complex mosaic, built in accordance with a definite scheme. It is not such an outpouring of the human heart, fluent but brimming over with learned memories, as must have proceeded from the pen of Gerson, such an outpouring as did in fact more than once come from his pen.

Moreover, not only is the date and spirit of composition against the theory that Gerson wrote the work, but the style itself has absolutely no point in common with Gerson's style, the style of a scholar, reminiscent at every turn of classical learning and the Latin philosophy of life.   Had Gerson written the *Imitation*, it would have contained, not some poor half-dozen echoes of classical thoughts, but a classical illustration in every paragraph.   That is Gerson's manner, but it is not the manner of the author of the *Imitation*.   It is probable, however, that Gerson's sojourn at his brother's monastery did in some way affect the history of the authorship of this work.   Copies of the *Imitation* were spreading over Europe after the year 1420, and it is more than probable that a copy came to the Celestine monastery at Lyons and was in later years attributed to the prior.   This seems the rational explanation of the Aronensis manuscript.   Gersen is certainly Gerson, and there is something unreasonable in the attribution of this manuscript to an abbot created for the purpose.   So many early manuscripts were attributed to the Chancellor of Paris, that it seems unreasonable in the extreme to argue that, because the "o" has become an "e" another author has to be found.   In fact two of the British Museum manuscripts have this peculiarity in an intensified form. In one of these manuscripts the Chancellor is called "Gerseem," and in the other "Gersem."   Other imaginary claimants would have been created, no

MS. IN THE BRITISH MUSEUM (HARL. 3216) OF THE TREATISE "DE IMITATIONE CHRISTI." THE MS. IS DATED "21 DEC., 1451." PART OF CAP. I. (LIB. I.) IS HERE REPRODUCED.

doubt, to fit these names, had it not been for the fact
that the word "Chancellor" in each follows. The
omission of the word "Chancellor" in the Aronensis
manuscript has led to one of the most inane
controversies, perhaps the most inane of mediæval
or modern times. There can be no reasonable doubt
that every manuscript that bears a variant of the
name Gerson was intended by the scribe to be attributed to the great Chancellor of Paris. That Gerson
was familiar with the work might possibly be adduced
from the fact that in his *De Laude Scriptorum* he
refers to the Canons Regular of Saint Augustine as
good copyists, if we couple it with the fact alleged
by M. Masson that one of the most ancient manuscripts of the *Imitation* was transcribed by, or by the
direction of, Thomas de Gerson, a nephew of the
Chancellor and a canon of Sainte Chapelle. In any
event it is certain that if the work did come Gerson's
way he would have read it with profound admiration,
for its attitude of humility accorded with the mental
and spiritual resignation of the broken statesman of
Constance. It may well have been at this time that he
wrote his *De Meditatione Cordis*—repeatedly in after-
times treated as an integral part of the *Imitation*—
and the fact that this work was known to be his may
have associated his name with the *Imitation*. In
any event Gerson, a voluminous author who did not
love anonymity, and whose works written during the
ten years of meditation and obscurity were for
the most part, at any rate, signed, never claimed the

D

authorship. The apparently very early date of the Burney manuscript in the British Museum which bears his name no doubt offers some difficulty if it was in fact written before his death. But the difficulty, as I have pointed out elsewhere, is not a very serious one, unless of course the origin of the manuscript can be traced to Lyons. There is no vestige of a claim by Gerson to have written the work. Indeed his time seems to have been filled with other labours, and continual introspection.

In 1423 he left the Celestine monastery and took up educational work in connection with the little church of St Paul at Lyons and still wrote on. He taught the children in the cloister beside the college of St Paul, and there they learnt also to pray for him in the pathetic words, "Mon Dieu, mon Createur, faites misericordes à votre pauvre serviteur Jean Gerson." Here Gerson wrote his mystic commentary on the Song of Songs. He finished it on July 9th, 1429, and immediately fell into an ecstatic trance from which he never came back to common day. His poor children were with him each day, repeating for him the prayer he had taught them. On July 12th, 1429, he passed away from the world in which he had played so great a part. "Notre père Jean Gerson" had ended his strange career— a mystic after all and not a politician. The spiritual aspirations and ideals that had inspired his earliest labours crowned his latest efforts. To instil into the education of youth the rapture of true religion was the solution that he offered first and offered last for the woes of the world. Such a conception is perhaps a better title to fame than the fruitless victories of the Most Christian Doctor in the Council of Constance.

Education is the only factor of progress, the future is in the hands of the little children, and it is in our power to make these children what we will. We may make them princes in all lands and give them power to change the very aspect of society. This Gerson fully recognised and ceaselessly preached. The poorest child was a child of God and an inheritor of the kingdom of Heaven, and therefore it was as great an honour to teach him as to teach the Dauphin. Gerson absolutely realised the relationship of education to the social problems of his day and of all days. He was in fact the first educationalist in our modern sense of the term. It is not possible fully to realise the age of Thomas à Kempis unless we obtain some conception of what education meant and whither it was drifting in that period of blood and iron, and also some appreciation of the mysticism or quietism which at this time lay beneath much, if not all, of the religious revivals in various parts of Europe. One particular combination of education and mysticism produced d'Ailly and Gerson, another Gerard Groote, Florentius, and à Kempis, and another the English mystics, and yet another visionaries such as Catherine of Siena and Bridget of Sweden. Education, on the other hand, uncombined with mysticism or any other form of earnest religion, was responsible for the cold and not very striking intellectuality of the average Paris doctor, the men who followed Jean Petit and justified the Burgundian reign of terror.   Education, moreover—the mediæval education of the mind alone—in no way checked the unrestrained lawlessness and debauchery of the Papal Courts at Avignon and Rome.   True education, then as now, comprised the training of the spiritual and moral as well as the purely intellectual faculties.   If either of these faculties were left untrained, there was a form of education that produced some abnormality of nature varying from the calculated degradation of Cossa to the ignorant but noble mysticism of Jeanne d'Arc.

It will be convenient to glance somewhat rapidly at the educational system in force about the year 1390.   In education, as in everything else, the decline had begun and mediævalism was fighting in strange, strenuous fashion against forces that it could neither understand nor adequately resist.   In the same way that mediæval armour in the fifteenth century—as illustrated in the sepulchral brasses both of England and the Continent—steadily increased in weight and complexity with the addition of grotesque devices for resisting the new mysterious gun, did the intellectual armour endeavour to meet new explosive ideas.

A desperate effort was made to carry the old educational ideals, the old strict training in the Trivium and the Quadrivium, into battle against the intellectual moral and spiritual unrest of the world. The Doctors of Europe, gathered together at Constance and elsewhere to do battle for old ideals, were cumbered by an intellectual armour that robbed them of all real strength. For a time it was possible by a continual increase of the outward strength of this armour to resist the new mysterious forces that were awakening in Europe. But the great century that saw the armour of the knight attain its most monstrous proportions, saw also its disappearance. The same is true of the armour of the Doctor. Knight and Doctor indeed vanished together. The gunpowder of the Reformation swept both away as the symbols of material and spiritual brigandage.

It must never be forgotten that the Roman Church performed a great work for education and culture during the Early and Middle Ages. Learning must inevitably have died after the decay and end of the Western Empire, had it not been for the efforts, first of the monasteries, and then of the popes and provincial councils. The names of the councils and popes who strove to keep alight the flickering torch of learning are forgotten to-day. Who remembers the *Capitulare Aquisgranense*[1] of the year 789 A.D., when the first Adrian was pope; the *Theodulfi Capitulare* (caps. 19 and 20) of the year 797, and the third canon of the Second Council of Chalons-sur-Soane of the year 813, both in the days

[1] Cap. 72 *de schola.*

of Leo III. ? Who recalls the thirty-fourth canon *De scholis reparandis pro studio literarum*, promulgated at the Concilium Romanum of the year 826, when Eugenius II. was pope, and who ever heard of the *Schola Cantorum* of Pope Sergius II. ? The seventeenth canon of the Council of Turin, held in the year 858, when the first Nicholas was pope, possibly only interests the antiquarian mind, while the reference to education in the same year at the Synodus Carisiaca (cap. 12) is probably too obscure for any notice, and the tenth canon (*de scholis sacrae scripturae, et humanae literaturae instituendis*) of the year 859 at the Council of Tullens is perhaps as dead as the rest. These and other instances of the scholastic activity of the Holy See and the bishops of the Church when all the world of thought and light seemed dead are, however, important as proving that in the dark eighth and ninth centuries there was a force in the world drawing men on to some far dawn.

Indeed the scholastic legislation of the Church in the ninth century is directly responsible for the educational organisation of the twelfth century. It is customary to attribute to the combined effects of the decrees of Third and Fourth Councils of Lateran [1] the establishment throughout Christendom of a diocesan system of schools. The Concilium Romanum of 826, however, in its thirty-fourth canon, really created this system. The canon runs : " We are

[1] Third Council of Lateran (cap. 18), 1179 A.D. ; Fourth Council of Lateran, 1215 A.D.

informed that in certain places there are to be found
neither teachers nor provision for the study of letters.
Therefore in all bishoprics and among subject peoples
and other places wherein the necessity arises, let all
care and diligence be exercised in the appointment
of such masters and teachers as shall have at heart
and diligently teach the study of letters and of the
liberal arts and the sacred doctrines. For in these
things are the divine commands most clearly mani-
fested and declared." The Fourth Council of Lateran
was but carrying this express provision into effect
when it declared, in 1215, that "in every cathedral
or other church of sufficient power the Dean or
Chapter must appoint a schoolmaster to whom the
revenue of a prebend should be given. In a
metropolitan church a theologian must also be
appointed. And if the church cannot support both
a grammarian and a theologian, it must provide for
a theologian out of its own revenues and see that
provision is made for the grammarian in one of the
churches of its state or diocese." These provisions
of the twelfth and thirteenth centuries were but a
re-statement of a recognised position made with
the view of encouraging and indeed of enforcing the
higher clergy to carry out their educational duties.
In the larger cities throughout Europe, however,
the diocesan system of education was and had long
been in force. It is more than probable that one of
the earliest permanent officials of a cathedral was
the *Magister Scolarum*, and that this official eventu-

ally became through the importance of his position the chancellor of the diocese. Mr A. F. Leach, dealing with the fact that the chancellorship of Southwell Minster was annexed to one of the first and most ancient prebends—Normanton—tells us that this is a " fact which suggests that here, as at York and Waltham, the *Magister Scolarum* was the earliest dignitary. All collegiate churches and cathedrals were bound to keep schools ; and the teaching of the grammar school was regarded in early days as an even more important part of the duties of the official, who afterwards was known as the chancellor, than his legal and clerkly business. It is indeed only through his scholastic functions that, at Southwell, we learn there was a chancellor at all, though when he appears in written evidence he no longer teaches school himself, but only sees that others do so. This he does not only in Southwell Grammar School itself, but throughout the county of which Southwell was the mother church. So the schools of the University of Oxford were, at first, under the superintendence of the Chancellor of Lincoln, as chancellor of the mother church of the diocese."[1] The diocese of Worcester gives us evidence as to the Magister Scolarum in that county,[2] while we get a particularly valuable instance of the powers of this official in the case of the diocese of London.

[1] *Visitations and Memorials of Southwell Minster*, Camden Society, 1891, p. xli.
[2] *Register of Worcester Priory*, pp. cx., 130 b, Camden Society, 1865.

As this is apparent in the very period with which I am dealing, it is desirable to refer to it somewhat fully. Dugdale, in his *History of St Paul's Cathedral*,[1] tells us that a charter of Richard, Bishop of London, in the time of King Henry I., "granted to one Hugh, the schoolmaster, and his successors in that employment, the habitation of Durandus at the corner of the turret (*id est* the Clochier or Bell Tower), where William the Dean of Paul's had placed him by his the said Bishop's command. To which Hugh succeeded in that place Henry, a canon of the same Bishop's, that had been educated under the said Hugh . . . which Henry had such great respect in those days that Henry de Bloys, that famous Bishop of Winchester (who was nephew to the King), commanded that none should presume to teach school within the whole city of London, without his licence, excepting the schoolmasters of Saint Mary Bow, and St Martin's le Grand." Newcourt, in his *History of the Diocese of London*,[2] adds a little to this information. He tells us that Henry the Chancellor of Paul's " was that Henry for whom Henry de Blois (who was Bishop of Winchester from 1129 to 1171 and nephew to the King) had such great respect, that by virtue of his legatine power he commanded the chapter of St Paul's and William the Archdeacon, and their ministers, by virtue of their obedience, that after three times calling, they should pronounce the

[1] Edition 1658, pp. 8-9.
[2] Edition 1708-9, p. 109 ; see Round : *Commune*, p. 117.

sentence of anathema against all those who without licence of Henry, the Master of the Schools, should presume to teach within the whole city of London, except those who were masters of the schools of St Mary le Bow and St Martin le Grand." The school was further endowed by Richard Nigel in the time of Richard I. I think, however, we must date the origin of the school earlier than the beginning of the twelfth century, for the educational canons of 826 A.D. promulgated by Pope Eugenius II. must have applied to an important cathedral church such as St Paul's, especially when we consider the fact that King Alfred is known to have initiated an educational revival on a large scale and must have been familiar with the specific educational provision of the English Provincial Council of Cloves-hoo and the Council of Rome in 826.[1] The school of Paul's, however, became a national factor under the patronage of Henry of Blois soon after the Norman occupation of England. During his occupation of the see of Winchester, Henry of Blois was an important social force in England. A contemporary writer,[2] under the date 1171, tells us : " Henry, Bishop of Winchester, than whom never was man more chaste or prudent, more compassionate, or more earnest in transacting ecclesiastical matters, or in beautifying

[1] *Concilium Cloveshoviense*, Canon vii., A.D. 747 (Wilkin's *Concilia*, vol. i. pp. 95-6, London, 1737).

[2] See *Annals of the Church of Winchester from the year* 633 A.D. *to the year* 1277, *by a monk of Winchester*, translated by Rev. J. Stevenson (*Church Historians of England*, vol. iv. part i., 1870).

churches, departed to the Lord, whom with his whole heart he had loved, and whose ministers, the monks and all other religious, he had honoured as the Lord Himself. May his soul repose in the bosom of Abraham." To the noble prelate, Alexander III., a great educational pope, wrote sometime after 1159 : " In future be more careful to see that nothing be demanded or even promised for the licence to teach anyone. If hereafter anything is either paid or promised, take care that the promise is remitted and payment restored, such charge being null and void— knowing what is written—'freely thou hast received, freely give.' Indeed if anyone by reason of such a prohibition delay the institution of masters in fit places, you may, by our permission, disregarding all gainsaying or appeals, appoint in such places for the instruction of the people, prudent, honest, and discreet men."[1] We may be sure that the bishop who had done so much for education in London did all that was possible to carry out this truly national policy. We know that even the reign of Stephen did not altogether check educational work,[2] and thirty years after the death of Henry of Blois the Council of Westminster ordained, "let nothing be exacted for licences to priests to perform divine offices, or for licences to schoolmasters. If it have been paid, let it be restored."[3] Alexander III. did not

---

[1] *Corpus Juris Canonici*, par. 2, col. 768 (Editio Lipsiensis secunda post A.L. Richteri, 1879-81).

[2] See *Sarum Charters and Documents*, Rolls Edition, p. 8.

[3] Johnson's *Laws and Canons*, vol. ii. p. 89.

restrict his educational efforts to England. In 1170 it was especially provided with respect to the Gallican Church: "pro licentia docendi pecunia exigi non debet, etiam si hoc habeat consuetudo " ;[1] and this provision was confirmed for the whole of Europe by the Third Lateran Council in 1179. From the middle of the twelfth to the middle of the thirteenth century, Rome indeed was doing all that was possible to secure the spread of education throughout Europe, and her efforts were admirably seconded in many cases, despite the disorders of the times, by great ecclesiastics like the Bishop of Winchester, and by a devoted clergy. The corruption of Rome in the fourteenth century did not undo her noble earlier work. We find that the great London school for which Henry of Blois had done so much had for the year 1190 become an educational centre of the greatest importance, and as in the two succeeding centuries the supremacy was maintained and the curriculum practically unchanged —save for the increasing application of Aristotelian scholasticism—I may quote William Fitzstephen's description of the curriculum,[2] as rendered by Stow. " Upon the Holydayes, assemblies flocke together about the Church, where the Master hath his abode. There the Schollers dispute ; some use demonstrations, others topicall and probable arguments, some practise Enthimems, others are better at perfect

---

[1] *Corpus Juris Canonici*, par. ii. col. 769.
[2] See *State Intervention in English Education*, by the present writer (Cambridge University Press, 1902), p. 43.

Syllogismes : some for a shew dispute, and for exercising themselves, and strive like adversaries : Others for truth, which is the grace of perfection. The dissembling Sophisters turne Verbalists, and are magnified when they overflow in speech ; some also are intrapt with deceitfull arguments. Sometime certaine Oratours, with Rhetoricall Orations, speake handsomly to perswade, being carefull to obscure the precepts of Art, who omit no matters contingent. The Boyes of divers Schooles wrangle together in versifying, and canvase the principles of Grammar, as the rules of the Preterperfect and Future Tenses. Some after an old custome of prating, use Rimes and Epigrams : these can freely quip their fellowes, suppressing their names with a festinine and railing liberty : these cast out most abusive jests, and with Socraticall witnesses either they give a touch at the vices of Superiours, or fall upon them with a Satyricall bitternesse. The hearers prepare for laughter, and make themselves merry in the meane time."

London at the end of the twelfth century was in the way to become, as Paris was becoming, one of the great Universities of Europe. The sudden development of Oxford and Cambridge checked the expansion of the ancient London school into a university, but the school itself remained famous and efficient, and was a type of the cathedral schools scattered all over Europe, some of which became universities in answer to some peculiar geographical or social demand, but all of which for two centuries, from the end of the twelfth century, remained centres of learning, sending forth travelling teachers possessing the licence to teach and actually teaching in the parochial schools of Europe—the A B C schools, the reading schools, the reading and writing schools—and in the important song and grammar schools that led directly to the universities, and possessing the curriculum —the very advanced curriculum — indicated by Fitzstephen. The Church, despite the terrible growth of ecclesiastical corruption in the fourteenth and fifteenth centuries, kept a firm hold upon the schools. We see this in all parts of Europe. At Beverley, at the opening of the fourteenth century, the independent schoolmaster is crushed out of existence.[1] At Dundee at the beginning, and at Glasgow at the end, of the fifteenth century, the same thing happens.[2]

In 1364 we have at Geneva an appeal to the Pope at Avignon, informing his Holiness that the titular canon of the chantry of St Peter, who was the *Magister Scolarum* of the city, had put up for sale the right to control the city and diocesan schools, and as no purchaser had been found, " quod scole ipse quasi ad nichilum sunt redacte." [3] The Pope ordered the canonical provisions on the subject

[1] *Memorials of Beverley Minster*, edited by A. F. Leach (Surtees Society, 1897), pp. lix.-lxv.

[2] *State Intervention in English Education*, p. 113.

[3] *L'Académie de Calvin*, par Charles Borgeaud, Genève, 1900, p. 6.

to be enforced. The dispute between educational authorities had, however, temporarily destroyed a flourishing local system. The schools in this case, as in many other cases from about this time forward, were taken over by the municipal authorities.

In London in 1393-4 we find the Magister Scolarum and the ecclesiastical authorities which controlled schools situated in Peculiars engaged in a desperate controversy. London was then so important, and the ecclesiastical courts so powerless, that the Church could not retain its control without the aid of the secular arm, and in consequence we have a petition to the Crown from the Archbishop of Canterbury, the Dean of the Free Chapel of St Martin le Grand, and the Chancellor of the church of St Paul's, relating a strange tale. The petitioners declared[1] that by the laws spiritual, and immemorial custom, the ordinance, the disposition, and examination of the masters of certain schools of the faculty of Grammar within the city of London, and the suburbs of the same, belonged to them, but that nevertheless strange unqualified masters of grammar held general schools in grammar in the said city, to the deceit and illusion of the children, and to the great prejudice of the King's lieges, and of the jurisdiction of Holy Church. The masters of the official schools of St Paul's, the Arches, and St Martin's had pursued their right against the intruders in the

[1] *State Intervention in English Education*, p. 41.

Court Christian, and the intruders in reply began proceedings in the secular court to secure a declaration of their right to teach grammar without ecclesiastical licence. The breath of the Reformation was in the bold demand. It was a deliberate attack in one of the greatest centres of Christendom on the immemorial claim of a Church now notoriously corrupt to control all and every form of education. The significant fact is that the attack was successful. The petition remained unanswered, and seventeen years later the English courts declared in the *Gloucester Grammar School Case*[1] that there was by the common law of the land, apart from prescriptive rights in particular cases, a perfect right to teach : " It is a virtuous and charitable thing to do, helpful to the people, for which he cannot be punished by our law."

This was in the year 1410, a date when new educational ideas were in the air, when the Brothers of Common Life had given their new conceptions of teaching to the world, when Gerson was proclaiming to Europe that education and the inner life alone could save society, when à Kempis was penning his immortal claim for the free intercourse of man with God, and the spiritual necessity for the following of Christ. The decay, the failure of the great mediæval educational system had begun, but the whole of its vast machinery was open to the new ideas, and they flowed in. The

---

[1] *Year Book, anno* 11, Henry IV., p. 47, Case 21.

University corporations of masters and scholars associated for this or that scholastic discipline, for the study of the liberal arts, of theology, medicine, or law, was gradually permeated with the new unrest that ran before the new learning. In Paris, with its faculties of arts, theology, and canon law—the very home of that study of Aristotle which from the end of the twelfth century had substituted dialectic and philosophy for the ancient Quadrivium—Gerson thundered forth the needs of the inner and the outer life. The life of Oxford was Wiclivism at this date, and the revival of Church authority as shown in Archbishop Arundel's Constitutions of 1408 was short-lived. In so far as the University was under the control of the Church, it slowly died during the fifteenth century, and the University of Paris about the middle of the century refused even to recognise Oxford as a seat of learning. Lollardism alone kept the flame of culture alive and made Oxford fit to receive the new learning at the end of the century. The mediæval system of education was in process of dissolution at the date when the *Imitation* first appeared, and the question for the world was whether the old machinery could be adapted to new needs, new methods of thought, new spheres of learning, new manners of life. The revolution in religion that accompanied the revolution in thought alone rendered this possible. The machinery of society was rapidly fitted to the new

E

ideas, and for this we have in some large measure
to thank the practical work of mystical thinkers
who did all that was possible to soften the rudeness
of revolution, and to make the hearts of men move
with their minds. The *Imitation* was, indeed, unconsciously enough, a representative of a force that
rendered possible the transition from mediæval to
modern manners without a disastrous loss of power,
and without a revolution that could only recreate by
virtue of destruction. That force was the Christian
mysticism which then as now lay beneath the
varying living forms of Christian profession.

In England the influence of mysticism was
peculiarly apparent. England gave to the world
extraordinary developments both of scholasticism
and mysticism. It was Anselm who first definitely
enunciated the principal of scholasticism in its
application to the interpretation of scripture. Had it
not been for his work, Petrus Lombardus could never
have created that logical structure which comprised
the whole dogma of the mediæval Church. These
men were realists and believed in the reality of
general ideas, and therefore in a sense made logically
possible the later extreme mystical position. Their
great descendants Albertus Magnus and Thomas
Aquinas were for this reason no opponents of the
mystic position. If general conceptions represented
real facts in nature, the general conceptions of the
mystic were real. The two Victorines—Hugo of
St Victor, a Saxon, and Richard of St Victor, a

Scotsman—had already realised this and evolved their mystic doctrine by the means of scholastic logic. Richard definitely built up a philosophical theory of contemplation as an intuitive fact distinguishable from cogitation (the ordinary power of reason) and meditation (the power of reflection upon a single subject). Another man closely connected with England, Bonaventura, carried the mystic doctrine into daily life and showed its practical application. At this stage, the mid-thirteenth century, the theory of religion was partly controlled by the Aristotelian logic and partly by the new transcendental logic of the mystics. One force or other was, however, certain sooner or later to dominate the religious world. The decision came in the fourteenth century. Another Englishman, Duns Scotus, gave the final development to scholasticism. He carried it beyond the bounds marked out by Albert and Aquinas. He forced it to its ultimate and logical conclusions, and justified Roger Bacon's appreciation of its essential unreality.

When Duns Scotus died in 1307, the final stage of mediæval scholasticism was in its prime. It was an intellectual triumph of the highest order, but it had ceased to have any relationship to life or religion. Throughout and beyond the fourteenth century, it was magnified as an intellectual weapon, but it had ceased to have any meaning in the life of the people. Realism vanished from the scholastic philosophy, and with realism the relationship of mysticism and scholasticism. Paris became the school of the nominalists, and formal theology was controlled by nominalism. Universals, she taught, were mere words, mere figments of the imagination. From that time the official faith of the Church became hard and materialistic, and the mystics alone represented the Invisible Church and alone carried on the Platonic conceptions of Saint Augustine. It was in England that the mystic movement was carried to its height. From early Norman times England had exhibited a vigorous Christianity that depended but little on the dictates of Rome. Even when Rome, in the reign of Henry III., possessed her maximun of power in England, the spiritual movements of the time seem to have developed quite freely. The monastic life from the time of Stephen appeared to offer singular attractions to English men and women, and in the twelfth century we get a curious mystic development, not so much among the thinkers, as among the people. The monastic discipline was not enough. An extraordinary desire for the eremitical life arose. The hermit was regarded as a person of peculiar and enviable sanctity. A desire to experience the fullest sweetness of religious contemplation became widespread. Men and women of all classes wished to live the mystic life. Mr Horstman tells us that " the chief conquests of the English mystics lay on the side of practical, moral, and popular theology, and gradually they—even more than Bonaventura—

absorbed the whole sphere of religion. They taught the way Godward, the way of perfection, the ruling of life ; and at the same time they undertook the edification and instruction of the people, of the poor and illiterate, taught them the elements of the faith, the commandments, the sacraments, etc., and took hold of the pulpit ; or they instructed the parish priests how and in what to teach the people, how to use the sacraments, etc., and made model sermons, festivals, legendaries, for their use. The sermon, the homily, the epistle, the religious tract became the mouthpiece of the mystics." [1]

It is in this mystical movement—of which a vast unprinted literature survives—that we find the origin of Lollardism and of the Reformation in England. It is in this movement that we find the leaders in their efforts to reach the people turning from Latin to the vernacular in England, Germany, and (later) France. Gerson, as we have seen, at the end of the fourteenth century wrote for the people in the vernacular ; à Kempis in at least one tract did the same ; but a century earlier, David of Augsberg (who died in 1272) and Meister Eckhart wrote in German, and in the first half of the fourteenth century Richard Rolle of Hampole, the great English mystic, wrote many of his tracts in the English tongue. Some mention must be made of Richard Rolle de Ampulla, for it would be difficult to over-estimate the indirect influence that he

[1] *Richard Rolle of Hampole*, by C. Horstman, vol. i. p. xii.

exercised over the development of religion in Europe. He was born about the year 1300 at Thornton, near Pickering, in the North Riding of Yorkshire. He died on September 29th, 1349, at Hampole. His life was an extraordinary exhibition of what appears to the ordinary mind as perverted holiness. He was sent to Oxford, and there he met scholasticism in its latest, its most brilliant, and its most arid stage of development. It filled him with horror, and after a brief sojourn at the University he fled at the age of nineteen. He returned home and, at an age when the pleasures of life seem most vivid, he decided to become a hermit. He found a patron who supplied him with a cell and the necessaries of life. He set to work to realise in his own person the mystic ideal. He passed through the stage of Purification, or Purgation, and was able to declare that he had reached that point of purification when even remorse is washed away. From that stage he passed to the second, the stage of Illumination, where the mind is kindled to the perfect love of God. Two years and eight months were spent in the exhausting exercises that could produce this subjective state. Then the hermit passed into his final stage, that of Contemplation, where man "sees into heaven, with his ghostly eye." In this extraordinary state he lay absorbed for a year, until he attained to the final goal of this type of mystic. He acquired the *Calor*—the inward spiritual warmth, almost indistinguishable, he tells us, from physical warmth—and

RICHARD ROLLE OF HAMPOLE (1300-1349) FROM COT-
TON MS. FAUSTINA B. II., PART II., FOL. 114ʙ—
BRITISH MUSEUM).

DR. C. HORSTMAN CONSIDERS THIS A CONTEMPORARY PORTRAIT, BUT
IT IS DIFFICUT TO DATE THE MS. EARLIER THAN 1400. IT MAY
WELL BE A COPY OF A CONTEMPORARY EFFIGIES

nine months later this was followed by the *Canor*—
an all-pervading melody of uncloyable sweetness.
These experiences were accompanied by the *Dulcor*
—a sense of spiritual happiness ineffable and divine.
A period of four years and three months had given
to Rolle these results. Henceforth, he declared,
they remained with him in various forms of intensity.
He laid claim to saintship as a being wholly
absorbed in the love of God, and he asserted that
the gift of Canor—that spiritual music, that invisible
melody, celestial sound, the greatest gift of God to
men—brought him within the select class of the one
or two " privilegiati." [1]

What is one to think of all this? It is certainly repellent, it is still more certainly dangerous. It shows us the road to that most
horrible of all heresies—Perfectionism—and it establishes, I think, the reactionary character of all excessive religious emotion. But nevertheless it is a
fact that has to be considered, very seriously to be
considered, in an age that promises to become as
mystical as the fourteenth century. It must be
remembered that Richard Rolle did not stand
alone. Some mystics went even further. It was
claimed that Saint Bernard actually saw God face
to face. We have to realise that there is in human
nature this extraordinary quality : the desire to
become unclothed of human · characteristics while
still in the flesh, and to take part in a life which is in

[1] See *Richard Rolle of Hampole*, vol. ii. (Introduction *passim*).

truth pure mentality. Rolle deliberately endeavoured to realise in his own person the transcen-
dentalism of Richard of St Victor, and he claimed
success. But the important point about this extraordinary mystic, for my present purpose, is his career
after he attained the summit of subjective holiness.
He returned to the world and became a wandering
preacher, and at last took up his pen. Here the
practical North Country Englishman came to light.
His treatises were treatises for the people ; treatises
of the practical mystic life; treatises of well-living
and well-doing, not untouched with the spirit of
social revolt that was to become a political factor in
his spiritual descendants—the preaching friars in
russet grey who filled the countrysides with
Lollardism. It is a curious story. This man was
not a monk. He was a layman who determined
to live the mystic life and inculcate it by word and
example. Having done his work, he settled down,
at the age of forty, at Hampole, as the spiritual
adviser of a community of nuns, and there nearly
ten years later he died, probably of the plague, which
was then raging in England. Wiclif was then twenty-
five years of age. Even a cursory examination of
Rolle's Latin writings show a remarkable unity of
ideas between him and the author of the *Imitation*.
His description of love and the true lover is almost
identical with the wonderful fifth chapter of the
book of Internal Consolations. Walter Hilton, of
whom I have written in another chapter, was a

follower of Rolle, and certainly those who are tempted to think that Hilton wrote the *Imitation* will find a measure of support in the influence that Rolle undoubtedly exercised over Hilton. It might well be contended that only one intimately acquainted with Rolle's writing could have written certain parts of the *Imitation*. The answer to such a contention is that the English and Flemish mystics had a common ground of thought and faith.

When we turn from England to Germany and the Low Countries, we find that mysticism had there, as in England, become a great though intangible force. Mechthild of Magdeburg, "prophetess, poetess, Church reformer, quietist,"[1] had stated the mystical case and its relation to social problems before the birth of Meister Eckhardt in 1260. This famous Dominican became Vicar-General for Bohemia in 1307, and from that date was engaged in preaching his transcendental doctrine of the God-head, "the universal and eternal Unity comprehending and transcending all diversity." A Neo-platonist, he gave a new currency to Plotinian conceptions, and though his doctrines were officially condemned in 1329, and he himself forgotten, his realistic conception of God had become part of the mystic creed. As Mr Inge points out, his philosophy "does not keep clear of the fallacy that an ascent through the unreal can lead to reality." But nevertheless he brought home to innumerable congregations the

[1] *Light, Life and Love*, by W. R. Inge, p. xi.

reality of God as an object of mystic contemplation. His successor was John Tauler, born about the same year, 1300, as Richard Rolle. He died in 1361, after a life of parochial work. To mystics of this type "everything, every event, every person, is a vision from the Unseen, a voice from the Inaudible. He lives in a world of parables, full of spiritual significance; and while for him there is a Real Presence everywhere, he finds it also most truly and effectively where it is most clearly discerned by faith. . . . In God's dealings with man from first to last he perceives a harmony that implies a foreshadowing of the last in the first, of the whole in the part; and in this way he can find an interpretation of spiritual value even in the thoughts of good men, who have pictured to themselves, inaccurately, it may be, as to matters of fact, God's earlier work in the creation of the world and of man."[1]   Tauler dwells continually on the oneness of man and God. "The soul is so nobly united to God, and, at first, in such a supernatural way, that man might justly shun, like death, every thought that could interfere with this union. The thought, which is to receive God into itself, can endure nothing strange. Therefore desire only invisible and inexpressible things" (Sermon on St Paul). The Plotinianism of Eckhardt is made into a practical mysticism by Tauler.

[1] See *The Inner Way, being thirty-six sermons for festivals by John Tauler*, with an invaluable introduction by the Rev. A. W. Hutton (p. xxxiii.).

God is not the only reality. Man is also a reality, but one that desires to merge into God. With Tauler we ascend through reality to reality. When we pass from John Tauler to Henry Suso (1295-1365), we meet a mystic more of the type of Richard Rolle—but possibly less spiritual and more sensuous and even more neurotic than was Rolle. He had something of the same influence over à Kempis that Rolle had over Hilton. John of Ruysbroek (*Doctor Ecstaticus*) is even of more importance in considering the spiritual heritage of Thomas à Kempis. He was a Fleming, born in 1293 at Ruysbroek, near Brussels. He founded the Abbey of Groenendael in the forest of Soignies, where he died in 1381, shortly after the birth of Thomas à Kempis. At Groenendael he was visited both by Henry Suso and Gerard Groote. These visits may be said definitely to connect à Kempis with the schools of the German and Flemish mystics. Ruysbroek's work has been carefully analysed by Mr W. R. Inge in his learned and brilliant Bampton Lectures for 1899.[1] In his abbey "he wrote most of his mystical treatises, under the direct guidance, he believed, of the Holy Spirit." He "was not a learned man or a clear thinker. He knew Dionysius, St Augustine, and Eckhardt, and was no doubt acquainted with some of the other mystical writers; but he does not write like a scholar or a man of letters. He resembles Suso in being more emotional and less

[1] *Christian Mysticism*, p. 167.

speculative than most of the German school." He elaborated the order of mystical evolution. He conceived a " Ladder of Love," the rungs of which were " (1) good will ; (2) voluntary poverty ; (3) chastity ; (4) humility ; (5) desire for the glory of God ; (6) Divine contemplation, which has three properties— intuition, purity of spirit, and nudity of mind ; (7) the ineffable, unnameable transcendence of all knowledge and thought." Still more elaborate is his analysis in his *Ordo Spiritualium Nuptiarum*. "The three stages are here the active life (*vita actuosa*), the internal, elevated, or affective life, to which all are not called, and the contemplative life, to which only a few can attain." He held with Rolle that there were *privilegiati*, and his analysis of life is not unlike that which Rolle endeavoured to realise. But his final position is more philosophic : " What we are, that we intently contemplate ; and what we contemplate, that we are ; for our mind, our life, and our essence are simply lifted up and united to the very truth, which is God. Wherefore in this simple and intent contemplation we are one life and one spirit with God. And this I call the contemplative life. In this highest stage the soul is united to God without means ; it sinks into the vast darkness of the Godhead." Here we have Eckhardt and Tauler mingled into one : but Rolle and Suso add some softening touches to this cold philosophic ending to the soul's spiritual journey. " We must be conscious of ourselves in God, and conscious of ourselves in ourselves.

For eternal life consists in the knowledge of God, and there can be no knowledge without self-consciousness." It was, we must believe, some such thought that drove Richard Rolle back to the world ere he reached the Ruysbroekian consummation of contemplation.

From John of Ruysbroek we pass to a figure who was destined to give a new and practical impulse to mysticism, and to create the means whereby the *Imitation* was given to the world. Gerard Groote was a contemporary of Wiclif, but unlike Wiclif and unlike Hus, he originated no political changes. An itinerant preacher, as Wiclif was, he nevertheless made no appeal, direct or indirect, to the spirit of social reform that then was stirring in the hearts of men. A spiritual descendant of the German and Flemish mystics, he went about preaching the doctrine of the inner life. The life story of Gerard Groote is a strange one, and it throws a vivid light on an important aspect of society in the days when the tide of time was turning from its ebb in the direction of the Reformation.

Groote was born at Deventer in the year 1340. Educated at the grammar school of that town and later at Aix-la-Chapelle and Cologne, he passed with a sound reputation to the University of Paris, where he drank deep of the well of scholastic learning and became a profound theologian and a nominalist of the recognised type. He left Paris perhaps twenty years before Gerson came to give the University new light and leading. Groote was a man of wealth, position, and learning, and was able to select his own career. He chose, after some experience of teaching and lecturing at the University of Cologne, that ecclesiastical career which was open to laymen. The choice appears to have been the result of a visit paid to the papal court at Avignon in the year 1366. That city must in many ways have impressed the mind of a man whose great gifts enabled him to see below the surface of things. St Bridget of Sweden in that very year was urging Urban V. to return to Rome. Rumours of the new mysticism, fear of all that it might mean, filled the papal court. There can be no doubt that at the very time when Groote was in Rome the mystic shadow lay on the soul of Urban—the shadow that was to drive him to Rome in the succeeding year, and was to brood over and haunt his death-bed. Gerard Groote had his first acquaintance with mysticism in the strange palaces of a dead faith. His immediate reward was scarcely spiritual. On his return to Deventer he found various benefices to his hand, as well as the canonries of Utrecht and Aix-la-Chapelle. In his new career he led a life of cultured and learned leisure, enjoying the present hour as his wealth and inclination dictated, and waiting for the further preferment that his gifts and his position were certain to secure. The turmoil of Europe, the struggle for temporal and spiritual power, meant as little to him as it meant to the average church dignitary of the eighteenth century.

He was a man who had great possessions—material, intellectual, and, as the sequel proved, spiritual. To him in due time, as to his prototype in the Scriptures, the call came, and, unlike that friend of Christ, he was not found wanting. From time to time he had been stirred by vague calls to life. He had heard them in the cathedral services and in the daily life of the church. But they came from other sources also. An unknown hermit came to him one day in the public street—did it recall the mystic rumours of Avignon—and cried, " Another man thou oughtest to become." Later in sore sickness he abjured his Parisian studies in astrology and magic. At last in 1374 the final call came, bringing inherited traditions of piety to light. A university friend, now a Carthusian prior, called upon him at Utrecht and eloquently bade him take up the following of Christ. There was little hesitation. The seed of mysticism suddenly germinated. Without hesitation or regret he renounced his benefices, his canonries, his ecclesiastical ambitions, and took holy orders as a deacon. Such were the contrasts of the fourteenth century : to take orders was to end the ambition of the Churchman. For five years he trained his heart. He visited the monastery of the Augustinian Canons at Viridis Vallis ; he communed deeply with John of Ruysbroek ; he entered the Carthusian House at Monichuysen. Under the influence of the ascetic life and of the mind of Saint Augustine he returned to the world in 1379, intent on its conversion. He became an itinerant preacher, and travelling on foot from place to place, might have been taken in his coarse grey robe for one of Wiclif's friars, who at this very date were tramping the roads of England and haranguing the multitude in churchyards and market-places.

But it was a very different though a not less wonderful work that he performed. He had three aims : one was to bring a sense of repentance home to the many; another was to introduce a new life into the work of the parochial clergy ; and the third was to make the education of the people a vital fact in the economy of the land. He devoted his wealth to this third aim, and not only intimately associated himself with the teachers in the chief schools, but also founded schools where they were needed. His itinerant preaching, which attracted multitudes, aroused ecclesiastical jealousy and suspicion. He, however, held the episcopal licence, and for five years continued his itinerant work. At last in 1383 his licence to preach was withdrawn on the ground that he was not a priest, but only held deacon's orders. His appeal to Urban VI. failed, and his labours henceforth were limited to educational work. But he was no longer alone. He had awakened spiritual life throughout the diocese of Utrecht and the work of preaching had in fact achieved its object. Centres of spiritual life, tiny congregations of humble Christians, had been formed in many places, and these congregations supplied him with a band of followers who could aid him in the great educational work that he had designed.

His educational and religious aims were well known, and young men seeking instruction came to him from all parts. We are told that as far as possible he educated them free of charge, and gave them copying work to do, for which he paid them. The result of his efforts was the formation of little bands of young men who lived together a life of simplicity, purity, and strenuous work. These were the Brothers of Common Life, and even in Gerard Groote's life there were several definite communities. He also founded a House of Sisters of Common Life at Deventer. Two of these communities are of particular interest to us, though they only formed part of a movement that spread throughout Germany and was vigorous until it was absorbed into the larger issues of the Reformation. It appears to have been Groote's first disciple, Florentius Radewin, who suggested the formation of communities entirely supported by the joint-earnings of the copyists, who in the days before the introduction of printing received good payment. Groote consented, and advised the drawing up of rules regulating the common life. The first community was that formed at Deventer under Florentius. It was immediately followed by the House of Sisters in the same town, while the community at Zwolle was probably formed about the same time. With this community Groote stayed, and made it an effective

F

mission centre. Groote felt that if the organisation that had suddenly come to life was to grow and prosper it must have a centre ; so, after consulting with John of Ruysbroek, he decided to found a central monastery to which all the scattered communities could look. The members of these communities were bound by no vow. Membership was from first to last voluntary. To pray, to preach, to teach, and to live by labour were the sole duties of the members. Gerard Groote did not live to see his work reach its prime. His desire to found a central monastery, a community of Canons Regular of the Order of Saint Augustine, to watch over the praying and teaching Order that he had founded, was, however, brought nearly to accomplishment. He could not himself found the monastery, for his great fortune had already been exhausted ; but at this very time a friend dying of the plague bequeathed the necessary money to carry out what he knew to be Groote's desire. Unfortunately Groote himself, waiting upon and consoling his dying friend, contracted the horrible disease and died. That was in the year 1384. His ministry had lasted, from the date of his call, some ten years. The results of that ministry are still felt throughout civilisation to-day.

Gerard Groote on his deathbed had exhorted his followers to found the monastery which he saw to be necessary as a rallying-point of the Brothers of Common Life. He had even indicated the place—" a waste and uncultivated spot lying between Deventer and Zwolle . . . afterwards called Windesem or Windesheim."[1] The monastery, after the lapse of some years, was founded, and among the first six brethren was John, the elder brother of Thomas à Kempis.

The foundation of the central monastery of Windesheim led to the establishment of various other houses, including that of Mount St Agnes, which was founded in 1398, on a site which had been chosen by Groote many years before, as a Brother House for the Brothers who had originally settled in the neighbouring town of Zwolle. After Easter 1398 Brother John à Kempis was elected Prior of the small band of Augustinian Canons now gathered on Mount St Agnes. This was the spot where Thomas à Kempis was destined to spend his long and holy life, and to become the spiritual light of a great movement which was quietly spreading through Central Europe.

It is almost startling to turn from the restless lives of men like Rolle, Groote, and Gerson to the serene placidity of the life of Thomas Haemmerlein, the only one of the innumerable writers of the late fourteenth and early fifteenth centuries besides Chaucer, who has survived to our day. Other writers of that period are read out of curiosity or for the somewhat idle purposes of book-making; but these two are read of necessity. Their works

---

[1] See *Thomas à Kempis and the Brothers of Common Life*, by the Rev. S. Kettlewell. It is a laborious and invaluable work.

are part of the spiritual heritage of the race.
"Thomas à Kempis was born in the year 1379 or
1380 at Kempen, a small but pleasant town in the
diocese of Cologne, and situated about forty miles
northward of this city, in the flat and fertile country
bordering the Rhine."[1] His parents were of the
laborious yeoman or citizen class, persons of some
education and much godliness, who apparently had
come under the influence of either Tauler or Gerard
Groote. There seems to be some evidence to prove
that the mother taught in a little school, but at any-
rate we are told that she was "sedulous in the
education of her children, attentive to the concerns
of her household, active in her habits, very
abstemious, not given to much talk, and extremely
modest in her behaviour." She is "especially
mentioned for her distinguished piety and for the
influence that she exercised over her son Thomas in
early implanting in his mind the love of holy things."[2]
Her sons certainly followed closely in her footsteps,
as she followed in those of her husband. All that we
are told of this simple household recalls the household at Nazareth. We only know of two children,
John and Thomas. John was born about the year
1364, and was probably one of Groote's earliest
scholars. He had been sent to the school at
Deventer probably before the birth of Thomas, and
had been helped by the community of Brothers of

---

[1] *Thomas à Kempis and the Brothers of Common Life*, p. 27.
[2] *Ibid.* pp. 30, 31.

Common Life there. He must have been a witness
of the foundation of Groote's first community, and
have been intimate with Groote himself. Long
before Thomas set out from home for Deventer, John
had joined the Brotherhood; and when, after the death
of Gerard Groote, the monastery was founded at
Windesheim, he had been chosen as one of the first
six Canons Regular. In due time, when Thomas
was about thirteen years of age, in the year 1392, he
was sent to Deventer to join his brother. His
parents did not know that John was already settled
at Windesheim. This has always seemed to me a
curious fact, and it is still more curious that Thomas
with all his gift of penmanship, makes scarcely any,
if any, definite reference to his parents. There
seems a certain want of human lovingness, an
absence of the love of kind, in the apparent
seclusion of these two men from the dearest
ties in life. Yet it is probable that the absence
of any reference is due to the loss of documents,
for we know from his biographical writings that
Thomas was peculiarly susceptible to human friendship, and when Lubert Berner was called away from
the House to visit his sick father, Thomas records the
incident with pleasure. Moreover, the brothers were
certainly devotedly attached to each other; so that
we may perhaps assume that in this instance quietism
was not guilty of the ingratitude with which it is so
often degraded and stained.

It was a long tramp from Kempen in the diocese of

Cologne to Deventer in that of Utrecht, but the farther march on to Zwolle in the same diocese was a smaller matter. There the brothers met, perhaps for the first time, and there was sealed one of those deathless friendships that give such a human aspect to the character of Thomas Haemmerlein. The elder brother determined that the boy should follow the course of education that had been so great a source of spiritual strength to himself and so many of his friends. He therefore gave him a letter addressed to the saintly Florentius, the Rector of the Brothers of Common Life at Deventer. Florentius, the chief disciple of Groote, and himself a contemporary of Ruysbroek and Suso, received the lad with many welcomes. "When I came," Thomas tells us, "therefore into the presence of this reverend Father, he, being at once moved with pity towards me, kept me for some little time with him in his own house, and there he prepared and instructed me for the schools, giving me, moreover, such books as he thought I might stand in need of. Afterwards he obtained a hospitable reception for me into the house of a certain honourable and devout matron, who showed much kindness both to me and to several other clerks."

Between Florentius and Boheme, the rector of the town school, the boy fared well. It was a notable age in this respect. Education was ever free to those who could show an intellectual or a moral title to it. In this dark and troubled age man's intellectual birthright was respected more fully than in later times. Thomas Haemmerlein remained at Deventer about seven years. The public school was in fact, if not in name, a song-school, with such local modifications as had been produced by the influence of Groote. The rector was one of the vicars in the parish church, and he in part drew his choir from the school. The song-school in the fourteenth century gave what we should now call a sound secondary education of the classical type, with special attention to the spiritual needs of the children. The part that they played in the cathedral or church services as choristers rendered a special training in matters of ritual essential. But the education given was also preparatory to the prolonged university course, and à Kempis had as his master a distinguished university scholar, while he had in Florentius an adviser who was acquainted with all Groote's educational views, and was moreover a scholar and a saint. These seven years were, therefore, spent in an environment of the most helpful kind. The House of the Brothers was in intimate touch with the school, and after perhaps five years à Kempis entered the House and became acquainted with the daily life of the Brotherhood—a life laborious and simple, modelled on the methods of the early Christian Church. Their life became the pattern of his life. Almost unconsciously he became a member of the community, joining in their labours, and learning to take a share of the copying work which then formed a main source of income. There he found his first personal friend—if we except his brother—a boy of his own age, Arnold of Schoonhoven, a youth of admirable piety, whose sweet and amiable nature played no mean part in determining the direction of the mind of à Kempis.

By the year 1400, when Thomas Haemmerlein was about twenty years of age, his future seemed clearly marked out. He had attained to a degree of scholarship that would have enabled him to have taken up the specialised work of a university; he had become a copyist of no mean ability; he had absorbed the spirit of the Brotherhood in which he had lived. The serenity of his environment had become a necessity of his life. In any other air he would have pined and died; in these high altitudes he could live and could rejoice. Florentius in daily intercourse had woven round him the subtle spell of the simple life, and when manhood came it seemed a matter of necessity, both to the disciple and his master, that the youth should pass into a monastery of the Community. At this date John à Kempis was at Mount St Agnes, and thither Thomas was sent with letters recommendatory. Florentius had completed his work. He had moulded this young son of a Flemish peasant on the very pattern of Christ, and had made it possible for him to write a handbook for the followers of Christ. The two were never to meet again. "The good Father and sweet Master Florentius," as à Kempis calls him,

" died on the Feast of the Annunciation in the same year." His life was written by his disciple, who describes the end in touching words : " The power of intense love compelled them to weep for so dear a father, when the light and mirror of all the devout, the solace of all the sufferers, was taken away from this temporal light. But the pious faith of those who loved him, reflecting on the sobriety and modesty of this most excellent priest, was consoled by the hope of celestial glory that would not be denied to him through Jesus Christ, Whom he loved with all his heart, to Whom he perseveringly clung unto death, by serving Him in the full devotion of faith. . . . For whose praiseworthy life praise and glory be to Christ for ever, Who adorned our times with a star of so bright a lustre."[1]

Mount St Agnes is a solitary hill near Zwolle. It is now known as Agnietenberg. In the monastery here of the Canons Regular of St Augustine, Thomas à Kempis lived, with one brief interval, for seventy years. Out of the world it lay, out even of the ecclesiastical world, to which it nominally belonged. It knew nothing of Avignon, nothing of Rome. " Raving Paris, roaring London " were not within the sphere of its contemplation. It knew nothing of ambition, nothing of controversy, nothing even of the great spiritual movement of which it was the heart. It was the silent, motionless centre of a whirling and incomprehensible world. It was like

[1] *Thomas à Kempis and the Brothers of Common Life*, pp. 112-13.

a cathedral shrine in a great city, shut in from all
the noise and strife of progress, but typifying the goal
of progress all the while. The poor little monastery
was composed of a tiny group of men who thought
only of Christ and strove to imitate Him ; whose sins
were minute fallings away from their ideal of the
Man of Nazareth—sins wept over and watched ;
whose hope lay on the other side of the grave that
offered them no terrors ; whose faith came so near
to the faith of the first Christians that the days of
Christ seemed to have returned. Mount St Agnes
was the Little Gidding of the fifteenth century. It
represented the noblest form of Christianity that
that or perhaps any age could produce. The Rule
of the Community inculcated the fundamental law of
love towards God and man ; the lessons of humility
as taught by Christ ; the preparation of body
and soul for orderly prayer, by proper and simple
attention to both body and mind. Nothing in
excess was the ideal of the community. The body
was to be made absolutely efficient for the purposes
of the soul, and the duty of man to his neighbour
was to shadow forth the duty of man to his God.
Perfect simplicity in dress and manners, food and
drink, work and play, was the ideal for the body ;
perfect charity to all men, to the young, to the sick,
to the sinful, was the ideal for the mind ; and the
love of God which passeth all understanding was
the ideal for the soul. No selfish faith dominated
the members of this little community. They did not

seek *Calor*, *Canor*, and *Dulcor :* but they walked with Christ.

But nevertheless their life had many pleasures —it had all the pleasures of simplicity. John à Kempis, who ruled it from its foundation in 1398 till 1407, in addition to superintending the erection of the buildings, planted an orchard of fruit trees, and an arbour, as well as laying out a herb and vegetable garden. There were guest cells, and there were many opportunities for converse, especially at meal times. The work of copying and illuminating manuscripts was ever at hand, while the many services were a continual refreshment from labour. During the rule of John à Kempis, seven clerical and three lay brothers were invested. On June 10th 1406, Thomas Haemmerlein and Octbert Wild of Zwolle were invested as Canons Regular, also a lay brother, Arnold Droem of Utrecht, who brought many gifts and was appointed Refectorarius. In the year 1408 the brothers were parted. John was directed by the Chapter of Windesheim to form a new community at Bommel on the Rhine. The movement was slowly moving south and east. Brother William Vorniken from Windesheim succeeded him. "A lover of poverty and discipline," he ruled the little house until 1425. He subsequently became Father-General of the Order. "He enlarged the boundaries of the monastery; he built a new house for the husbandmen, and folds near at hand for the flocks; he planted divers sorts of trees, and among them those bearing fruit, in many places in the grounds belonging to the community; the rougher portions moreover of the mountain, which for the most part had been as yet untouched, he planted, and reduced the sandy tracts to service. He decorated the sacrarium with pictures, wrote books for the choir, and good copies for practising; he also illuminated many books." [1]

Such a life, with its simple pleasures and unassuming godliness, offered many attractions to the pious, and we find that in 1408 the first convent for Sisters of Common Life was established at Dieppenheim near Deventer. On April 8th 1412 the church on the Mount, dedicated to St Agnes, was consecrated. It had been many years a-building and the brothers had done much of the work themselves.

In the year 1414, Thomas à Kempis was ordained priest. Mr Kettlewell thinks that it was about this time that the *Imitation* was begun. There is some evidence that before this Thomas had written certain tracts. But certainly up to this date his time was full enough, and it is difficult to think that the four tracts of the *Imitation*, or any of them, were written by a man under thirty years of age. On the other hand, as is pointed out in another chapter, the manuscript evidence, for what it is worth, seems to point to an earlier date than 1414. This evidence requires consideration. It is at any rate certain that a complete copy of

[1] *Thomas à Kempis and the Brothers of Common Life*, p. 239.

the first three books was available by the year
1425. We know that à Kempis visited the mother
House at Windesheim in 1425, and Mr Kettlewell
suggests that he did so for the purpose of depositing
there the first three tracts of the *Imitation*. It is
certainly remarkable that a manuscript formerly
at Kircheim, and now in the Royal Library at
Brussels, should have the following important
attestation clause attached to it : " Notandum quod
iste tractatus editus est a probo et egregio viro,
Thoma Magistro de Monte Sanctae Agnetis et
Canonico Regulari in Trajecto, Thomas de
Kempis dictus, descriptus ex manu auctoris in
Trajecto, anno 1425, in sociatu provincialatus."
Mr Kettlewell translates this passage as follows :
" Let it be observed that this treatise has been
composed by a pious and learned man, Master
Thomas of Mount St Agnes, and Canon Regular
of Utrecht, called Thomas à Kempis. It has been
copied from the manuscript of the author in (the
diocese of) Utrecht, in the year 1425, and in the
Society's House of the Provincialate." It is in truth a
very striking coincidence that à Kempis should have
visited the house of the Provincialate—Windesheim
—at this very date, and certainly the fact appears
directly to connect this, the earliest dated copy, with
à Kempis. The copy itself is not in the handwriting of Thomas, but it may well have been
copied out at Windesheim from a copy deposited
there by à Kempis. What has become of this copy ?

In 1425 he began a lengthy work—the copying of the whole Bible in Latin. This laborious undertaking occupied him until 1440. About that year he began the final copy from his pen of the four books of the *Imitation*, and of others of his writings. This work was finished in the following year. " The venerable codex is now preserved among the manuscript treasures of the Royal Library at Brussels, where it is numbered 5855-5861. It is a small volume, composed of 192 leaves of paper, intermixed at irregular intervals with leaves of vellum, and written entirely by the hand of Thomas à Kempis, as is attested by the following inscription which ends the manuscript :—' Finitus et completus anno domini MCCCCXLI. per manus fratris thome Kempis in monte sancte Agnetis prope Zwollis.' The writer has placed at the beginning of the volume a table of the treatises therein contained, all of which are of his own composition. It is as follows :—

' In hoc volumine hi libelli continentur.
Qui sequitur me non ambulat in tenebris.[1]
Regnum Dei intra vos est dicit Dominus.[2]
De Sacramento. Venite ad me omnes qui laboratis.[3]
Audiam quid loquatur in me Dominus Deus.[4]
De disciplina claustralium. Apprehendite disciplinam.
Epistola devota ad quemdam regularem.

[1] First Book of the *Imitation*.   [2] Second Book.
[3] Fourth Book.   [4] Third Book.

Renovamini autem spiritum mentis vestre.
Cognovi Domine quia equitas judicia tua.
Recommendatio humilitatis. Discite a me.
De mortificata vita. Gloriosus apostolus Paulus.
De bona pacifica vita. Si vis Deo dignus.
De elevatione mentis. Vacate et videte cum
ceteris.
Brevis ammonicio. Ab exterioribus.'

"Although the different treatises are written on separate sheets of paper, and divided by one or two blank leaves, the manuscript is quite homogeneous. The whole is transcribed by the same hand, and no doubts have ever existed as to its authenticity and integrity. The date affixed to the last page is therefore applicable to the entire volume : it was finished and completed in the year 1441." [1]

The only other manuscripts that we have now extant from the pen of Thomas are (1) another collection of treatises composed by him and written out in 1456, "and removed from Mount St Agnes to the House of the Jesuits at Courtrai, and afterwards to that of the same society at Antwerp. It is now in the Royal Library at Brussels." (2) "A volume containing the "Sermones ad Novitios" and "Vita sancte Ledewegis," now preserved in the University Library at Louvain."

[1] *The Imitation of Christ, being the autograph manuscript of Thomas à Kempis ... reproduced in facsimile ... with an introduction,* by Charles Ruelins, Keeper of the Department of Manuscripts, Royal Library, Brussels.

The Autograph manuscript has had a curious history. It lay at St Agnes' until after the destruction of the House in 1559. It was found there in 1577 by Johannes Latomus, the Visitor-General of the congregation of Windesheim, and taken by him to Antwerp. It passed from him to Jean Bellère, a famous printer of Antwerp, who died in 1595. In 1590 Bellère gave the volume to the House of the Society of Jesus in Antwerp. On the suppression of the Society it was transferred to the Burgundian Library at Brussels.

These two manuscripts, the Kirchheim manuscript of 1425, and the Autograph manuscript of 1441, form what I may call the fundamental evidence for the authorship of Thomas à Kempis ; but, as we shall see in subsequent chapters, this evidence by no means stands alone. There is one piece of evidence inherent in the text of the autograph manuscript which is of great importance. It was first noticed by Dr Carl Hirsche of Hamburg. This is the use of a peculiar system of punctuation for the purpose of indicating a peculiar rhythm or musical cadence running through the entire work. This elaborate system is described by M. Ruelins as follows. We have "the full stop followed by a small capital, the full stop followed by a large capital, the colon followed by a small letter, the usual sign of interrogation, and, lastly, an unusual sign, the *clivis* or *flexa*, used in the musical notation of the period." This system

THE BEGINNING OF CHAPTER XI ("DE PAUCITATE AMATORUM CRUCIS JESU") OF THE SECOND BOOK OF THE TREATISE "DE IMITATIONE CHRISTI." FROM THE MANUSCRIPT OF 1441 IN THE HANDWRITING OF THOMAS A KEMPIS. (ROYAL LIBRARY, BRUSSELS, MS. 5855-5861.)

PART (BEGINNING "ET MUNERA QUAE POTES DARE ET INFUNDERE,") OF CHAPTER XXI OF THE THIRD BOOK OF THE TREATISE "DE IMITATIONE CHRISTI" FROM THE MANUSCRIPT OF 1441 IN THE HANDWRITING OF THOMAS A KEMPIS. (ROYAL LIBRARY, BRUSSELS MS. 5855-5861)

is used in a systematic fashion : " it indicates the external structure of the sentence, marks its out-line, and establishes the most complete harmony between the sentence and the internal structure of the ideas."

Now the importance of this question can hardly be over-estimated. In a subsequent chapter I have dealt very fully with a class of manuscripts of the *Imitation* that include only the usual first three books and are always entitled *Musica Ecclesiastica.* As will be seen, these manuscripts are particularly numerous in England, and were from very early times attributed to Walter Hilton without there being any idea that the *Musica Ecclesiastica* and the *De Imitatione Christi* were the same work. Specimens of this class of manuscript very rarely occur on the Continent.   There is, however, one in the Royal Library at Brussels entitled : " Hic est libellus qui vocatur musica ecclesiastica."   It ends : " Explicit liber interne consolationis id est tertius libri Musice ecclesiastice."   It is evidently of the English type.   How can we account for the title. Dr Bigg is clearly baffled by it.   He includes the whole of the four books under it, and tells us that " The meaning of this title is to be sought, not in the rhythmical character of the style—how could a book be said to be "about music" because it is musical ? —but in the subject.   The music is the Inner Life, or, more especially, the *melifluum Nomen* of the Redeemer."   This explanation, interesting though it

G

is, is nevertheless founded upon a misapprehension. The title of manuscripts of the class is not "de Musica Ecclesiastica"—though in some corrupt manuscripts the "de" may occur—but "Musica Ecclesiastica." It is a descriptive title, and most scribes took it in that sense, as may be seen from the illustration at the beginning of this volume reproduced from the manuscript "qui vocatur musica ecclesiastica" in the British Museum. The Four Latin Fathers are producing the ecclesiastical music. The title is taken partly from the cadence of the text, and partly perhaps from the Divine Music—the *Canor*—that sustained the mystic. But how can he connect Thomas à Kempis with this curious title? M. Ruelens has supplied the missing link. Adraan de But, a Flemish chronicler contemporary with à Kempis, writing under the year 1480, says: "Hoc anno frater Thomas de Kempis de monte Sanctae-Agnetis, professor ordinis regularium cano-nicorum, multos, scriptis suis divulgatis aedificat; hic vitam sanctae Lidwigis descripsit et quoddam volu-men metrice super illud : *Qui sequitur me*." The "volumen metrice descriptum" beginning *Qui sequitur me* was of course the "*Musica Ecclesiastica*" or the "*De Imitatione Christi.*" This, however, still leaves obscure the relationship of England to this par-ticular type of manuscript. It does not of course entirely dispose of Hilton's claim, but it does as-sociate à Kempis as well as Hilton with this par-ticular type of the *Imitation* manuscripts.

I must briefly conclude my account of the life of Thomas à Kempis. In 1425, Brother William Vorniken was promoted to be prior of Windesheim. The sub-prior of St Agnes, Brother Theodoric Clive, succeeded him as prior on the Mount, and in the same year Thomas à Kempis was chosen as sub-prior. Four years after his election happened the only event of public interest that occurred during his long residence at St Agnes. The people of Zwolle and Deventer refused to accept as the bishop of the diocese Sweder de Culenborgh, who had been confirmed Bishop of Utrecht against the wishes of the majority of the electors. The towns were placed under an interdict, and as the Canons of St Agnes decided to observe the interdict, they were driven out of their monastery by the enraged people. It was a melancholy exodus. The little army of martyrs stayed one night at Hasselt, and took ship for Friesland on their way to the House at Lunenkerc : this was in 1429, the year in which Gerson died. Between two and three years they were absent. For two years of the time à Kempis was with them. But in August or September 1431 he was called away to his brother John, who lay sick at the House of Bethania near Arnheim. For fourteen months he nursed him assiduously, till his death at midnight on November 4th, 1432. Thomas à Kempis is almost garrulous about the virtues of others in his records of the brethren. Of this beloved brother he says little.

He loved him too well to praise him. He baldly recites his various charges—his rectorship of the House at Arnheim, his priorship at St Agnes, at Bommel, at Haerlem, his rectorship of the House at Bronopia near Campen. "At length he came to the House of Bethania, which, being interpreted, is the House of Obedience, where he ended his days happily *in obedience*, and in a good old age, and was buried within the cloisters after vespers, when I was present, since I had closed his eyes." John à Kempis was sixty-seven. Forty years were to pass before the brothers were united beyond the grave.

Thomas returned from Bethania to St Agnes, for the House was once more open. He did not continue his office as sub-prior, but in later years he filled it once again and also served as procurator. In 1447 Prior Theodoric Clive resigned his office, since he was bowed with age. He was succeeded by Brother Henry Wilhelm of Deventer after a contested election. Thomas succeeded him as sub-prior. Three years later a terrible outbreak of the plague at Cologne called forth special exertions of the St Agnes Brothers, who took over a House of the Regulars in that town and served the people. By this date à Kempis was approaching old age, and he seems to have attained a certain fame, singularly displeasing to him, as a man of peculiar holiness. But though he avoided anything in the nature of assumed saintship, he laboured hard with pen and voice and took his pleasures gladly, reading his "little book in a little nook," or meditating in his cell or in the garden. It was about this time that he finished his second volume of treatises still extant. It ends, "*Anno Domini M.CCCC.LVI. finitus et scriptus per manus fratris Thomae Kempensis.*" He was then seventy-seven years of age. The years that followed, calm and beautiful as they are, are marked with the inevitable sadness of great age. Friend after friend died. Notice after notice he writes, in his book of records, of friends—many of them friends of his youth with whom he had lived in continual brotherhood. But what implies sadness to us, in an age when doubt seems to so many to have chilled the promises of death, was not perhaps a source of sadness to him. As life passed by he became more and more rapt in the mystic vision : " His cell was made to him a Paradise, the Church or choir a Heaven ; while the Word of God was his food, and the bread of angels his hidden manna to feed upon." He did not expect rest or peace in life, and therefore he found it. But he did not find it only in his visions. He declared, "In omnibus requiem quaesivi, sed non inveni, nisi *in Hoexkens ende Boexkens.*" The "little book in the little nook" still as years passed gave him pleasure and insight into divine things. But to him, as to every true mystic, age brought its consolation. " The bush is bare." At last the full conception of God dawns upon the watchful soul.

" The poet's age is sad : for why ? "

Browning answers the critic's question. The apprehension of God makes life fuller and not less full as the end draws near. It is not true to say

"And now a flower is just a flower."

But the poetry of nature is absorbed into the poetry of nature's Creator.

". . . the purged ear apprehends
Earth's import, not the eye late dazed :
The Voice said 'Call my works thy friends !
At Nature dost thou shrink amazed ?
God is it who transcends.' "

These last words of one of the greatest of modern poets have an application to the saintly mystic of St Agnes. The dying years passed swiftly on. The things of nature, the clamour of the outer world, the ceaseless stir of awakening Europe in no way break the things that belong to his peace. He had given his message to the world, and now he was realising his message in his own life. He still kept in touch with all that happened in the House, though he had long ceased to be its sub-prior. He still jotted down its chronicles. The last entry was made under the date January 17th, 1471 : " Died early in the morning after high mass, a devote laic, John Gerlac, a native of Dese, near Zwolle, nearly seventy-two years old. He had lived with us for more than fifty-two years in great humility, simplicity, and patience, enduring much toil and penury. And

among other virtues which he possessed he was pre-
eminent chiefly for that of taciturnity, so that through
a whole day he would say very little : also in his
labours, and while performing other duties, he was
an example of silence." Silence was about to fall
upon the Saint of the Mount. An entry in the
Chronicle tells us that on July 26th, 1471, "at the
close of a long summer's day, after *compline*," he
died. His long eventless life of more than ninety
years was over. The "purged ear" long had
caught the heavenly music. The rest is silence :
but such a silence, we may believe if we hold
the mystic faith, as is full of harmony and ripe
with eternal life. Not in vain had he cried in the
Oratio Aurea,[1] "*Protege et conserva animam servuli
tui inter tot discrimina vitae corruptibilis, ac,
comitante gratia tua, dirige per viam pacis ad per-
petuae patriam felicitatis et claritatis.*"

The age of Thomas à Kempis was one of contrasts vivid and significant. We pass from the
depths of wickedness to the heights of saintliness
and spiritual rapture within the confines of the same
Church. On the one hand we see atheism avowed
and shameless, on the other an intensity of belief'
that would seem to make even reasonable doubt poor
and naked. At this distance of time we see clearly
enough into the strata of religion in the fifteenth
century. We see a Visible Church claiming to base

[1] Lib. iii. cap. 59. So-called in MS. note to Ulm edition (B.M.).

its authority on its corporate position, its immense wealth, and its immemorial traditions. We see in fact that it is supported by an Invisible Church which preserved the faith that alone makes the existence of a Church tolerable. Had the Invisible Church ceased to exist, the organised forms of Catholicism must have passed away. It was this Invisible Church that made the Reformation possible, and so preserved the organisation of Christianity in Europe from dissolution. In this, from the social point of view, lies the value of the all-pervading mystic movement that resulted in the Reformation and found its spiritual crown in *The Imitation of Christ*. Certainly there are lessons for to-day in the spiritual history of the fourteenth and fifteenth centuries. Now as then we are on the verge of great changes : then it was the Renaissance of Letters that was coming, coupled with the Reformation and the discovery of the Far West. To-day a different Renaissance, a different Reformation, a different discovery are at hand. Science takes the place of Letters, a social Reformation takes the place of a political and religious Reformation, the discovery of the Far East—the awakening of Japan and China—take the place of the discovery of the Far West. History does not repeat itself, but the same principles are at play. Mysticism too is now as widespread, as deep-rooted as when the German mystics taught and thought. Europe and the Churches of Europe have before them much the same problem that was before them in the fifteenth century. How will they solve it? Will practical mysticism conquer once more as it conquered four centuries ago, or will all-pervading Doubt take the place of the unwavering Faith that alone rendered modern Europe possible?

SOME FIFTEENTH CENTURY MANU-
SCRIPTS AND EDITIONS OF THE
IMITATION

THE British Museum manuscripts of the *Imitation* are six in number. They offer some features of considerable interest and are in excellent condition. Two are of very early date and are possibly the earliest extant manuscripts of the work. One of these early manuscripts should play an important part in any adequate discussion as to the authorship of the four treatises, for it is attributed to John Gerson. None of these manuscripts appear, however, to have been used with effect by any of the many militant writers on this vexed question. Mr Kettlewell cursorily examined them, but with so little care that he even misdates one that is specifically dated. They probably interested him little, since they offer no direct support to the authorship of Thomas à Kempis. The oldest manuscript is one of the Royal Manuscripts and is indexed under Codex 8 C. vii. This Codex begins with lives in Anglo-Saxon of St Agatha and St Agnes. On folio 22b begin a series of theological treatises (such as the *De Contemplacione* beginning on folio 121b), all in ecclesiastical hands of about the

PART OF THE FIRST CHAPTER OF THE FIRST BOOK OF THE TREA-
TISE "DE IMITATIONE CHRISTI." FROM THE IMPERFECT ROYAL
MS. OF THE FIRST BOOK. 8.c.vii. (BRITISH MUSEUM)

THE MANUSCRIPT IS UNDATED BUT IT BELONGS TO THE BEGINNING OF THE FIFTEENTH
CENTURY AND IS PROBABLY THE EARLIEST EXTANT MS. OF THIS WORK (CF., MS.. BODL.,
758, DATED 1405).

same date and prefixed by the following' rubric :
"In hoc versu ostendit quadrupliciter debemus
laudare beatam virginem Mariam videlicet, quia
est utilis, nobilis, mirabilis, amabilis, et quod prima
laus invitat nos ad ejus honorem. Secunda ad ejus
timorem. Tercia ad laborem. Quarta ad amorem."
The *De Imitatione Christi* manuscript begins on folio
149, and follows straight on without any break from
a short treatise of the usual theological type. The
manuscript consists only of twenty-four chapters of
the first book and the greater part of the twenty-
fifth or last chapter of the same book. It ends
abruptly at the bottom of a folio and presumably
continued on succeeding folios now lost. There is
nothing to show whether there was only one of the
four treatises or more, or even all. It is not, however, an unreasonable suggestion to make, that whoever tore off the succeeding folios did so with the
purpose of securing some other work beginning on
the next folio. Now the place where the manuscript
ends is almost the end of the first treatise. Therefore at the top of the next folio there began either
the second treatise of the *Imitation* or some other
work. No one would have any reason for separating
the second treatise from the first, but a person may
well have had some reason for separating some
independent treatise from the treatise beginning *de
imitatione Christi et contemptu mundi*. For this
reason I think that this was a manuscript of the first
treatise only, which in all probability was current

before the other treatises.   We know that in fact
this first treatise does occur by itself, for we have
a manuscript at the Bodleian Library and very early
printed editions of this first book only.   It is therefore not at all unlikely that an early draft of the
first treatise was current before the others, and was
thus incorporated in this collection.   This fact is,
I think, confirmed by the date of the manuscript.
The Museum authorities date it as early fifteenth
century.   This may mean any date between 1400
and 1440.   The latter date appears to be almost
out of the question.   A somewhat careful search
has not revealed any middle or late fifteenth century
manuscript written in a hand that in the least
resembles this ecclesiastical hand.   The nearest
manuscript so far as the formation of letters goes is
a manuscript in the Bodleian Library (MS. Bodl.
758) on *The Passion of our Lord* by Michael de
Massa, an Austin Friar, and dated 1405.[1]   There is
a distinct resemblance between the two hands, but it
must be noticed that one manuscript is in English
and the other in Latin, so that it is perhaps not a
proper test to compare them.   On the other hand,
it might be said that a resemblance in handwriting
which appears in two languages ought not to be
neglected.   Of course, if the hands are the same,
it does not follow that the dates of the manuscripts
are the same.   A man's age makes very little difference to his handwriting, and it might well be that the

[1] See *Paleographical Society*, Series II. Plate 134.

Massa MS. was written when the style was current, and the *Imitation* MS. by a scribe who retained in his old age a style then out of fashion. As against this, however, it must be noted that the Massa manuscript appears to be the latest dated manuscript in this particular style, and the law of probabilities is as much in favour of the earliness of the *Imitation* as of the Massa manuscript. The latter might be the late survival, and the former an example of a current style. In that event the *Imitation* manuscript would belong to the fourteenth century, and this would render possible the argument in favour of the authorship of Walter Hilton. This, however, is not likely, and we may take it that the manuscript is not earlier than the Massa manuscript. It may therefore be as early as 1405, and it may also be as late as 1440. On the whole it seems not unreasonable to adopt an approximation to the earlier rather than the later date, in view of the possibility that this manuscript only consisted of the first of the four treatises. That would point towards an early origin and therefore an early date of copying into this Codex. It is to be noticed that this manuscript varies in some ways from the accepted text. The title of the first chapter usually runs : *de imitatione Christi et contemptu omnium vanitatum mundi*. The title in the Royal manuscript runs: *de imitatione Christi et [vanitate et] contemptu mundi*. The words in square brackets have been added by a somewhat later hand. Another difference is that the opening quotation from St John's Gospel, *Qui sequitur me non ambulat in tenebris* usually given, is varied and completed by the addition of the words *sed habebit lumen vitae.* The manuscript does not in fact belong to the type of manuscripts usually associated with the Autograph manuscript of 1442. Neither, however, does it belong to what I may call the "Hilton" type, of which the best dated instance is the Magdalen manuscript of 1438.[1] It is on the whole not absurd to contend that this British Museum manuscript is the oldest extant manuscript of the *Imitation.* It is true that it may possibly be as late as 1440, but the probabilities seem to indicate that it was written between 1405 and 1420.

But whatever its age may be, it is probably not much older than the next manuscript to which I shall refer. The manuscripts themselves cannot be compared, as they are in hands incapable of comparison, the one being a peculiarly ecclesiastical and the other a purely literary hand. This second manuscript is numbered 314 in the Burney collection of manuscripts. The Burney catalogue of 1840 refers it to "*Sec.* 15 *ineuntis.*" The view that this manuscript belongs to the "beginning" of the fifteenth century makes it an important document. The authorities are at present inclined to confirm the view of the specialists of 1840. At any rate it cannot be later than 1440, and there is really very

---

[1] This type is represented in the British Museum under the usual title—*Musica Ecclesiastica.*

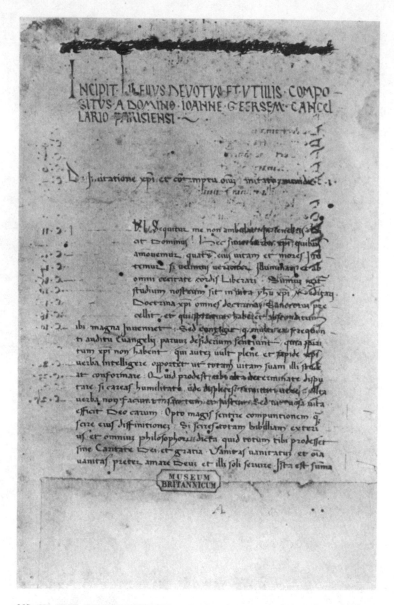

MS. IN THE BRITISH MUSEUM (BURNEY 314) OF THE TREATISE "DE IMITATIONE CHRISTI." THE MS. IS UNDATED BUT IT WAS WRITTEN PROBABLY NOT LATER THAN 1420. PART OF CAP. I. (LIB. I.) IS HERE REPRODUCED.

little reason to suppose that it is as late as this. It is in a small or minuscule humanistic Italian hand. It is written on paper, and has many points of resemblance to a manuscript of Terence also on paper in a renaissance hand and dated 1419. The observations as to the fixing of dates of manuscripts made above apply generally, and it would of course not be safe to say that this manuscript can also be dated 1419. But the probabilities are equally in favour of an earlier or a later origin within a short range of years. The specialists of 1840 plainly gave it an earlier origin, for to anything later than 1420 we could not apply the phrase " Sec. 15 ineuntis." This document is clearly one of the earliest manuscripts of the *Imitation*. If it was written before 1419, it is earlier than the manuscript in the Royal Museum at Brussels, which has the following passage at the foot of the first page : " Notandum quod iste tractatus editus est a probo et egregio viro, magistro Thoma, de Monte Sanctae-Agnetis et Canonico regulari in Trajecto, Thomas de Kempis dictus, descriptus ex manu auctoris in Trajecto, anno 1425, in sociatu provincialatus." If we take this to mean that in the year 1425 the work was attributed to à Kempis, we must in the weighing of evidence set up this British Museum manuscript against the Royal Brussels Museum manuscript. The former manuscript is probably the earlier of the two, and yet it is absolutely explicit as to the authorship, for it begins : "Incipit libellus devotus et utilis compositus a domino

Joanne Geersem Cancellario Parisiensi." This manuscript was almost certainly written in the lifetime of
Jean le Charlier de Gerson, who ceased to be Chancellor of the University, of Paris about 1419 and
died in 1429. If it was written in his lifetime, it is
probable that it was written before he retired from
the Chancellorship of the University, for the scribe,
one may surmise, would not call him the Chancellor
of the University if he had ceased to occupy that
position. This to some extent corroborates the
early date of the manuscript. It is noticeable
that the word "compositus" is used with respect
to Gerson, while it is used in no manuscript with
respect to à Kempis. It is also noticeable that
the *Imitation* should have reached Italy at so early
a date if it was written by à Kempis.

The manuscript offers difficulties that do not seem
to me to have been cleared up by the advocates of
the à Kempis authorship. As an advocate of that
authorship, as one who has practically no real doubts
as to that authorship, but who also believes that the
case against à Kempis should be stated in all its
strength, I am inclined to explain this manuscript as
follows. The debates at the Council of Constance
had made Gerson perhaps the most notable figure
in the religious world of Europe. His flight after
the Council was ended, and his retirement into a
purely contemplative life, added to the interest that
attached to any works that came from his tireless
pen. This work suddenly appeared without the

name of any author attached. The very anonymity seemed under the circumstances to indicate the authorship. It may very well be that a copy of the work fell into the hands of an Italian scribe directly after the sessions at Constance had ended, and Gerson had fled from the vengeance of his Burgundian enemies. If that were so, the scribe would very naturally have attached Gerson's name to his copy —the name of the most famous religious thinker in Europe, now suffering exile and persecution—and so may have given us the copy that lies in the British Museum to-day. In any event the fact that this very early copy bears Gerson's name as the undoubted composer is one that has to be reckoned with in any adequate discussion of the problem. It shows that before the date of the autograph copy Gerson was supposed to be the author, and the fact of the authorship is stated with a clearness which does not appear in any early manuscript that supports the claim of the Augustinian canon. I am convinced on other grounds that Gerson was not the author, but I can only account for the early attribution of the work to him by the explanation that it was the persistent practice in the Middle Ages to attribute anonymous works to certain popular writers. Everything in England of a mystical character was attributed first to Rolle and later to Hilton ; and Gerson, as the greatest contemplative writer on the Continent, was naturally accepted as the author of the *Imitation*. Fine distinctions of style

H

did not trouble the scribes—a work from the pen of the Most Christian Doctor was worth more than a work from the unknown pen of a monk in the far-off independent diocese of Utrecht.

The remaining British Museum manuscripts of the *Imitation* can be dealt with more briefly. The Harleian manuscript number 3216 is dated at the end, "21 Dec. 1454." No author is named in the manuscript, but a much later, probably a modern hand has added on the first folio "Thomas de Kempis de Imitatione Christi." The only real point of interest about this manuscript is the fact that it proves that as late as 1454 the work was passing from hand to hand unrecognised. The Hilton class of manuscripts—the *Musica Ecclesiastica* class—are further evidence of this, but they have a different origin. The fourth manuscript I shall notice is the Additional Manuscript, number 11,437. This is undated, but was probably written between 1465 and 1470. It is in a German hand much larger than but somewhat resembling the hand of Thomas à Kempis himself. This manuscript attributes the work to "Cancellarius Parusiensis" (*sic*). It contains two books only of the *Imitation*—not *three* books, as stated in the British Museum manuscript catalogue of 1905—and is a bad copy in the way of text and spelling—cf. *Parusiensis*. It begins on folio 110 of the codex. A fifth manuscript is an interesting example of the *Musica Ecclesiastica* type. It is a Royal Manuscript (7 B viii.), with a magnificently illuminated frontispiece. It is in a Flemish hand of the late fifteenth century, not later than 1480 or earlier than 1460. The superb frontispiece—which is reproduced as a frontispiece to this book—represents the ecclesiastical music as given to the world by the four Latin Fathers. Gregory the Great as Pope is playing a two-manual organ, the bellows of which are pumped by Saint Jerome dressed as a Cardinal. Two bishops (Augustine with book and crook, and Ambrose with a cross) are apparently singing to the music. We look through an open window to a green landscape. The work which follows the illumination is attributed to no author. After the *Registrum* the work begins as follows : " Incipit liber interne consolacionis qui vocatur musica ecclesiastica. Et dividitur in tres partes. Prima pars continet xxv capitula principales Capitulum primum de imitacione Christi et contemptu omnium vanitatum mundi." The first book ends as follows : " explicit prima pars libri interne consolacionis qui vocatur musica ecclesiastica." The second book begins: "Incipit secunda pars ejusdem libri," and ends : "explicit secunda pars libri interne consolacionis qui vocatur musica ecclesiastica." The third book begins : "Incipit tercia pars ejusdem libri," and ends : "explicit tercia et ultima pars libri interne consolacionis : qui vocatur. musica ecclesiastica." Of this type of manuscript I have written somewhat fully in a subsequent chapter, and shall not deal with it further here except to note the fact that there is no author mentioned, and that there is nothing in the title to identify the manuscript with the *De Imitatione Christi*. This and the quite independent title probably led to the fact that throughout the Middle Ages the *Musica Ecclesiastica* and the *De Imitatione Christi* were always regarded as different works by different authors.

There only remains one other British Museum manuscript of the *Imitation* to be noted. It is the second Harleian manuscript (number 3223) of the four treatises. It has one point in common with the Magdalen manuscript of 1438 and the Autograph manuscript of 1441 : it is dated. John Dygoun, a recluse of Sheen, wrote part of the Magdalen manuscript—the original of the *Musica Ecclesiastica* type. Thomas à Kempis of course wrote the Autograph manuscript. This Harleian manuscript was finished " 1478 ex floreto." " Ex Floreto " seems to refer to some bad Latin verses that end the MS., though one would like to find in the phrase the name of the scribe. This was seven years after the death of Thomas à Kempis, and eight years after the issue from the press of the first edition of the work under his name. Yet the scribe—presumably an Italian—seemed to have no doubt as to the authorship. The manuscript begins : " Incipit libellus devotus et utilis compositus a domino Johani. Gersem cancellario pariensis de Imitatione Christi et contemptu omnium vanitatis (*sic*) mundi." It is interesting to notice that three of these six manuscripts attribute the work to Gerson. The Burney manuscript (*circa* 1419) calls the author

END OF INDEX OF CHAPTERS OF THE FIRST BOOK AND PART OF
THE FIRST CHAPTER OF THE FIRST BOOK OF THE TREATISE "DE
IMITATIONE CHRISTI' FROM THE HARLEY MS. 3223 (BRITISH MUSEUM)

THIS MS. CONTAINS THE FOUR BOOKS, AND IS DATED 1478. THE DATE IS FOLLOWED BY
THE WORDS "EX FLORETO;" POSSIBLY REFERRING TO THE SCRIBE, OR TO THE VERSES
WHICH FOLLOW.

Dominus John Geersem, Chancellor of Paris; the Additional Manuscript (*circa* 1465) calls him simply Chancellor of Paris; while the Harleian manuscript (1478) calls him Dominus John Gersem, Chancellor of Paris. No manuscript refers in any way to Thomas à Kempis if we except the modern or almost modern attribution on the Harleian manuscript numbered 3216. It should be noticed that Gerson is spelt Gersem and Geersem in this manuscript, and this spelling is associated with the Chancellor of Paris. This alone entirely disposes of the attribution of the work to the imaginary John Gersen of Vercelli.

The bulk of the English manuscripts are of the *Musica Ecclesiastica* type. Five of those mentioned above are, however, not of this type, and to these we may add three Bodleian manuscripts. Two are in dexed with a curious note of doubt as to their origin. One is included in the Digby codices (37.5) and is dated *circa* 1450. It is indexed as follows: " liber primus tractatus Tho. à Kempis, sive cujuscunque sit, ' De Imitacione Christi et contemptu vanitatum mundi.' " The book or tract concludes as follows: " explicit libellus de Imitacione Christi et contemptu vanitatum mundi." This is apparently an instance of the first book only, and accounts for the printed editions containing only one tract. The second is among the Laud MSS.,[1] and belongs to the sixteenth century. It is indexed as follows: " Johannis Gersoni sive Johannis

---

[1] The third MS. is *Marshall*, 124 (lib. ii. cap. 12, in Dutch).

à Kempis sive cujuscunque sit de imitatione Christi libri quinque, cum tabula capitum unicuique libro praefixa." The reference to John à Kempis is so late that it adds nothing of value to the controversy as to the authorship of the *Imitation*. Neither of these fragments contain any reference to the author, though Bernard has referred the latter to à Kempis. The first, however, appears for some reason to have been indexed under the title *Musica Ecclesiastica* in the early eighteenth century. Hatton's correspondent[1] in 1706 declared that it bore that title. Possibly there are other manuscripts in the country that are not of the *Musica Ecclesiastica* type, but I have seen no note of them.

A consideration of some of the more important fifteenth-century printed editions of the *Imitation* will be found to throw a good deal of light upon the authorship of the work as well as on its early and extensive popularity. The first edition was issued, it is thought, the year after the death of its author, 1471, from the Augsburg press. This famous and interesting edition, an edition older than many of the manuscripts, attributes the work to Thomas à Kempis, and is important because of the very early date of issue. This edition on examination dispels a curious error adopted by some students of the *Imitation*, the belief that the title *De Imitatione Christi* was first adopted for the whole collection of treatises in the well-known

[1] See chapter iii.

PART OF THE FIRST CHAPTER OF THE FIRST BOOK OF THE TREATISE
"DE IMITATIONE CHRISTI:" FROM THE "EDITIO PRINCEPS" ISSUED AT
AUGSBURG ABOUT THE YEAR 1471.

THE PREFATORY NOTE AS TO THE TITLE IS POSSIBLY FROM THE PEN OF THOMAS A KEMPIS
HIMSELF. THIS EDITION ATTRIBUTES THE WORK TO THOMAS A KEMPIS.

Nuremburg edition of 1494. I think the title is practically implied if not directly used in some early manuscripts, and it is actually used in late manuscripts, such as the Harleian manuscripts numbered 3223. But this question of title is directly dealt with in the Augsburg printed edition of 1471. The work begins with this statement : " Incipit libellus consolatorius ad instructionem devotorum Cujus primum capitulum est de imitacione Christi et contemptu damni [sic] vanitatum mundi. Et quidam totum libellum sic appellant scilicet libellum de imitatione Christi. sicut evangelium Mathei appellatur liber generacionis Jesu Christi Eo quod in primo capitulo sit mentio de generacione Christi secundum carnem. Incipit primum capitulum." Here we have quite a fascinating item of literary history. We find the first publisher discussing in the year 1471 this vexed question of the title, and actually poking fun at those who call the whole book "libellus de imitatione Christi" from the title of the first chapter. It is as absurd, he says, as if we were to call the Gospel according to St Matthew the genealogy of Jesus Christ because mention is made in the first chapter of our Lord's genealogy according to the flesh. This statement makes it quite clear that even in the lifetime of Thomas à Kempis and before the days of printing the work was known as the *Imitation of Christ*. The quiet humour of the analogy tempts one to believe that this introductory note was from the pen of à Kempis. It has his manner and his style, and justifies the belief that he had adopted the title which has for centuries struck the imagination of the world. Whoever the editor was, and despite his humour, it is clear enough that the title is adopted in this first edition. The first book in the edition of 1471 ends as follows : " Explicit primus liber de imitacione Christi et de contemptu omnium vanitatum mundi." The second book ends : " Explicit liber secundus de imitatione Christi scilicit de ammonitionibus ad interna trahentibus." The third book begins : "Incipit tercius liber de imitacione Christi qui tractat de interna consolacione Christi ad animam fidelem," and it ends : " explicit liber interne consolationis qui est tercius de imitacione Christi." The fourth book opens with the title and ends, "explicit liber quartus de imitatione Cristi in quo specialiter tractatur de venerabili sacramento altaris." The volume concludes as follows : " Viri egregii Thome montis sanctæ Agnetis in Trajecto regularis canonici libri de Christi imitatione numero quatuor finiunt feliciter, per Gintheum zainer ex reutlingen progenitum literis impressi ahenis." The *Imitation* was therefore ushered into the world of printed books under the name of the famous though unofficial saint of Mount St Agnes.

A consideration of the more notable editions of the fifteenth century shows us that the title rapidly became settled. It will be convenient to consider these editions for this and other reasons. The Metz edition of 1481 came from one of the early monastic presses, "impresse in civitate Metensi per fratrem Johannem Colini ordinis fratrum carmelitarum. Et gerhardum de nova civitate. Anno domini mille° cccc°LxxxII." The book consists only of the first treatise and follows the title of that treatise as given in the autograph of 1441 : "incipiunt ammoniciones ad spiritualem vitam utiles." It seems to show that manuscripts of the separate treatises were abroad without any name of the author attached. This view is in accordance with the evidence of English manuscripts.

In the following year, 1483, there was issued from the Venice press the first printed edition, so far as I am aware, that attributed the work to Jean Gerson. The edition begins : " Incipit liber primus Johannis Gerson cancellarii parisiensis." It names the chapters, and gives a special title to the last book or treatise. The four books are named as usual, and are numbered thus: Liber primus, Liber secundus, Liber tertius. But the last book ends as follows : " Explicit liber quartus et ultimus de sacramento altaris." The colophon is in these words : " Johannis Gerson cancellarii parisiensis de contemptu mundi devotum et utile opusculum finit M.cccc.Lxxxiii per Petrum löslein de langencēn alemanum Venetiis feliciter impressum. Laus Deo." The title in this edition is "de contemptu mundi." This may have led to its confusion with some other work by Gerson, but it is probable that the attribution to Gerson was in the copy used by the printer.

Another edition of the *Imitation* was issued at Venice in 1485. In the British Museum copy of this edition there is written on the fly-leaf, in an old manuscript hand, "Thomas de Kempis de Imitatione Christi Johannis de Gerson Tractatus de Meditatione cordis, Venetiis 1485." This is the earliest edition that I have seen in which these two works are printed together. It should be compared with the remarkable but very late manuscript in the Bodleian Library referred to above among the Laud MSS. which is indexed as follows : "Johannis Gersoni, sive Johannis a Kempis, sive cujuscunque sit, de imitatione Christi libri quinque, cum tabula capitum unicuique libro praefixa." The work begins : "Incipit libellus devotus et utilis. De imitatione Christi et contemptu omnium vanitatum mundi." In this manuscript the "de Meditatione Cordis" of Gerson has been treated as a *fifth* book of the *Imitation*—a unique error so far as I am aware, either in manuscripts or printed books of the *Imitation*, but one that shows how ready the mediæval mind was to confuse the works of these very dissimilar writers.

The Venice edition of 1485 begins : "Incipit liber primus Joannis Gerson cangellarii [sic] parisiensis. De imitatione Christi et de contemptu omnium vanitatum mundi." The second book begins : "Incipit secundus. De interna conversatione." The third book begins : "De interna Christi locutione ad animam fidelem." The fourth begins : "Devota

exhortatio ad sacram corporis Christi communionem,"
and ends, "explicit liber quartus et ultimus de
sacramento altaris. Johannis Gerson cancellarii
parisiensis, de contemptu mundi devotum et utile
opusculum finit MCCCC.LXXXV per Dionysium et
Peregrinum ejus sotium bononienses. Deo Gratias.
Amen."

It is perhaps a matter of controversial interest to
point out that this book was printed from a manuscript curiously akin to the Codex *de Advocatis*,
which gave rise to the still living but extremely
futile controversy as to the authorship of an
imaginary thirteenth-century Abbot of Vercelli. I
am inclined to think that this edition was actually
printed from that manuscript, with small changes
necessitated by the condition of the text and the
views of the editor. This Venice edition contains
the titles of the second and fourth books used in the
Aronensis manuscript. The second book in the
manuscript begins : "Incipit liber de interna conversatione." The fourth book is headed "de devota
exhortatione ad sacram corporis Christi communionem." The titles of the first and third books
differ, but the likenesses are very striking, and it is
allowable to conjecture some relationship between
the Gerson edition and the so-called Gersen
manuscript.

The next edition that I notice is one of unusual
interest. It was published by Jacobus Britannicus
at Brescia, on June 6th, 1485. It begins with

the usual table of contents. This is followed by a unique prefatory devout address or sermon, and then follows the following curious statement, which proves that the controversy as to the authorship was already acute in the late fifteenth century : " Incipit opus Beati Bernardi saluberrimum de imitatione Christi : et contemptu mundi : quod Johanni Gerson cancellario Parisiensi attribuitur." This is apparently printed from the same manuscript as the Venice edition of the same year. The second book is entitled, " De interna conversatione"; the third book, " De interna Christi locutione ad animam fidelem"; and the fourth book, " Devota exhortatio ad sacram corporis Christi communionem. Vox Christi. . . ."

John de Westfalia's edition, issued at Louvain probably in the same year, begins : " Incipit liber primus Johannis Gerson cancellarii parisiensis. De imitatione Christi et de contemptu omnium vanitatum mundi." The books have the above titles, and the volume ends : " Johannis Gerson cancellarii parisiensis de contemptu mundi devotum et utile opusculum finit. Impressum per me Johannem de Westfalia."

From Louvain we pass to Cologne, where a curious little undated edition of the first book only, without any indication of authorship, appeared probably in 1486. The table of chapters is followed by the phrase " incipiunt ammoniciones ad spiritualem vitam utiles," and the book concludes, " expliciunt ammoniciones ad spiritualem vitam utiles: Deo gracias."

From Cologne we cross the Alps to Venice, where what seems to be the third Venetian edition of the *Imitation* appeared in 1486. It begins: "Incipit liber primus Joannis gerson cancellarii parisiensis. De imitatione Christi et de contemptu omnium vanitatum mundi." The books have the usual titles. The last is also named as usual "de sacramento altaris." The volume concludes with Gerson's *De Meditatione Cordis*. The colophon runs as follows: "Johannis Gerson cancellarii parisiensis: de contemptu mundi libri quatuor una cum tractatu de meditatione cordis felici numine finiunt. Impressum Venetiis impressis Francisci de madiis M.CCCC.LXXXVI."

The Argentine edition of 1487 is, I think, the first dated edition in which the work is attributed to à Kempis. There is, however, very little doubt that the Augsburg edition may be dated 1471. In this edition we have on the fly-leaf, in bold black type, "Tractatus de imitatione christi cum tractatulo de meditatione cordis." This again disposes of the theory that the title "De Imitatione Christi" was not given to the collected work before 1494. In this edition, after the very full table of contents, the work begins as follows: "Incipit liber primus fratris Thome de Kempis canonici regularis ordinis sancti Augustini." The usual titles are prefixed to the books. This treatise ends: "explicit liber quartus et ultimus de sacramento altaris." The volume concludes as follows : " Fratris Thome de Kempis de imitatione christi : et de contemptu mundi devotum et utile opusculum finit feliciter. Incipit tractatus de meditatione cordis magistri Johannis gerson. . . .

" Tractatulus venerabilis magistri Johannis Gerson de meditatione cordis : Argentine impressus par Martinum flach Anno domino M.CCCC.LXXXVII. finit feliciter."

There is another edition of 1487, but this has no printed place of issue.[1] On the fly-leaf we read in bold type, " Tractatus de ymitatione cristi cum tractatulo de meditatione cordis." There follows a full table of contents with folio references—a rare convenience to the mediæval reader. The work begins : " Liber i. Tractatus aureus et perutilis de perfecta ymitatione Christi et vero mundi contemptu." The last book is named as usual : " Explicit liber quartus de sacramento altaris. Incipit tractatus de meditatione cordis." The volume ends : " Tractatus aureus et per utilis de perfecta ymitatione Christi et vero mundi contemptu cum tractatulo de meditatione cordis finiunt feliciter anno MCCCCLXXXVII."

John Zeiner published an edition in 1487. There is in the British Museum copy a manuscript note in an early hand on the fly-leaf. There is a table of contents with folio references. The treatise begins : " Liber i. Tractatus aureus et perutilis de perfecta ymitatione Christi et vero mundi contemptu," and ends : " explicit liber Quartus de sacramento altaris.

[1] British Museum, I. A. 9267.

Incipit tractatus de meditatione cordis." The volume ends : "tractatus aureus et perutilis de perfecta ymitatione Christi et vero mundi contemptu Cum tractatulo de meditatione cordis finiunt feliciter Per Johannem zeiner Ulment. Anno. LXXXVII." This is identical with the previous edition with the addition of the name of John Zeiner, of Ulm, and they are successive editions from the same press.[1]

A fourth Venice edition was published in 1488. In the British Museum copy there is a Latin verse on the fly-leaf in an old hand. On the next leaf we have "Joannis Gerson de contemptu omnium vanitatum mundi." This is followed by a table of chapters, and then stuck on a further fly-leaf is a tiny woodcut of the Crucifixion. The work begins: "Incipit liber primus Joannis Gerson cancellarii parisiensis, de imitatione Christi : et de contemptu omnium vanitatum mundi," and ends : "explicit liber quartus et ultimus de sacramento altaris. Incipit tractatus de meditatione cordis Johannis Gerson." The volume ends : "Johannis Gerson cancellarii parisiensis : de contemptu mundi libri quatuor uno cum tractatu de meditatione cordis felici numine finiunt. Impressum Venetiis arte et impensis Bernardini de Benalus MCCCCLXXXVIII."

The Milan edition of 1488 is of some interest. The treatise begins with a rubric : "Incipit liber primus Joannis Gerson cancelarii parisiensis. De

---

[1] John Zeiner also issued in the same year a German translation of the *Imitation*.

imitatione Christi et de contemptu omnium vanitatum mundi," and ends : " explicit liber quartus et ultimus de sacramento altaris. Incipit tractatus de meditatione cordis Johannis Gerson." The volume ends, " Johannis Gerson Cancellarii parisiensis de contemptu mundi libri quatuor una cum tractato de meditatione cordis felici numine finiunt. Impressum Mediolani impensis Leonardi Pachel de Alamania. MCCCCLXXXVIII mensis Julii." Then follows the index of chapters.

The Paris edition of 1489 begins : " Incipit liber Johannis Gerson cancellarii parisiensis. De Imitatione Christi et de contemptu omnium vanitatum mundi," and ends : " explicit liber quartus et ultimus de sacramento altaris. Johannis Gerson cancellarii Parisiensis : de contemptu mundi devotum et utile opusculum finit. Laus omnipotenti Deo. Sequitur tractatus de Meditatione Cordis a Magistro johanne de Gersonno." This is followed by a Table of Chapters of both works, and the volume ends : " Liber Magistri Johannis Gerson Cancellarii Parisiensi de Imitatione Christi et contemptu omnium vanitatum mundi : una cum de meditatione cordis unicuique religioso ac devoto necessarius. Finit feliciter impressus parisius per Higman Almanum. In vico clausi brunelli ad intersignium leonum prope scolas decretorum anno domino millesimo quadringentesimo octuagesimo nono, die vero decima octava januarii."

The Augsburg edition of 1488 calls for some notice. It begins : " Incipit liber primus Johannis Gerson cancellarii parisiensis de Imitatione Christi et de contemptu omnium vanitatum mundi"; and ends: "explicit liber quartus et ultimus de sacramento altaris Johannis Gerson cancellarii parisiensis de contemptu mundi devotum et utile opusculum impresium Auguste arte et impensis Erhardi ratdolt viri solertis anno domini MCCCCLXXXVIII. sequitur tractatus de Meditatione cordis a magistro Johanne de Gerson. . . ."

The Lyon edition of 1489 is very important, since it attributes the work to à Kempis. On the fly-leaf we read in bold type: "Tractatus de imitatione Christi cum tractatulo de meditatione cordis." After the Table of Chapters we have "incipit liber primus fratris Thome de Kempis canonici regularis ordinis sancti Augustini de imitatione Christi et de contemptu omnium vanitatum mundi." The treatise ends: "explicit liber quartus et ultimus de sacramento altaris. Fratris Thome de Kempis de imitatione Christi: deque contemptu mundi devotum et utile opusculum finit feliciter. Incipit tractatus de Meditatione cordis magistri Johannis Gerson. . . . Tractatulus venerabilis magistri Johannis Gerson de Meditatione cordis Lugduni impressus per Johannem Trechzel artis impressoriæ magistrum anno nostrae salutis MCCCCLXXXIX. die vero XI. mensis octobris finit feliciter."

The Argentine edition of 1489 has on the fly-leaf the words, "Thomas de Kempis De imitatione christi, de contemptu omnium vanitatum mundi.

I

De interna conversatione. De interna locutione Christi ad animam fidelem cum quanta reverentia Christus est suscipiendus. Item Johannes Gerson de meditatione cordis." A very curious woodcut is printed on the other side of the fly-leaf. The work begins : " Liber primus. Incipit liber primus fratris Thome de Kempis : canonici regularis ordinis sancti Augustini De imitatione Christi et de contemptu omnium vanitatum mundi " ; and ends : "explicit liber quartus et ultimus de sacramento altaris. Fratris Thome de Kempis de imitatione christi, et de contemptu mundi devotum et utile opusculum finit feliciter. Incipit tractatus de meditatione cordis magistri Johannis gerson. . . . Tractatulus venerabilis magistri Johannis Gerson de meditatione cordis Argentinus impressus. Anno domini M.CCCC.LXXXIX. finit feliciter."

The Paris edition of 1491 has an illustrated fly-leaf with the words, " Gerson de Imitatione Christi et de Meditatione cordis." This is the first case in which we have the works definitely associated in this way. The book begins : " Incipit liber primus Johannis Gerson Cancellarii parisiensis. De Imitatione Christi et de contemptu omnium vanitatum mundi"; and ends : "explicit liber quartus et ultimus de sacramento altaris. Johannis Gerson Cancellarii parisiensis de contemptu mundi devotum et utile opusculum finit. Sequitur tractatus de Meditatione cordis ab eodem Magistro Johanne de Gersono." The colophon runs : " completum est opusculum

TITLE PAGE OF THE PARIS EDITION OF THE TREATISE
"DE IMITATIONE CHRISTI" ISSUED BY THE BROTHERS
MARNEF IN 1491.

(THE DEVICE OF ENGUILBERT, JEAN, AND GODEFROY DE MARNEF.)

exoratumque Parisii per Philippum Pygouchet. In vico cithare. In locagiis collegii vulgariter nuncupati de Dainville Anno domini millesimo quadragentesimo nonogesimo primo die vero ultima mensis martii."

An edition of 1492, imprinted without place of origin, is interesting. On the fly-leaf is printed: "tractatus de Ymitatione Christi cum tractatulo de meditatione cordis." The work begins: "Tractatus aureus et perutilis de perfecta Ymitatione Cristi et vero mundi contemptu"; and ends: "explicit liber quartus de sacramento altaris. Incipit tractatus de Meditatione cordis Johannis Gerson. . . . Tractatus aureus et perutilis de perfecta Ymitatione Christi et vero mundi contemptu cum tractatulo de Meditatione cordis finiunt feliciter anno domini MCCCCLXXXXII." It will be noticed that in this edition, while the *Meditation of the Heart* is attributed to its author Gerson, no mention is made of the authorship of the *Imitation*. It is clear from this that there was a doubt at this time as to the authorship. It was no longer possible to assert the identity of authorship of the two associated works—*The Imitation* and *The Meditation of the Heart*.

The Luneborch edition of 1493 is practically identical with the Argentine edition of 1489. The only real difference is the abbreviations of Latin words. It is of course an important edition, for it definitely states that à Kempis is the author of the *Imitation;* "Incipit liber primus fratris Thome de

Kempis canonici regularis ordinis sancti Augustini."
The volume includes *The Meditation of the Heart*
and concludes : "Tractatulus venerabilis Magistri
Johannis Gerson de meditatione cordis Luneborch
impressus per me Johannem Luce, anno domini
MCCCCXCIII., XXII. die mensis maij finit feliciter."

Another à Kempis edition of about this date is both
undated and without place of issue (1496 ?).[1] It is
entitled "Tractatus fratris Thome de Kempis canonici
regularis ordinis Sancti Augustini de imitatione
Christi et de contemtu omnium vanitatum mundi.
Cum tractatulo Johannis Gerson de Meditatione cordis
et complures alii tractatus pulcri." This is a kind of
expansion of the Argentine and Luneborch editions.
The *Imitation* in this edition ends : "Fratris Thome
de Kempis de imitatione Christi et de contemptu
mundi devotum opusculum finit."

The Venice edition of 1496 is of some interest.
In the British Museum copy there is a loose fly-leaf
bearing the words : "Joannis Gerson de contemptu
omnium vanitatum mundi." It appears not to
belong to the book. It will be sufficient to quote
the ending of the volume : "Joannis Gerson cancelarii parisiensis de contemptu mundi libri quattuor
uno cum tractatu de Meditatione cordis felici numine
finiunt. Impressum venetiis. MCCCCXCVI. die ultimo
Januarii."

The Paris edition of 1496 is more important. It
has a fly-leaf with a very curious woodcut. Above

[1] I. A. 10955 (Magdeburg, or Thanner at Leipsic (?), Hain, 9081).

the woodcut are the words : " de imitatione Cristi et contemptu mundi magistri Johannis Gerson cancellarii parisiensis," and below it the printer's name, Georgius Mittelhus. On the reverse side of the fly-leaf is another woodcut representing the Magi worshipping. The work opens in common form and ends : " explicit liber quartus et ultimus de sacramentis altaris. Johannis Gerson cancellarii parisiensi de contemptu mundi devotum et utile opusculum finit. Sequitur tractatus de Meditatione cordis ab eodem magistro Johanne de Gersono." The colophon states that the work of printing was completed by George Mittelhus at Paris on March 1st, 1496.

The Florentine edition of 1497 bears on the fly-leaf the words : " Johannis Gerson de contemptu omnium vanitatum mundi." It begins in the common form : " Incipit liber primus Johannis Gerson cancellarii parisiensis," and ends as usual with the " de Meditatione cordis." It was completed by Master John Peter de Maganza at Florence, on November 10th, 1497. The Paris edition of 1498 has a fly-leaf with the words " de Imitatione Christi," and a woodcut of the Crucifixion. It begins in the usual form : " Incipit liber primus Johannis Gerson cancellarii parisiensis de Imitatione Christi," and ends with the " de Meditatione cordis ab eodem magistro Johanne de Gersono." The new century opens with an à Kempis edition issued in 1501 at Cologne. It follows the common form. On the fly-leaf are the words : " Liber de Imitatione Christi cum tractatu de Meditatione cordis." The edition contains a woodcut in duplicate, and ends with the little tract, *Doctrina pulcra pro religiosis et solitariis.* It begins in the usual form (substituting à Kempis for Gerson) : "incipit liber primus egregii viri Thome de Kempis de Imitatione Christi. . . ." There is, however, a variant in the ending : "explicit liber quartus et ultimus . . . de Imitatione Christi ab egregio viro Thoma de Kempis editi." It is curious to find the word *compositus* used with respect to Gerson and *editus* with respect to à Kempis. It seems to reflect a feeling that à Kempis was a compiler and Gerson an author. The literary world seems to have felt that if Gerson wrote the work he composed it, but that if à Kempis wrote it he compiled it.

I have referred above to some twenty-six independent issues of the *Imitation* between 1470 and 1501. During the period of thirty years there were in all about, and probably above, eighty editions issued. The editions given above are, however, probably representative, as they are those of which copies exist in the British Museum. One and twenty of these editions have some author named. One edition is referred to St Bernard, with Jean Gerson as a possible alternative. Seven editions—Augsburg, the two Argentine editions, Lyon, Luneborch, Cologne, and one unplaced and undated (Leipsic ?)—attribute the work to Thomas à Kempis. But these places are all west of the Alps and comparatively unimportant. On the other hand, thirteen editions (independent of the Brescia edition that names Gerson as an alternative to St Bernard) attribute the work to Gerson. These include five editions issued at Venice, four at Paris, one each at Louvain, Milan, Florence, and Augsburg. The great centres of culture and literary movement with one voice rejected à Kempis and adopted Gerson. It was not necessary to make inquiry. A book by Gerson the famous chancellor and theologian would sell, but the name of Thomas à Kempis was no voucher of literary merit. The same principles did not apply in the small towns. The book was printed there because of a demand for a work of the particular type and character of the *Imitation*. In such a case it was worth while to ascertain who was the true author. The Augsburg edition of 1471 gave this information, and it was emphatically repeated in the volume that issued from Nuremberg in 1494, giving to the world the collected works—including the *Imitation*—of Thomas à Kempis. The *Notabilia* concerning the Canon given on folios lxxxiiii. and lxxxv. of the edition conclude : " Et quia multos tractatus scripsit et dictavit in vita, et pauci sciunt quo modo intitulantur vel vocantur : ideo tabulam de ejus tractatibus et libris hic intitulare et scribere intendo ut omnes qui legunt vel audiunt possunt scire quot sunt." The *Registrum* gives "Tituli operum librorum venerabilis patris Thome de Kempis," including of course the four books of the *Imitation*. It is unfortunate, however, that this great edition of the works should have introduced into the volume writings attributed to Gerson and to Gerard Groote. The fourth book of the *Imitation* is immediately followed by the *De Meditatione cordis* of Gerson, without any textual break. It is not, however, claimed for à Kempis. The text runs : " explicit liber quartus de sacramento altaris. Incipit tractatus de meditatione cordis Johannis Gerson." The tract is almost regarded as part of the fourth book.[1] It ends as follows : " Tractatus aureus et perutilis de perfecta imitatione Christi et vero mundi contemptu cum tractaculo de meditatione cordis finiunt feliciter." Since the editor of the authorised version of the works could be so foolish as to introduce a work known throughout Europe as from Gerson's pen into intimate and physical connection with a work of doubtful authorship, no one could complain at the controversy being obscured. If the works were inseparable, the *Meditation of the Heart* was entitled to import its undoubted authorship into the title-page of the *Imitation*. Nothing in fact was done to break down the French tradition in favour of Gerson, and that tradition is as strong as ever to-day, though it is impossible to bring forward in its favour a single argument based upon the internal or literary evidence of the *Imitation* itself.

When such a tradition is abroad, it is hard to kill.

---

[1] It fills folio 27a to folio 28b in the 1494 edition.

It rapidly extended from the Continent, though, as we shall see in another chapter, England had her own tradition as to authorship, and had in fact possessed, when the first English edition was issued in 1502-3, for perhaps sixty years an English version, still extant, of the *Following of Christ*. But the tradition of the French and Italian press was too strong for any local tradition. So when Dr Atkinson in 1502 translated into English the *Imitation* from a manuscript of the *Musica Ecclesiastica* type—he only translated *three* books, and this fact settles the type—the printer gave Gerson's name to the work. The colophon to the 1503 edition runs as follows : " Here endeth the thyrde boke of Jhon Gerson : Emprynted in London by Rycharde Pynson, in Flete strete at the Sygne of the George. at the commaundement and instaunce of the ryght noble and excellent prynces Margarete moder to our soverain lorde Kynge Henry the. VII. and Countesse of Rych mount and Derby. The yere of our lord MD.iii. The. xxvii. day of June." Atkinson had evidently no manuscript containing the fourth book. As has been shown above, such manuscripts are very rare in England. He clearly had to use a manuscript of the *Musica Ecclesiastica* type containing only three books. But the reading public were aware of the fourth book, and Princess Margaret herself gave the public an English version, not from the Latin, but from an early French version. The fourth book "was translated oute of frenche into Englisshe in

fourme and maner ensuinge. The yere of our lord
god MDiiii." by the Princess, and was published
in the same year by Pynson. He appears to have
bound up some copies with Dr Atkinson's translation
of the first three books issued the previous year.
Our present point, however, is that the whole work
was issued under the name of Gerson and the
French tradition imposed upon the English
printers. I shall show later that the tradition in
no way affected the position of the English bibliophiles who persistently attributed the first three
books of the *Imitation* to Walter Hilton.

MASTER WALTER HILTON AND THE AUTHORSHIP OF THE IMITATION

THE controversy as to the authorship of the *Imitation* — Tractatus aureus et perutilis— has now been for all practical purposes at rest for some thirty years. Dr Hirsche's discovery in 1873 that the work is written in a species of rhythm peculiar to Thomas à Kempis was the last step in an ancient argument based on internal evidence that has at last overwhelmed even those who are still troubled by the really weighty claims of Jean Le Charlier de Gerson, Doctor Christianissimus. Few to-day are so critically poor as to do reverence to that Ignisfatuus of theological literature, Gersen of Vercelli. All other putative authors have been ruled out of court. It is true that the claims of Saint Bernard are still arguable, but the weight of manuscript evidence with respect to the final passage of chapter fifty (or chapter fifty-five if that method of division is adopted) of Book III. bears so heavily against him that no one to-day will adopt the case of the Saint. Indeed the *Imitation* is so clearly a philosophical phenomenon of the late fourteenth or early fifteenth century, that there is critical weakness in attributing it to a much earlier age. Nevertheless controversialists must bear in mind that the work was attributed to Saint Bernard in the mid fifteenth century, and that his claims received a volume of French support that at one time threatened seriously to compete with the fascination that Gerson the Most Christian Doctor exercised over those engaged in finding authors for the anonymous works of that day. Ludolph of Saxony, the Carthusian; Ubertinus de Casalis, head of the "Spiritualists," and named "The Mystical Antichrist"; Peter Rainaluzzi of Corbario, afterwards the Anti-Pope Nicholas V., emerged from the mists of the early fourteenth century, only to be speedily forgotten; and with them may be dismissed Pope Innocent III., whose work *De contemptu mundi* was for a time confused with the *Imitation* when the latter work was copied or printed under the former title.

Johannes de Canabaco belongs to a different class, for he was an author of the fifteenth century and possessed personal qualities consistent with the authorship of the *Imitation*. His works were current in Europe at the date when the golden tracts were in the making, and not only do we find them in the library of the good Duke Humphrey, but in the monastery where à Kempis laboured. But there is no evidence that he wrote the *Imitation*, and his chief title to fame may well be that his *Consolations of Divinity* was one of the "little books" that Thomas read in the "little nooks" at Mount St Agnes. The case for John à Kempis, the elder brother, was

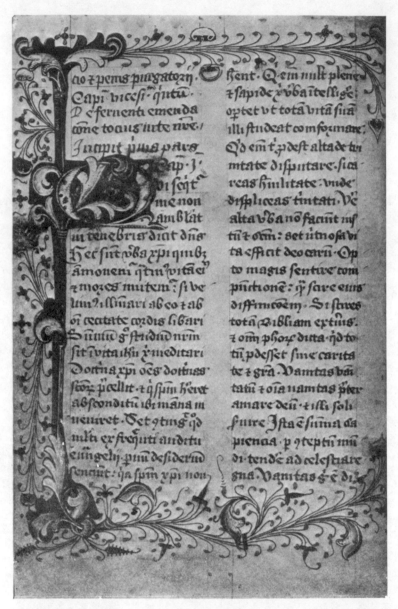

END OF THE INDEX OF THE FIRST BOOK AND PART OF THE FIRST
CHAPTER OF THE FIRST BOOK OF THE TREATISE CALLED "MUSICA ECCLES-
IASTICA:" FROM MS. 475 IN THE LAMBETH PALACE LIBRARY. THIS MS.
CONSISTS OF THE FIRST THREE BOOKS OF THE TREATISE "DE IMITA-
TIONE CHRISTI" AND BELONGS TO THE MID-FIFTEENTH CENTURY.
ON THE FLY-LEAF ARCHBISHOP SANCROFT (?) HAS ATTRIBUTED THE WORK TO WALTER HILTON.

likewise based on grounds that have little to do with evidence. Three names are left. The *Imitation* was produced, written, compiled, put it how we will, by Thomas à Kempis, by Jean de Gerson, or by the one man yet unmentioned—Walter Hilton. It is true that Walter Hilton, an Augustinian Canon like à Kempis, is dismissed as summarily as the rest by Mr Samuel Kettlewell in his pleasing and invaluable work upon the authorship of the *De Imitatione Christi* published in 1877. Mr Kettlewell, however, has not considered this aspect of the general problem with the care that it deserves, and in addition to inaccuracies that might perhaps have been avoided, he has not placed before the reader all the available evidence. It will be therefore of interest to English readers to re-examine Walter Hilton's claims. It is indeed desirable to do so from another point of view. As I have said, the controversy has now been at rest for thirty years. It has been at rest long enough. The period of repose threatens to exceed the limits of time laid down by precedent. This controversy has now in one shape or another interested the world of literature and moved the world of theology for more than four centuries and a half, with occasional pauses or breathing intervals such as that in which we now find ourselves. It is time in the interests of literary and theological polemics for the great cause to be re-opened, though we are not likely to find again at large the superb and unreasonable loyalty of a Constantine Cajétan.

Nevertheless the modern Shakespeare-Bacon logo-machy shows us that there are spirits abroad who will risk all on behalf of what they consider literary justice. The cause of Walter Hilton is a more worthy one than the cause of Francis Bacon ; for while it is absurd on a priori grounds to suppose that Bacon wrote the plays of Shakespeare, it is most reasonable on a priori grounds to suppose that Hilton wrote three of the four famous devotional treatises of Thomas à Kempis. Though it would, in my opinion, be extremely rash, or extremely patriotic, to assert that the evidence is capable of enthroning Hilton and reducing à Kempis to the respectable level of his other admirable works, yet it seems to me clear that the evidence does create a literary problem of some magnitude that deserves consideration at the hands of experts. That problem is simply this : what was the relationship between the *Imitation* and the English school of theological enthusiasts and mystics whose work survives dimly for the serious minded reader of to-day in Hilton's *Ladder of Spiritual Perfection*. So far as the general reader goes, Hilton's name in literature is forgotten. Mr Saintsbury has not thought fit to give him a place in his gallery of English authors despite the number and the literary interest of his reputed works and his great position in mediæval theological literature. If he is forgotten, we need not expect any-one but German scholars and heroic editors of early English texts to remember William Flete, living in 1380, when English mediæval scholarship was approaching its height ; William Exmeuse, Richard Rolle de Ampulla, John Hilton, Walter Shirlaw, Lowys de Fontibus of Cambridge, John Pery, and others.

It is not my present purpose to attempt to penetrate into the difficult literary problems that these English mystic writers present. It will be sufficient to state a little more fully than has yet been stated the evidence upon which those who wish to advocate the English authorship of the *Imitation* will have to rely. The question was first raised in England in a definite controversial form in the year 1707, when was published "The Christian Pattern, or the Imitation of Jesus Christ, Vol. ii. Being the genuine works of Thomas à Kempis. Containing four books, viz. :—

   I. The sighs of a penitent soul, or a treatise of true compunction.

   II. A short Christian Directory.

   III. Of spiritual exercises.

   IV. Of spiritual entertainments, or the soliloquy of the soul.

Translated from the original Latin, and recommended by George Hickes, D.D., to which is prefix'd,

A large account of the author's life and writings."

This book is a singular production and worthy of study. It is recommended by that very learned nonjuror George Hickes, sometime Dean of Worcester, and that is a guarantee of its literary value. The account of the controversy as to the authorship is quite admirably done, and the life of à Kempis is from the original sources. The curious point is the text. Mr Kettlewell seems to me to assume, as any one who had not closely perused the text might assume, that it is a translation of the four books of the *Imitation*. In fact it is nothing of the sort, and this might perhaps have been anticipated from the use of the word "genuine" on the title-page. Mr Kettlewell, assuming, I think, that the text was a translation of the *Imitation*, read carefully all that is stated with respect to Hilton, and particularly the assertion at the end of the book that the argument in favour of Hilton "will no wise invalidate the authority of the blessed Saint [à Kempis], from whose more certainly genuine works the present volume is compiled in *English*." In fact the anonymous author, Dr Lee, compiled a new *Imitation* from the undoubted works of à Kempis, in the belief that the Augustinian Canon did not write the *De Imitatione Christi*.

It is singular that Mr Kettlewell should have been misled by Dr Lee. However, partly on this ground, partly on the ground that no specialist believes in Hilton (a dangerous form of argument), and partly on the erroneous assumption that Hilton died in 1433, Mr Kettlewell dismisses the case with these words: "It is probable that Walter Hilton had introduced the 'de Imitatione,' for it was beginning to be well known in his day, and this might be the cause of its being attributed to him, since the author's name has not been put to the book." Had Mr Kettlewell thought it desirable to extend his well-known powers of painful research to the personality of Hilton, he would have found that this writer died on March 24th 1395, and that therefore if the *Imitation* "was beginning to be well known" in England in Hilton's day, the work was certainly not written by Thomas à Kempis. However, before dealing with the question fully, it will be convenient to consider the views of the writer of 1707, who says, after considering with admirable judgment the claims of eleven candidates for authorship, "but after all there remains another, who has not yet been taken notice of, as I find, by any. And this is an Englishman, and an eminent light of religion in his day: I mean *Walter Hilton*." The writer goes on to state the facts as to Hilton set forth by John Pits in his account of illustrious English writers published in Paris in 1619. Pits is erroneous in his facts. Hilton was not a Carthusian, he did not live in the house at Sheen called Bethlehem, he did not flourish in 1433. But our editor, in spite of or because of the errors of Pits, has little doubt of Hilton's claim. Mr Kettlewell adopts the same errors, and on those errors, bases his refutation. We must consider the grounds on which the editor of 1707 came to his conclusion, for these facts were before Mr Kettlewell. The editor publishes a letter from the Hon. Charles

K

Hatton, dated December 2nd 1706, which refers to a discussion between the two as to Hilton's claim. Hatton states that fruitless search has been made in the University libraries for Hilton's treatise *De Musica Ecclesiastica*. In default of the manuscript he thinks it desirable no longer to delay stating the grounds for believing " Walter Hilton to have been the genuine author of that justly celebrated pious book *De Imitatione Christi*, which hath most generally been ascribed to Thomas à Kempis."

Hatton goes on as follows :—" Nay, more colourable pretences may be alledg'd in behalf of Walter Hilton, than have been produc'd in favour of Thomas à Kempis, whose justification to be Author of the book de Imitatione Christi depends chiefly on the authority of an M.S. thereof in which it is not said that he is the Author, but only *Finitus et completus A.D.* 1441, *per Manus Thomae A. Kemp. in Monte S. Agnet. prope Zwoll*, which might have been asserted, if he had only transcrib'd it. Now it is apparent out of Pitseus his *Relationes, Historicæ de Rebus Anglicis*, and from the Authority of other Authors, that Walter Hilton flourish'd before the date of that M.S., for he was famed for his eminent Piety and learning A.D. 1433, and 'tis to be observ'd, that the like strain of devotion with that in the book *de Imitatione Christi*, runs through his highly esteemed pious Treatise stil'd Scala Christianæ Perfectionis, of which Walter Hilton is undoubtedly the Author : and tho' that be the only book I cou'd ever meet with compos'd by him yet *Joan. Jacobus Frisius*, in his *Epitome Biblothecæ Gesnerianae* and our countryman Pitseus (as undoubtedly Theodorus Pitreius and others who give an account of the Carthusian Writers, tho' I have not seen any of them) do enumerate several other devout books writ by him, and among them one stil'd, *de Musica Ecclesiasticâ*, which begins Qui *sequitur me non ambulat.* . . .

" I shall now only add, that some years ago, being in conversation with *Mr Obadiah Walker*, he happened to cite an Expression out of his favourite book (as he term'd it) *de Imitatione Christi*, omitting the name of T. à Kempis, to whom 'tis most commonly ascrib'd, which occasion'd a discourse about the eminent controversie Who was the author thereof; and upon my remarking to him, that Joan Jac. Frisius in his epitome of *Gesner's Bibliothecæ*, and Joan. Pitseus renumerating the works of *Walter Hilton* make mention of a book compos'd by him, stil'd, *de Musicâ Ecclesiasticâ*, and recites the first words thereof, Qui sequitur me non ambulat, etc., which are the initial words of the book *de Imitatione Christi*, and enquiring of him whether he had ever taken any notice thereof in those Authors, he not only told me he had, but did positively aver to me that he had seen, perus'd and compar'd the M.S. of *Walter Hilton, de Musicâ Ecclesiasticâ*, with the book de Imitatione Christi, most generally ascrib'd to *Thomas à Kempis*, and that throughout, it exactly agreed therewith, abating some literal *Errata*, and some few Words and Expressions which did not in the least vary the Sense. Whilst we were thus discoursing, some Persons, strangers to me, intervening, with whom Mr Walker declared he had some private concern, I left him, and to my great regret, never had an opportunity of seeing him afterwards, which if I had, I should not have fail'd to enquire of him, where he saw that M.S. of Walter Hilton? What was the date thereof? And if he cou'd inform me where it might now be found?"

In fact two hundred years ago Mr Hatton stated the exact problem that we have to solve, if it is solvable, to-day. When our friend was on the very brink of the great discovery the intervention of persons of importance played its wonted part in literature.

However, Mr Hatton was satisfied in his own mind. The evidence of Mr Obadiah Walker, the learned and distinguished Master of University College, Oxford, was sufficient; and his positive averment was supported by the more or less respectable authority of Pitseus, Pitreius, and Frisius. As we shall see directly the case as stated by Hatton is but a bald recital of a much stronger case. Hatton's correspondent did what he could. He wrote to Oxford for confirmation, and received the following statement :—

" According to your order we have consulted *Theod. Pitreius,* in his catalogue of the writings of *Wal. Hilton* he reckons his book *de Ecclesiastica Musica,* and cites for his authority Possevinus and Simlerus. We consulted the Titles of the treatises of this latter contained in our publick library, and finding nothing that promised any account of Hilton ; we had recourse to Possevinus, who attributes *Musica Ecclesiastica* to Hilton ; Possevin's book was published about the year 1603, under the Title of Apparatus Sacer Ecclesiasticorum Scriptorum. As for the manuscripts there are none either in Merton or Lincoln College according to the printed catalogue. In Magdalen College we found one entitled, *Musica Ecclesiastica,* the same with the book *De Imitatione Christi,* but ascribed to no particular author. The Bodleian library has two manuscripts with the same title of *Musica Ecclesiastica.* One contains only the first book *de Imitat. Christi* and no more : the other contains the whole book *de Imitat.* etc. except the first chapter, with a little of the beginning of the second, which are wanting, but the Author is mentioned in neither of them. As for the birth and death of Hilton, neither Possevin nor Petrius say anything of it ; only the former has this expression, *Aiunt vero eum floruisse Henrico sexto anglorum Rege* which *Petreius* repeats out of him with this addition, licet Cartusiam in qua vixerit, non exprimant."

The conclusion finally come to by the anonymous

writer (who is now identified as Dr Francis Lee) of
whom Hickes thought so highly was, "there is little
doubt but that Hilton must have been the Author, if
not of the whole Four Books at least of one of them,"
but that the work as we have it was "compil'd,
digested and improv'd" by Thomas à Kempis. This
is of the nature of a feminine ending and unworthy
of the masculine force of Mr Obadiah Walker.
However, in an *Advertisement* at the end of the
volume we are told that there are "several other
arguments yet behind," and though they are not set
out it is clear that the anonymous friend of Dr Hickes
had a full belief, which he was afraid to express, in
the authorship of Walter Hilton.

This was the evidence before Mr Kettlewell, and
he supplemented it by referring to further manuscripts entitled *Musica Ecclesiastica*, including one
at Cambridge, which is a fifteenth century English
version or rendering of the *Imitation*. As we
have seen he rejected as in duty bound the claims
of the Englishman. No doubt he was right in
so doing, but it is only proper that Hilton's case
should be stated as clearly and fairly as it can be
stated, and judged on grounds quite other than
those that Mr Kettlewell used. I cannot hope to
state the case as it should be stated, but this chapter
may induce some enthusiast to do what I am unable
to perform.

First, then, as to Hilton himself. It is possible
to add a little, though not much, to the useful

account given in the *National Dictionary of Biography*. He was possibly the son of a man of the same name (see MS. 9259 in Bernard's list of English MSS., published at Oxford, 1697), not a particularly illuminating fact. Whether he was in any way related to the Franciscan John Hilton of Norwich, a voluminous writer who died in 1376, is not known. His name is variously given. He is sometimes called Walter de Thurgarton. Bale, in his "A Registre of Wryters," [1] calls him Gualtherus de Hylton, but the "de" is dropped in his Index of British and other writers. The most usual name is Walter Hilton, but we also get Hylton. In the fifteenth-century Cambridge MS. of Hilton's translation into English of St Bonaventura's *Stimulus Amoris* we have the statement that the translation was made by "Maister Walter Hilton chanon and governaire of the House of Thurgarton biside Newark." [2] He was a man famed for his devotional zeal. "A ful devoute man" he is called in the Cambridge fifteenth-century MS. of the *Scala perfectionis*. In the British Museum MS. (Harl. 3852 f. 182*b*) of the *Speculum de Utilitate Religionis Regularis* he is described by the phrase Magister *Beatus*. Hilton, so far as I am aware, shared with à Kempis exemption from beatification, and it is remarkable that this word should have been added to the manuscript. This very work is called elsewhere *Epistola Aurea*. John Bale, Bishop of Ossary, calls him *vir pro sua*

[1] Printed in 1549, London.   [2] See also Royal MS. 8.A. vii.

ætate eruditus. Thomas Tanner, following John
Pits, declares that he was a Carthusian of Sheen
and afterwards a doctor of Theology and Canon of
Thurgarton. A manuscript in New College seems
to suggest that Hilton was Vicar of St Mary
Magdalen, Oxford. The Dictionary of National
Biography makes it clear that he was an Augustinian.
To sum up, he was a man with the highest reputation for sanctity, who became the head of the
Augustinian House at Thurgarton. An examination
of his works shows that he wrote as freely in English
as in Latin, and that he translated Latin authors
into English for the use of the faithful. It is
difficult, indeed, to tell whether his works were
originally written in Latin or English, but the
evidence seems in favour of English. Among his
translations were English renderings of Lowys de
Fontibus on *Perfection*, and Bonaventura's *Stimulus
Amoris.*

There is some difficulty in settling the canon of
his works, for even so well-known a book as the
Ladder of Perfection is occasionally attributed to
Richard Rolle de Ampulla. The date of his death
is fixed by two possibly independent manuscripts.
The first is a manuscript (Harley, 330 f. 126*b*) of the
Scala Perfectionis—a Latin version by a Carmelite,
Thomas Fishlake, from the original English, and it
concludes with the statement that the work was by
Walter Hilton, Canon of Thurgarton, who died on
March 24, 1395-6. The other is a late Cambridge

manuscript of the same work, which concludes :
" explicit libellus magistri Walteri Hilton Canonici
de Thurgarton qui obiit anno domini MCCCXCV
decimo kalendas Aprilis circa solis occasum." If any
further evidence is wanted to show that this is the
probable date of his death it is to be found in the
fact that Adam Horsley, to whom Hilton addressed
his work in praise of the Carthusian order, was an
officer of the Great Exchequer, and was employed
in the county of Gloucester in the year 1370.[1]

The date of Hilton's death excludes the explanation that he translated the *Imitation*. He died
when Thomas à Kempis was fifteen years of age.

The questions that have to be considered are these :
How are we to explain the fact of a persistent English
tradition that Hilton was the author of the *Imitation*,
the fact that the greatest English bibliophiles of the
sixteenth and seventeeth centuries were absolutely
satisfied that he was the author, the fact that among
the list of Hilton's works there always occurs a
work entitled *Ecclesiastica Musica*, which is identical
with the first three books of the *Imitation*, that
this title is exclusively English and appears in no
printed edition of the fifteenth century and in only one
Continental manuscript *quod sciam*, and that manuscripts so entitled occur frequently in England ?
First, we must consider the English literary authorities
that support Hilton. Charles Hatton's letter and

---

[1] See Issue Roll of the Exchequer, 44 Edw. III., pp. 404-5, edited
by F. Devon, 1835 ; and Patent Rolls, 1 Ric. ii., p. 202.

the Oxford letter of 1706-7 give us the following
data : Petrius, Frisius, Possevinus, and Pits include
the *Ecclesiastica Musica* in Hilton's works, and
identify it with the *Imitation*.   Obadiah Walker had
carefully considered the question of the authorship
and had no doubt about Hilton's claim.   Three
Oxford manuscripts entitled *Ecclesiastica Musica*
were in fact the *Imitation*, but had no author's name.
This evidence can be considerably enlarged.   Bishop
Tanner is a late but important addition to the literary
authorities that accepted Hilton.   John Bale, Bishop
of Ossory, is a still more important addition, for his
opinion is almost overwhelmingly weighty as well
as early.   He was born in 1495—only twenty-five
years after the death of à Kempis—and died in
1563.   In 1540, on the fall of Thomas Cromwell, he
fled to Germany, and did not return until 1552, when
he was nominated Bishop of Ossory.   By this date
he had acquired his unique knowledge, and his large
collection, of mediæval manuscripts.   When he was
hunted out of Ireland he fled to Zeeland and afterwards to Basle, returning to England in 1558.   A
year later he became Prebendary of Canterbury.
Bale must have been familiar with both Continental
and English manuscripts of the *Imitation*, and with
the Continental opinion as to the authorship—at
that time strongly in favour of Gerson.   Yet he is
absolutely clear on the point.   He gives an elaborate
list of Hilton's works with the place where he had
seen each manuscript, and among these he includes:

"de Musica Ecclesiastica, Li. i. 'qui sequitur me non ambulat,' *Ex Bonham et Wolfio*."[1] Bale possibly refers to the *Imitation* as the work of Hilton when he says of him " Gualtherus Hylton, vir pro sua etate eruditus, inter alia preclarum edidit opus, cui titulum addidit . . . claruit," A.D. (No year given.)

William Bonham was apparently a bookseller of whom nothing else is known ; but Reiner Wolfius, the other source referred to by Bale, was the well-known London printer and publisher of German origin, who came to London at Cranmer's invitation before 1537, and who died in 1573. His copy of the *Ecclesiastica Musica* may have come from Leland's collection. Bale's evidence appears to me to amount to this, that there was in existence in England in the first half of the sixteenth century manuscript evidence which convinced authorities such as Bale, Wolfius, and probably Leland, that Walter Hilton was the author of the famous work. Was this the same evidence that convinced Obadiah Walker ?

We seem to be able to take back the attribution of the work to Hilton to an even earlier date, though not with the same certainty that exists in the case of Bale.

We shall have occasion directly to refer to the Catalogue of the Syon Monastery at Isleworth[2] in dealing with the MSS. entitled *Musica Ecclesiastica*, but for the moment we must note the following point.

---

[1] *John Bale's Index of Bishop and other Writers*, edited by Reginald Lane Poole, with the help of Mary Bateson (Oxford 1902), p. 106.

[2] Edited by Miss Mary Bateson (Cambridge 1898).

In that library was a manuscript entitled *Ecclesiastica Musica*, given by Johannes West, and numbered in the Catalogue M. 26. In the imperfect index to the Catalogue (made at the end of the fifteenth or beginning of the sixteenth century) there is given a list of Hilton's works contained in the library. This list does *not* include the *Ecclesiastica Musica*, but it refers to various works of Hilton as occurring in the Codex M. 26, beginning respectively on Folios 41, 51, and 113 of the Codex, and it also mentions the *Scala* as included in the same Codex. It seems not illegitimate from this to assume that M. 26 contained a set of Hilton's writings, and that the *Ecclesiastica Musica*, which is catalogued under M. 26, was at the date of the catalogue regarded as Hilton's work. On the other hand, it might be contended that this catalogue is the origin of the whole matter; that this work was regarded as Hilton's, because it was bound up with Hilton's undoubted works. This view is supported perhaps by the fact that the other MSS. of the *Ecclesiastica Musica* are not included in the Index of Hilton's catalogued works. It is also perhaps a fact to be noted that this library contained a MS. entitled *Tractatus de Sacramento Altaris*, against which the author of the Index puts a note of warning. Now this title *De Sacramento Altaris* is the title of the fourth book in the earliest manuscripts of the *Imitation*—of the book that is *not* included in the *Ecclesiastica Musica*. It is notable that this fourth book is entitled as if it were a separate work, and indeed there seems to be internal evidence to show that the three books of the *Ecclesiastica Musica* and the book *De Sacramento Altaris* are to some extent independent works.[1]

Codex M. 26, and the Index to the Catalogue, do seem to show on the whole that the *Ecclesiastica Musica* was regarded in the fifteenth century in England as the work of Hilton. The fact that the Index does not refer to the other MSS. may be explained by the fact that it is very imperfect.

Now, the House at Isleworth was founded in 1415, and it is at present impossible to say at what date subsequently to this John West gave the manuscript. It was almost certainly in the first half of the fifteenth century, though possibly the fact that no copy of the *Ecclesiastica Musica* seems to occur in Duke Humphrey's bequests to Oxford of 1439 and 1443 may be adduced against this conclusion. On the other hand the Codex *Librum commonitorium de Contemptu Mundi*, in the bequest of 1443, might possibly be this very book, for *De Contemptu Mundi* is one of the earliest titles of the *Imitation*, and, as we shall see, one that occurs in connection with the title *Ecclesiastica Musica*. However, I am inclined to think that this codex, once in the possession of Duke Humphrey, is the manuscript now in Lincoln College, Oxford, which begins, " Beati pauperes spiritu."

However, this may be, there is a *primâ facie* case

---

[1] But see British Museum MS. *de Sacramento Altaris* (Arundel 214).

for the proposition that long before, perhaps half a century before the death of Thomas à Kempis, the first three books of the *Imitation* were current in England under the title *Ecclesiastica Musica*, and with the reputation of having as their author the saintly Augustinian Canon Walter Hilton. It is certainly a remarkable fact that such a statement can be seriously made, and it is one that needs very definite explanation. But explanation is not made any easier by the fact that the manuscripts entitled *Ecclesiastica Musica* are not only comparatively numerous, but also possess the peculiar characteristic of so much of Hilton's work, the co-existence of both Latin and English manuscript editions. Speaking for myself only, I must confess that if I knew that Hilton had flourished at the date that Pits says that he flourished, namely 1433, I should despair of any solution. The case would be as conclusive for the authorship of Hilton as it is for the authorship of à Kempis. However, Hilton almost certainly died in 1395.

Mr Kettlewell adds several to the *Ecclesiastica Musica* group of manuscripts referred to in the inaccurate and misleading Oxford letter of 1706-7. References to manuscripts so entitled are, however, much more numerous than Mr Kettlewell realised. Even my own necessarily incomplete examination of the subject makes this clear, as the following list will show. It may be that specialists will be able to add to the number. In making the list it will be convenient first of all to refer to all such manuscripts, wherever mentioned, keeping in mind the fact that the first six manuscripts mentioned are possibly included in the others which are all extant.

The Syon Catalogue gives four with the following titles :

(1) Musica ecclesiastica (M. 26. given by John West).

(2) Musica ecclesiastica de Imitacione Christi et de contemptu mundi. Multi sermones cum aliis. fo. 48 (M. 86).

(3) Musica ecclesiastica cum aliis (M. 112. Given by John Lawisby, Vicar of Ware, who died 1490).

(4) Tractatus qui intitulatur *Musica ecclesiastica* solitariis et contemplativis utilis fo. 109 (N. 37. Given by one Pynchbek, who was possibly a Doctor Pinchbeck who flourished 1457).

With respect to (1) Miss Bateson suggests that it may be identical with MS. 475 in Lambeth Library (see p. 160 below).

With respect to (2) Miss Bateson says, "Owing to this title Hilton has been called the author of the De Imitatione, *cf.* M. 26." The Catalogue, however, does not attribute any of these four MSS. to Hilton.

(5 & 6) John Bale refers to two copies of the *De Ecclesiastica Musica* from the shops of Bonham and Wolfius.

(7) The British Museum (Royal MS. 7 B. viii) has a fine copy in a Flemish hand which may be dated 1460-80. It begins : "Incipit liber interne

consolacionis qui vocatur musica ecclesiastica et dividitur in tres partes principales. Prima pars continet xxv capitula capitulum primum de imitatione Christi et contemptu omnium mundi," and ends : " explicit tercia ultima pars libri interne consolacione qui vocatur musica ecclesiastica." With this MS. may be ranked

(8) The Coventry School MS., described for Bernard's Catalogue of 1697 by the illustrious Humphrey Wanley. He catalogues it as follows :— " This wants a Title page and author's name, which is not mentioned in it.

" It is divided into three parts, which are thus called :—

1. Musica ecclesiastica.
2. Admonitiones ad interna trahentes.
3. De interna consolatione.

" It is wrote in parchment, about the time of King Edw. IV., as I guess by the hand."

Wanley makes no suggestion of authorship, but Bernard indexes the MS. under Thomas à Kempis at the very date when Obadiah Walker made his declaration against the authorship of à Kempis.

We may next notice the Lambeth Palace Library MSS. (Numbers 475 and 536).

(9) Folios 1 to 90 b of MS. 475 comprise a work (according to the Catalogue, by Walter Hilton), "*Qui Vocatur Musica Ecclesiastica*, in three books. This is followed in the Codex by the treatise *De Utilitate*

PART OF THE FIRST CHAPTER OF THE FIRST BOOK OF THE TREATISE
"MUSICA ECCLESIASTICA:" FROM THE MANUSCRIPT IN THE LIBRARY OF
EMMANUEL COLLEGE, CAMBRIDGE

THIS MS. CONSISTS OF THE FIRST THREE BOOKS OF THE TREATISE "DE IMITATIONE CHRISTI,"
AND PROBABLY BELONGS TO THE FIRST HALF OF THE FIFTEENTH CENTURY. THERE IS A
SECOND MS. AT EMMANUEL CONSISTING OF THE THIRD BOOK ONLY.

Tribulationis, which has always been recognised as Hilton's, and the juxtaposition of the two works raises a presumption that the *Musica* was at the date of transcription considered to be by Hilton. What is the date of transcription ? The catalogue states that the MS. *de Utilitate* (in the same hand) is a *fourteenth* century manuscript, and if this is so the claims of Thomas à Kempis are finally disposed of. It seems, however, to be the better opinion that it is a fifteenth century manuscript, and I should place it rather late in that century. On the fly-leaf of the Codex is the signature, Johannes Bark-ham, A.D. 1612. Under this is written : " In hoc volumine continetur 1° Gualteri Hilton Musica Ecclesiastica sive De Imitatione Christi in tres partes seu libros divisa, 2°. . . ." On the face of it these words seem strong evidence of Hilton's claim. In fact they are worth about as much as the opinion of Pitseus, for they were probably written by John Barkham, and indeed the words " Gualteri Hilton " and " de imitatione Christi " must be by a later hand, probably Dr Sancroft's hand, as they have been added after the rest of the passage was written.

This passage is, however, clearly not the origin of the Hilton case, as Bale had long before advocated Hilton's claim. I see, moreover, no grounds for identifying the Codex with M. 26 of the Syon Monastery Library. Indeed it is obviously not that Codex which contained works not in this Lambeth MS.

L

(10) The Lambeth MS. 536 is on parchment, and is attributed to the fifteenth century. I should be inclined to place it earlier than MS. 475. It may possibly be dated early in the century. The manuscript begins : " Hic libellus qui vocatur musica ecclesiastica omnibus in virtute proficere cupientibus valde necessaria et dividitur in tres partes." It is the second MS. in the Codex, and is described in the catalogue as follows:—

" 2. Musica ecclesiastica libris III. Incipit, *Qui sequitur me non ambulat in tenebris.* Nihil habet de Musica praeter Titulum, sed agit de praecipuis virtutibus Christianis. Tres sunt primi Libri de Imitatione Christi, qui Kempensi vulgo ascribuntur, fol. 4."

Three Cambridge MSS. may next be noticed.

(11 § 12) The Emmanuel College parchment Codices are indexed as follows :—

" 77. De interna Christi locutione ad animam fidelem ";

" 83. Augustini Soliloquia, cum Thomae à Kempis Musica ecclesiastica, item Imprecationes ecclesiae contra inimicos suos." The manuscripts give no author's name. The first MS. consists of the third book only. The second MS. begins *qui sequitur me non ambulat in tenebris* and consists of the three usual books. The work concludes : "explicit liber interne consolationis et tertia pars Musicae Ecclesiasticae." This is followed by six folios of directions for each day of the week. The college authorities regard it as a fifteenth century manuscript. It is

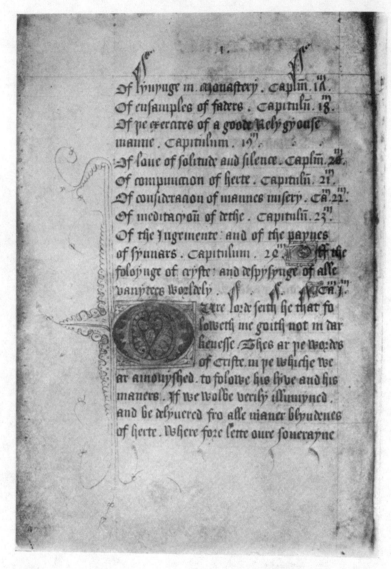

Of the folowynge of cryste : and despysynge of alle vanytees worldely . capła.
Are lorde seith he that folowethe me goith not in darkenesse. Thes ar þe wordes of Criste. in þe whiche we ar amonyshed. to folowe his lyfe and his maners. If we wolde verily illumyned. and be delyuered fro alle maner blyndenes of herte. Where fore sette oure soucrayne

INDEX OF CHAPTERS 17-25 OF THE FIRST BOOK AND PART OF THE FIRST CHAPTER OF THE FIRST BOOK OF THE FIFTEENTH CENTURY ENGLISH VERSION OF THE TREATISE "MUSICA ECCLESIASTICA:" FROM MS. G. G. I. 16, IN THE CAMBRIDGE UNIVERSITY LIBRARY. THIS MS. IS IMPERFECT BUT CONTAINS MOST OF THE FIRST THREE BOOKS OF THE TREATISE "DE IMITATIONE CHRISTI." IT BELONGS TO THE FIRST HALF OF THE FIFTEENTH CENTURY.

apparently in one hand throughout, but the same hand probably did not write the other works contained in the Codex.

(13) The manuscript catalogued as G. g. 1. 16 in the Cambridge University Library is described in the published catalogue as follows : "a quarto, on vellum, containing ff. 171 . . . *date about* 1400. An English translation of the first three books of the treatise de Imitatione Christi." If in fact the manuscript can be dated "about 1400," it disposes of the claim of Thomas à Kempis almost as effectually as the Lambeth MS. 475 would have disposed of them had the cataloguer's date been correct. However, there seems little doubt that G. g. 1. 16 is a good deal nearer 1450. The MS. begins: "Here begynneth the tretes called Musica Ecclesiastica"; and ends after the *Oratio Aurea :* "Here ends the boke of inwarde consolacion." This MS. must be classed with the two following MSS.

(14) An MS., in 1697 in the College of Physicians, Dublin, is now in the library of Trinity College, Dublin, and has been collated with (13) above and brilliantly edited for the Early English Text Society (1893) by Dr J. K. Ingram. It is catalogued by Bernard as follows :—

"The works of Tho. à Kempis in an ancient hand, in old English, on vellom, containing only three books, the fourth commonly printed with the three first, being falsely called his as some think."

This entry reflected a particular class of opinion at the end of the seventeenth century. While some scholars claimed three books for Hilton and one only for à Kempis, others, as we see, considered the *de Sacramento Altaris* as not belonging to à Kempis at all.

It should be noted that there is no old English MS. in the Bodleian.

The Bodleian contains, however, to use Bernard's descriptions :—

(15) " De interna consolatione tractatus imperfectus " [this MS. (Laud. 215 (1), 15th cent.) has lost the first chapter of the first book and the last chapter (59) of the third book. It has only three books]; and

(16) " Liber de Musica ecclesiastica ita scilicet, inscribitur sed sensu allegorico, agit enim totus de rebus ad Pietatem spectantibus. Cap i. est de imitatione Christi et contemptu omnium vanitatum mundi " (Bodley 632).

(17) " Musica ecclesiastica, alias de imitatione Christi, tribus partibus, scriptus erat liber iste A.D. 1469," et an. octavo, Edward IV. Regis Angliae etc. per Tho. Kempis " (Arch. Seld. Bodley 93).

Bernard appears to have recognised that (16) was the *Imitation*, though he has added a note similar to that written a hundred years later by the cataloguer in the Lambeth MS. 536. Perhaps it should be noted that (17) is of the same date and class as the British Museum (7) and Coventry School (8) MSS. The last manuscript that I shall note is a famous Oxford one, namely :—

(18) The Magdalen College MS. (xciii.), Novem-

ber 29th, 1438. The first book was written by
John Dygoun, a recluse of Sheen ; the other two
books were from the pen of Dygoun, aided by some
anonymous scribe.

It may be that the solution of the mystery is
involved in the origin and history of this manuscript.
I have noted that there were no less than four
copies of the *Musica Ecclesiastica* in the Library
of Syon Monastery. The Carthusian House at
Sheen called Jesus of Bethlehem was, as Miss
Bateson points out, founded about the same time
as the House of the Monks and Nuns of the
Brigettine Order at Syon, Isleworth (circa 1415),
and "the two Houses frequently acted together."
One may therefore suspect some common origin
of the Magdalen MS. and the manuscript of Syon.
Had Hilton been a member of the Carthusian
Monastery at Sheen, as alleged by Pitseus, we
should bring him into almost direct relationship with
the earliest manuscripts of the *Ecclesiastica Musica*,
but, fortunately or unfortunately, he died, if the
British Museum and the Cambridge manuscripts
are to be believed, twenty years before the House
at Sheen was founded.

There can be no manner of doubt that Hilton held
the Carthusian Order in great veneration, for there
is at Magdalen a work attributed to him entitled *De
utilitate et prærogativis Religionis et praecipue ordinis
Carthusiensis* (by accident or design in the same
Codex (93) with the copy of the *Musica Ecclesiastica*) ;
and at Merton there is a manuscript of the same

treatise also addressed to Adam Horsley, a Baron of the Exchequer. The work was in fact a trumpet-call to swell the ranks of the Carthusian Order. This Magdalen manuscript was (probably) once in Syon Monastery. It certainly seems to me to play an important part in the mystery that surrounds the origin of the belief in the Hilton authorship. It is therefore not impossible that when, in the first quarter of the fifteenth century, the House at Sheen secured an anonymous copy of the first three books, they attributed the work to a man who was already popularly known as Beatus, and was in fact the most prolific author of theological treatises of his day.

Meanwhile an embargo was, for some ecclesiastical reason, laid upon the fourth book—assuming of course that the *De Sacramento Altaris* of the Syon catalogue and the fourth book of the *Imitation* are the same works. This seems to me a reasonable explanation of the facts. The only way to reconcile the claims of Hilton and à Kempis, if Hilton did in fact write the *De Ecclesiastica Musica*, is to suppose that Hilton wrote the work in English and that à Kempis translated it into Latin; but this would assume a knowledge of the English vernacular that à Kempis could hardly have possessed.

If the House at Sheen did in fact issue a manuscript in Hilton's name, it is not difficult to understand the very positive position adopted by Bale and Walker. But the existence of the early English translations, though in accordance with Hilton's usual practice, seems to me entirely explicable on

PART OF THE ALPHABETICAL INDEX OF THE THIRD BOOK AND
PART OF THE FIRST CHAPTER OF THE FIRST BOOK OF THE TREATISE
"MUSICA ECCLESIASTICA,' (DE IMITATIONE CHRISTI), FROM THE MS.
NUMBERED 93 AT MAGDALEN COLLEGE, OXFORD

THE MS. IS DATED NOVEMBER 29TH : 1438. IT CONTAINS THE FIRST THREE BOOKS. THE FIRST
BOOK IS FROM THE PEN OF JOHN DYGOUN, A RECLUSE OF SHEEN. THE SECOND AND THIRD
BOOKS CONTAIN ALSO THE HAND OF AN ANONYMOUS SCRIBE.

other grounds; for the Carthusian monks of Sheen, if they attributed the work to Hilton, would naturally have followed his practice of issuing an English as well as a Latin edition.

What is remarkable is the rarity of manuscripts of the *Imitation* which are not of the *Ecclesiastica musica* type. The House at Sheen was obviously the only English source of copies in the early fifteenth century, and this perhaps accounts for the fact that Humphrey, Duke of Gloucester, had no copy. A cursory examination of sources shows eight manuscripts of the *Imitation* that are not of the Sheen type—five in the British Museum and three in the Bodleian. One Bodleian manuscript is very late, and presumably includes the *De Meditatione Cordis* of Gerson, for it is described as being in *five* books.

The British Museum manuscripts are interesting, and in them, I think, we must look for the source of the Sheen type. The earliest MS. is the Royal MS. 8, C. VII., and it is, one can scarcely help believing, very early fifteenth century in date, lying between the dates 1405 and 1420. It consists of not quite the whole of the first book. The rest of the MS. has been lost, but we have no right to assume that it did not consist of the whole work. The Burney MS. 314 is certainly also very early fifteenth century, not later than 1440 and perhaps as early as 1420. Its particular value is that it is probably the earliest MS. that attributes the work to Gerson. The Harleian MS. 3216 is dated 21st December 1454, not 1464 as Mr Kettlewell has stated in error. The additional MS. 11,437, which is probably not later than 1470, and the Harley MS. 3223 which is dated 1478, both attribute the work to Gerson.

The manuscript of interest in this present discussion is the Royal MS. 8, C. vii. Its date suggests that it may have been the original from which the monks of Sheen or Syon copied, and one is tempted to infer (as an alternative to the explanation previously suggested) that the remaining copy having been secured and attributed to Hilton, an attempt was made to detach the MS. from the Codex, but that this was done so as accidentally to leave most of the first book intact.

If the monks of Sheen and Syon were desirous of appropriating the work of Mount St Agnes to their own country, they had a large measure of success. The first edition printed in England by Pynson in 1503 consisted *only* of the first three books. Dr Atkinson had, it is clear, access to a MS. with only these books, and it was necessary to supplement the work with Princess Margaret's translation from the French vernacular version. Moreover, as we have seen, the keenest bibliophiles of the sixteenth and seventeenth centuries were entirely deceived. Hence, while it is, as I think, impossible to believe that Walter Hilton wrote the *Imitation* or any part of it, yet the relationship of his name to the work forms an interesting chapter in the history of European literature.

Those, however, who wish to prove that the *Imitation* was written by an Englishman need not despair. The case for Hilton is a strong one if his death can be placed a little later. Perhaps it can, though I confess that it is difficult to get over the evidence as to Adam Horsley. It would be strange, however, if the authorship of the *Imitation* were to turn on the identity of an English Exchequer official of the baser kind in the year 1370. Still, even if Hilton has to be abandoned, there is his School to consider—work enough for a century of polemics. Meantime I am content to believe that the work was written at Mount St Agnes about the year 1410. The view is confirmed, as I have shown above, by the fact that Thomas à Kempis is definitely connected by Adriaan de But (writing in 1480) with a work, "*Metrice descriptum*." De But in fact connects the *Musica Ecclesiastica* with the name of the Flemish Augustinian Canon. The musical marks used by à Kempis for purposes of punctuation also seem to connect him with this title.

I may perhaps finally note here, before I pass from the question of the manuscripts, that the work, or part of it, became popular in Holland at a very early date. Among the Marshall MSS. at the Bodleian Library (MS. 124) there is a Codex of about the middle of the fifteenth century which contains ten short religious pieces in Dutch. The sixth piece is a translation of the twelfth chapter of the second book, and is entitled, "Van den conincliken wegh des Heilighen Cruce, ende hoe ons selfs cruce sullen draghen."

THE STRUCTURE OF THE IMITATION

THE material that goes to the making of the four books of the *Imitation* calls for some analysis. These devotional works seem the soul of simplicity. Their fresh springs of aspiration and prayer appear to gush forth in spontaneity from the ground of the heart. If any force draws them, it is the affinity between man and God. The operations of the mind, the literary instinct of man, the intellectual building up of a great work seem to have no place here. Yet in truth art can so closely approach nature that it is difficult to distinguish their operations. The author of the *Imitation* was an artist of the highest rank, and he built his work, sentence by sentence, with an indefinable skill, with a constructive genius that defies analysis. His height of art does not simulate, but actually produces the cry of the child to the Father which is in Heaven. With an unerring judgment he has gone to the literary sources and fountains where is to be found that yearning "of the alone for the Alone," which he adopts and teaches. Not as a philosopher or as a creed worshipper has he gone to those sources, but as a man seeking for words that would touch the hearts of men, and he has transferred these

living words into the structure of his work : the
ipsissima verba that living souls had long ago
poured out to the living God, not dead summaries
of what dead men believed and thought. His art
consisted in the inspired borrowing of phrases and
in bringing phrases so borrowed into vital organic
union one with another : inspired selection, inspired
combination, and the spiriting away of all traces of
art. The *Imitation* was a new work, a book born
into immortality, and yet it contains hardly an
invented phrase. This is indeed the very virtue of
the work. No phrase that time had not proved to
be a living force in the instinctive spiritual life
of man was allowed any place in it. It was intended to represent the spiritual experiences of past
generations, and to bring them into the lives of
generations yet unborn. It was tacitly assumed
that all possible spiritual experiences had been
exhausted since the time of Christ, and that if they
could be crystallised into words, the follower of
Christ would at any rate know the road eternally
set aside for the following of Christ. The words
that time had proved to be alive, words that had
been the life and death cry of unnumbered millions,
the cry of the saint as well as of the sinner, these
words, the author of the *Imitation* seemed to think,
might well be recombined into the λογος of the
spiritual life, as that life was conceived before the
Dawn of the Renaissance. Hence we see in the
very structure of these little books the spiritual

limitations that they lay down.   Spiritual experience
was not exhausted in the beginning of the fifteenth
century, it is not exhausted now.   Then, as now, it
was approaching a new place of departure, was
evolving a new method of approaching the Divine.
But Thomas à Kempis, looking out upon the night
of his time, saw nothing but the stars.   He gives
us no hint of the dawn.   He is living at the end of
the night, not only of his age, but of the Middle Ages,
and the darkness before the dawn is very deep.   He
is fulfilling his duty, and he believes that he is stating
the whole duty of man when he crystallises into
perfect literary form the Godward yearning of
humanity through fourteen centuries of time.   He
was not even the modernist of his own age.   The
mysticism of the fourteenth century is not fully
reflected in his work.   It is not possible for the
literary critic to say, this bears beyond all doubt
the mystic stamp of the late fourteenth century.
Competent critics have been prepared to carry
it back to the days of St Bernard without any
sense of literary or spiritual incongruity.   The
author felt nothing of the reform movement so
busily at work in his time.   No touch of Wiclivism,
no taint of Lollardy appears in the little books, yet
the writer is so immersed in the best thought of all
the Christian ages that there is no touch or taint of
superstition.   An unconscious reformer, he adopts
unconsciously as part of his calm spiritual outlook
all that, from his point of view, the Reformation and

the Counter-Reformation had to teach. It was not necessary to disorganise or reorganise the civilised world in order to teach him the unfettered right of man to approach his Creator. On the other hand, no social upheaval could have taught him other lessons that the Reformation had in hand. The best of the past was his already, but as to the future, he looked for it, as he would have looked for it in the days of Gerbert when the thousand years were about to be accomplished, in another and a heavenly country.

He made little of the promise of this life; he looked eagerly for that which is to come. The following of Christ was the matter that he had in hand, and diligently he mapped the journey. The material wherewith to fill in the ground-plan of his map he found in the New and Old Testaments, and he selected it with the aid of the most spiritual thinkers and dreamers that had lived between his time and the time of the Apostles. Through a mind of singular humility and receptive power, a mind already saturated with the German mysticism of the Middle Ages, there passed in patient detail the great book from Genesis to the Revelations of St John the Divine. With his own neat and unhastening hand he copied out the Bible from cover to cover. The mind retained what the mind looked for, what was already half its own. What did the Bible mean to Hämmerlein? Did it mean the message of the Catholic Church? Perhaps. But first and foremost it meant that men should follow, not this or that creed, but Christ. The fourth book, the *de Sacramento Altaris*, was a supplement. The three books are an entity without it, though it can be fitted in, as à Kempis himself fitted it in, after the second. The author, be he à Kempis or another, is concerned with life rather than with doctrine, with life eternal, as exhibited in the Bible, and seen by the men who followed Christ in the school of St John of Patmos.

The books are a marvellous mosaic, largely compiled from the actual text of the Bible. There are more than one thousand direct references to the Bible in the four little treatises. In the first treatise of twenty-five short chapters there are at least one hundred and seventy references ; in the second treatise with its twelve brief chapters, at least one hundred and three ; in the third and longest book of sixty-three chapters, there are as many as five hundred and fifty ; while in the last treatise containing eighteen chapters we have as many as two hundred and three. From every part of the Bible they come in lavish profusion. There is hardly a book unrepresented. The great sources of inspiration are first, not the New Testament, as we might expect, but the Psalms, and secondly, the Epistles, and then the Gospels. In the first book—the admonitions useful for a spiritual life—there are some seventy-seven passages referable to the Old Testament, and ninety-three passages referable to the New Testament. Of the former, eighteen are from the Psalms and seventeen from Ecclesiasticus, whilst we have also references to Genesis, Numbers, Deuteronomy, Joshua, Kings, Chronicles, Job, Proverbs, Ecclesiastes, Isaiah, Jeremiah, Tobit, Judith, Esther, the Wisdom of Solomon, and first book of the Maccabees. There are twenty - seven references to the Gospels, namely, eleven to St Matthew, one to St Mark, seven to St Luke, and eight to St John. There are sixty-six other definite references to the New Testament, to the First Epistle of St John, the Epistle to the Ephesians, the First Epistle of St Peter, the Epistle to the Romans, the Acts of the Apostles, the Epistle to the Galatians, the Epistle of St James, the two Epistles to the Corinthians, the two Epistles to Timothy, the Epistle to the Philippians, the Epistle to the Colossians, the Epistle to the Hebrews, and the Epistles to the Thessalonians.

The second book—the treatise of admonitions tending to things internal—gives us forty-seven references to the Old Testament and the Apocrypha, of which eighteen are to the Psalms. There are quotations from Genesis, Deuteronomy, Kings, Chronicles, Job, Jeremiah, Isaiah, Proverbs, Micah, Tobit, the Song of Solomon, Joel, Wisdom, Ecclesiasticus, and Judith. In the New Testament there are ten references to St Matthew, eleven to St Luke, and five to St John. We have also references to the Epistles to the Romans, the Hebrews, the Corinthians, the Thessalonians, the Galatians, the Philippians, and to the Acts, the Epistle of St James, the First Epistle of St Peter, and the Revelations. There is no quotation from St Mark. The author quotes him but rarely. There are in all only eight quotations from St Mark in the whole of the *Imitation*, as against sixty-seven from St Matthew, fifty from St Luke, and sixty-eight from St John. The only reference in the first book is the second paragraph in the first chapter, where the phrase " Ab omni caecitate cordis liberari " may be referred to St Mark (iii. 5) and the Epistle to the Ephesians (iv. 18). In the third book we get in chapter vi. a reference—*immunde spiritus*—to St Mark (v. 8), and in the same chapter another reference — *Tace et obmutesce* — to the previous chapter of St Mark (iv. 39). This same verse is again referred to in chapter xxiii. verse 21, where St Mark's phrase *tranquillitas magna* is used. In the fourth book, chapter iii., we seem to have references to St Mark (i. 34, and viii. 1 *seqq.*). In the twelfth chapter we have a direct reference to St Mark (xiv. 14, 15). For some reason the Gospel according to St Mark did not appeal to the author of the *Imitation* in the way that the other Gospels, the Epistles, and the Psalms appealed to him. We have forty-three references to the Epistle to the Romans, sixty-six to the Epistles to the Corinthians, twenty-two to the Epistle to the Hebrews.

When we turn to the long third book we find that there are three hundred and fourteen references to the Old Testament and Apocrypha (including one hundred and thirty-four to the Psalms, twenty-two to Job, and twenty to Isaiah), ninety-five references to the Gospels, and one hundred and forty-one to other books of the New Testament.   In the Old Testament and Apocrypha there are references to Genesis (fifteen), Exodus, Leviticus, Numbers, Deuteronomy, Kings, Job, Proverbs, Isaiah, Jeremiah, Ezekiel, Daniel, Nahum, Tobit, Baruch, Wisdom, Esdras, Judith, Maccabees.   In the New Testament there are references to the Epistles to the Corinthians, the Romans, the Galatians, the Ephesians, the Philippians, the Colossians, the Thessalonians, the Hebrews.   There are thirty-five references to St Matthew, three to St Mark, seventeen to St Luke, and forty to St John.   There are references to the Acts of the Apostles, the Epistle of St James, the Epistles of St Peter, the Epistles to Timothy, the Epistle of St Jude, and the Revelation of St John the Divine.   It is noteworthy that in this third book the references to the Old Testament considerably exceed those to the New, while the references to the Psalms alone are half as numerous again as those to the Gospels.   The references to the Epistles are, however, almost as numerous as those to the Psalms.   When we turn to the fourth book we find that there are about one hundred and thirteen

M

quotations from or allusions to the Old Testament, of which thirty-five are from the Psalms. There are some forty-five references to the Gospels—eleven to St Matthew, four to St Mark, fifteen each to St Luke and St John. The references to the Old Testament and Apocrypha include the books of Genesis, Exodus, Leviticus, Numbers, Deuteronomy, Kings, Chronicles, Job, Isaiah, Jeremiah, Ezekiel, Daniel, Proverbs, The Song of Solomon, Hosea, Ecclesiastes, Habakkuk, Malachi, Ecclesiasticus, Esdras (i), Wisdom. The references to the New Testament include the Epistles to the Hebrews, the Ephesians, the Corinthians, the Philippians, the Colossians, the Galatians, the Romans, and the Epistles of St Peter, St John, and St James, the Epistles to Timothy and Titus, the Acts of the Apostles, the Revelation of St John the Divine.

These thousand or more direct or indirect references to specific passages in the Old and New Testaments and the Apocrypha—of course the numbers given are only approximate—in no way complete the author's debt to the Bible. Every phrase is haunted with Biblical reminiscence. One curious consequence of this is patent to the English ear. No modern translation of the *Imitation* wholly satisfies the expectation of the reader or the hearer. The roll of an Elizabethan version, of one contemporary with the Authorised Version of the Bible, is the demand of ear and heart. The Biblical reminiscence is partly lost, unless we hear the

cadence that belongs beyond divorce to our English
Bible.

The peculiar tenets and the peculiar limitations
of the *Imitation* are woven into a groundwork of
Biblical phrases, and they take from those phrases
their colour and tone. The chief of these limitations
is that the reader of the *Imitation* must look at the
Bible as à Kempis and his spiritual predecessors
looked at it, if the full significance of these little
treatises is to be felt. They appeal to our nature,
but not to our whole nature. Save in so far as à
Kempis anticipated the cleansing forces of subsequent
spiritual developments—and he did to a considerable
extent anticipate these forces—we can only place
ourselves in touch with the mind behind the *Imitation*
by neglecting the lessons of the Renaissance and
the Reformation, and the even deeper lessons of
modern research into the mysteries of mind and
matter. The Bible, as à Kempis and his spiritual
ancestors read it, is the groundwork of the *Imitation*.
The modern mind must in many ways read it differ-
ently, and therefore again and again we feel ourselves out of touch with the *Imitation* as a whole.
Yet this fact does not materially militate against
the lasting power of the work, for while the books
taken as a whole are wanting in much that belongs
to modern spiritual experience, yet the individual
chapters have not, as a rule, this defect ; they may
well appeal to the entire nature in a particular mood ;
and in fact their appeal to all classes of society

is as powerful to-day as it has been at any time in the past five centuries.

Into the Biblical groundwork à Kempis weaved the thoughts of men to whom, as to himself, the Bible was ultimately the main source of inspiration and spiritual direction. But these same men were for the most part familiar with the great thinkers and writers of the pre-Christian ages. These thinkers did not appeal at all directly, and with the exception of Plotinus hardly appealed at all to Thomas à Kempis. He was not conscious of the debt that he owed both to Plato and the Neo-Platonists, or of the influence that Aristotle's philosophy had upon his own philosophy of life. Once, or at the most twice, does he quote Aristotle. The only notable instance is in the opening words of the second chapter of the first book, where he says, "Omnis homo naturaliter scire desiderat sed scientia sine timore Dei quid importat?" This is from *The Metaphysics* (lib. i., cap. i.). Monsignor Puyol has traced the quotation to the Latin version of Cardinal Bessarion,[1] where the words used are ' Omnes homines natura scire desiderant.' Thomas à Kempis immediately corrects the Aristotelian statement of the natural aspiration of man with its spiritual equivalent : of what avail is knowledge without the fear of God? Truly, he adds, a humble serf who serves God is better than a proud philosopher who, neglecting himself, studies the courses of the stars. We shall

[1] Tom. ii. page 1269, ed. Lugd., 1581.

see directly that this is only one of various direct attacks on the Aristotelian School as represented by Abelard and others. In chapter twenty-five of the first book we have the phrase, "subtrahere se violenter ad quod natura vitiose inclinatur," and Dr Bigg is inclined to think that perhaps there is here a reference to Aristotle's *Ethics* (ii. 9). It may be so, but it must be remembered that in the fourteenth century Aristotelian concepts were much in the air, and were unconsciously adopted by many who had no sympathy with Aristotle as presented by the Schoolmen. The Augustinian Canon may have obtained both passages direct from Bessarion, but it is more probable that they were drawn from some monastic commonplace book. This was almost certainly the case, as Dr Bigg has pointed out, in the solitary instance where Seneca is quoted. This is in the sixth paragraph of chapter twenty of the first book, where we read, "Dixit quidam: quoties inter homines fui, minor homo redii."

This is a paraphrase of a passage in Seneca's Seventh Epistle: "Avarior redeo, ambitiosior, luxuriosior, immo vero crudelior et inhumanior, quia inter homines fui."

We have several quotations from the Latin poets, but there is only one doubtful reference to the deified Virgil. The first quotation is from Ovid's *De Remedio Amoris* (lib. ii. 91), and occurs in the twenty-first paragraph of chapter thirteen in the first book. The passage runs :—

"Unde quidam dixit:
Principiis obsta, sero medicina paratur
Quum mala per longas convaluere moras."

It is a note that à Kempis strikes often.   He that
is whole needeth no physician, therefore resist the
beginnings of sin.   The remedy comes too late when
the sin is well rooted.   In the eleventh chapter of
the same book he sounds the same warning: "Resiste
in principio inclinationi tuæ, et malam dedisce
consuetudinem, ne forte paulatim ad majorem te
ducat difficultatem."

It was perhaps with a gleam of the latent humour
which is ever peeping out in this most serious call to
humanity that the saintly canon went to Ovid for
the purpose of driving home the lesson.   In the
thirty-third chapter of the third book we seem to
find, Dr Bigg has pointed out, a further reference to
Ovid.   The passage runs in Dr Bigg's version: "It
is rare to find one who is wholly free from the mole
of self-seeking" ("et raro totus liber quis invenitur a
nævo propriae exquisitionis"), and Dr Bigg tells us
that "there is probably a reference to Ovid.   Tristia
v. 13, 14: "Nullus in egregio corpore naevus
erit."   This view is, however, very doubtful, for the
identification turns on the use of the word *naevus*.
Now the Codex Aronensis—an excellent text as
edited by Monsignor Puyol, whatever we may think
as to its alleged authorship—has no such word.   It
has *nervus*, which, if used, as it is colloquially used in
the Latin comedies, to mean a prison, fits in well

with the word *liber*, and makes a simpler text than if the word *naevus* is used. It is difficult also to see why the expression should be translated "the mole of self-seeking." It is not so much self-seeking as personal impulse in opposition to acting under the inspiration of the divine will. " The prison of wilful impulse" seems nearer to the meaning of the mystical writer.

The shadowy reference to Virgil occurs, according to Gence, towards the end of the ninth chapter of the third book. There we have the statement, "Vincit enim omnia divina caritas, et dilatat omnes animae vires." This certainly recalls, by way of a commonplace book doubtless, the famous words of the tenth eclogue (69), "Omnia vincit Amor." Chaucer, a contemporary of à Kempis, it will be remembered, quoted them also.

We have in chapter fifty-four of the third book one possible reference to Horace. The passage runs : " Omnes quidem bonum appetunt, et aliquid boni in suis dictis vel factis praetendunt : ideo sub specie boni multi falluntur." Monsignor Puyol refers this to the phrase "decipimur specie recti" in the *De Arte Poetica* (v. 25). This seems somewhat far fetched, but the idea is the same, and it is possible that here again we have a commonplace - book version.

The only other Latin authors from whom à Kempis quotes are Pliny and Lucan. In chapter twenty-five, of book three, we have the passage that tells us where true peace is to be found. " In surrendering thyself with all thy heart to the divine Will : not seeking thine own in great matters or in small, in time or in eternity ; so that with unchanged countenance thou abide in thanksgiving, amid prosperity and adversity : weighing all things with equal balance " ("omnia aequa lance pensando"). Dr Bigg refers this to Pliny (i. 7) : "Is demum profecto vitam aequa lance pensitabit, qui semper fragilitatis humanae memor fuerit." There is a likeness of phrase that is possibly not accidental, and may again be referred to the commonplace - book. Dr Bigg is also inclined to find a reference to Pliny (i. 10, 49) in the sentence at the end of chapter twenty-seven of the same book : "Quia haec magna sapientia est, non moveri omni vento verborum nec aurem male blandienti praebere Sirenae, sic enim coepta pergitur via secure." The similarity can hardly be accidental.

The reference to Lucan's *Pharsalia* is apparently quite direct (i. 135). It is a famous phrase, "the shadow of a great name." It occurs in chapter twenty-four of book three : [1] "Non sit tibi curae de magni nominis umbra et non de multorum familiaritate, et de privata hominum delectione." Hirsche, however, thinks that the phrase is borrowed, probably from the first of St Bernard's sermons on the Circumcision, where we read "non est in eo [Jesu] magni nominis umbra, sed veritas." [2]

---

[1] It is also used by à Kempis in his *Chronicles*.
[2] See the Paris edition of 1494.

In addition to these direct quotations we find in the *Imitation* one or two classical proverbs. Thus in chapter twenty-four of the first book we have " in omnibus rebus respice finem"; and at the end of chapter twenty-six of the third book we have "inter haec quaeso manus tua me regat et doceat, *ne quid nimium* fiat." These may once more be referred to a commonplace - book. The classical references are, it is clear, sparse and obscure enough. They are mere driblets from the classical reading, now growing sadly narrow, of the religious in the Middle Ages. They give no hint whatever of the Renaissance, and their form is evidence enough, if evidence of this type were needed, that Thomas à Kempis was absolutely unconscious of anything of the nature of a Revival of Letters. They also seem to me to indicate that the book was actually written at the beginning of the fifteenth century. Had it been later, we might perhaps have expected more references. Had it been earlier, we certainly should have had an abundance of quotations, for the early thirteenth century had a large acquaintance at any rate with polite letters. All that we actually get are echoes of echoes, the murmur of culture that reverberated fainter and more faint till it was lost in the remotest monasteries.

When we turn from classical to mediæval literature we find, not indeed an abundance of quotations, but a pervading atmosphere of that literature from end to end of the *Imitation.* St Augustine and St

Bernard are the two great sources from which à
Kempis drew, or rather let me say the two great
influences under which he worked. But the influence
of the Schoolmen, when their philosophy melts into
faith, can also be traced. Thus it is just possible
that à Kempis, in chapter fifteen of the third book,
has been influenced by Scotus Erigena: "In manu
tua ego sum, gyra et reversa me per circuitum."
("I am in thy hand: spin me forward or spin me
back"). Dr Bigg thinks that there may be here a
reference to the Vulgate version of Ecclesiastes (i. 6),
to which the Subtle Doctor also refers in the words
"Gyrans gyrando vadit spiritus et in locum suum
revertitur." The Vulgate version runs: "Gyrat per
meridiem, et flectitur ad aquilonem: lustrans universa
in circuitu pergit spiritus, et in circulos suos
revertitur." Whether à Kempis had or had not
the text of John Scotus in mind the passage is an
interesting and characteristic example of his method.
The Scriptural idea, almost the very words of
Scripture, are used, but both are applied to new uses
and are organically introduced into a new connection.

Dr Bigg has detected two references to St
Thomas Aquinas, both in the thirteenth chapter of
the fourth book. The first is the passage, "O, quam
suavis est spiritus tuus, Domine, qui ut dulcedinem
tuam in filios demonstrares, pane suavissimo de
Caelo descendente illos reficere dignaris"—"Oh
how sweet, Lord, is Thy Spirit; who to show forth
Thy loving-kindness toward Thy children, dost deign

to refresh them with the bread of sweetness which cometh down from Heaven." Bigg and Hirsche both refer the passage to the Angelic Doctor.[1] Hirsche further notes that à Kempis employs the same quotation in the *Three Tabernacles*. The passage, however, is in fact a combination of passages from the Book of Wisdom and St John's Gospel. Thus in the twelfth chapter of Wisdom we have " Dulcedinem tuam, quam in filios habes, ostendebat,"[2] and in the sixth chapter of the Gospel of St John (verse 50) we have, " Hic est panis de Caelo descendens." Here again then we have an instance of Biblical phraseology and ideas brought into a new and a living connection. The combination appears, however, in this case to have been made by the great mind of Aquinas, and to have been adopted by à Kempis. This well illustrates what has been said above as to the Augustinian's use of the Bible and of living phrases drawn from it, or from commentators upon it. The phrase, the form is the thing, though no one would more stoutly have denied the insinuation than the worthy Canon, sitting " little book " in hand in his "little corner," and enjoying a life of letters in a way and to an extent that few other men have done. His phrase, " Multa verba non satiant animam " (i. 2), does not exclude the supposition that he believed in the spiritual efficacy of " the few best words in the best order." A word in due season how good it is.

The Angelic Doctor is again quoted in the same

[1] *In Off. Sacr. vesp. ad magnificat.*   [2] See also cap. xvi. 21.

chapter :[1] "Quae est enim alia Gens tam inclyta sicut plebs Christiana." Aquinas took the form of this direct from Deuteronomy :[2] " Quae est enim alia gens sic inclyta?" The phrase is adopted by à Kempis, and developed and expanded. If there are no such people as the people of Christ there can be no creature so beloved as the Christian soul, fed in the sacrament by God Himself.

Turning from Aquinas to other mediæval writers, we find (according to Dr Bigg) two possible references in chapter four of the second book to two Latin hymns. The chapter opens with the phrase "Duabus alis homo sublevatur a terrenis, simplicitate scilicet, et puritate." Does this allude to the hymn *Ecquis binas columbinas Alas dabit animæ?* Certainly the trick and jingle of words in this mediæval hymn were likely to catch the mind of Thomas à Kempis, which was peculiarly susceptible to any interplay between sound and sense. It is also suggested that the later sentence in the same chapter—"si rectum cor tuum esset, tunc omnis creatura speculum vitæ, et liber sanctae doctrinae esset"—is drawn from the hymn by Alain de Lille beginning :—

> " Omnis mundi creatura
> Quasi liber et pictura
> Nobis est et speculum."

Certainly the idea and the phrasing is very similar, and in neither case has the image or the phrase

[1] *Off. Sacr.* Lect. 5.　　　　[2] iv. 8.

been traced to the Bible. À Kempis, a continual student of books, must have gathered phrases from all quarters, and it is probable that most of the passages that have no scriptural authority will be found to be echoes of striking words in the devout literature of the Middle Ages. It is, however, noticeable that the service books supplied the writer with very little material—other, of course, than scriptural material. In the fourth book, *De Sacramento Altaris*, we have four references to the Gelasian Sacramentary,[1] and one reference in chapter fifty-seven of the third book. We have also at the end of chapter fifty-five of the third book the *Oratio* for the sixteenth Sunday after Pentecost : " Tua ergo me Domine gratia semper praeveniat et sequatur, ac bonis operibus jugiter praestet esse intentum." This is, of course, the English collect for the seventeenth Sunday after Trinity : "Lord we pray that Thy grace may always prevent and follow us, and make us continually to be given to all good works, through Jesus Christ, our Lord. Amen."

The sentence immediately preceding this collect is a good instance of the manner in which à Kempis selected his phrases from various biblical sources. It runs : " Quid sum sine ea, nisi aridum lignum, et stipes inutilis ad ejiciendum." The text is unsettled. The autograph of 1442 has *stips*, while the Codex Aronensis has *stipes*. Dr Bigg suggests that *stirps* is the only possible reading, while Hirsche

[1] See caps. 1 and 3, *Bigg's Edition*. See also *lib. iii. cap.* 48 *and lib. iv. cap.* 3.

prefers to retain *stips*. *Stips* is, however, an impossible reading. It is a rare Latin word with which à Kempis could hardly have been familiar, and its meaning—a gift or profit—is incompatible with the context. *Stipes*—the reading of the Codex Aronensis—seems at first sight the best reading, for it means, in classical Latin, *a log*, and this fits in with and carries on the conception of *lignum*, which conveys the idea *wood* rather than *tree*. On the other hand *lignum* is translated *tree* when used in St Luke's Gospel (xxiii. 31), where in the sentence "For if they do these things in a green tree what shall be done in the dry?" the word *dry* is the rendering of *aridum lignum*. If *lignum* is intended to mean *tree* rather than *wood*, then *stirps* is a more reasonable reading than *stipes*, for it means the stock or trunk of a standing tree. The passage would then run : "Without it [truth] what am I but a dry tree and a trunk, fit only to be cast away?" This view is confirmed by a passage from Isaiah (xiv. 19), which was almost certainly in the mind of à Kempis when he wrote the sentence. It runs as follows : "Tu autem projectus es de sepulcro tuo quasi stirps inutilis pollutus." Here we have the very phrase *stirps inutilis*, while the connection with *tree* is emphasised by the fact that the phrase *velut lignum aridum*, with that meaning, occurs in Ecclesiasticus (vi. 3). Of course the difficulty may have arisen in consequence of the practice pursued by à Kempis of playing with words. He may have written *stips,* having the idea of a valueless reward in his mind, while he still desired to carry on the conception of dead wood or a dead tree (conveyed by the word *lignum*), by the words *stipes* or *stirps.* The literary artist who plays with words habitually runs the danger of such a slip. The really interesting point, however, is that there we get a combination of phrases from Ecclesiasticus, Isaiah, and St Luke—a combination that brings out all the peculiarities of the literary methods pursued by the author of the *Imitation.*

There are still other sources to be considered before we turn to St Bernard and St Augustine. We have in chapter nine of the second book the account given by St Maximus of Turin of the martyrdom of St Laurence and Pope Sixtus under the Emperor Valerian in 258 A.D.[1] The value of the reference is in the light it throws on the works read by à Kempis. The choice of such an obscure illustration by an obscure writer would seem to indicate a mind steeped in the less obvious literature of the Middle Ages. But that à Kempis had any knowledge of the *Apocalypse of Peter* can perhaps hardly be inferred from his statement of the doctrine so fully developed by Dante, that each sin is punished by the thwarting of the desire that lies behind the sin. But the twenty-fourth chapter of the first book shows that à Kempis was fully familiar with the doctrine—"In quibus homo peccavit, in illis

---

[1] See Bigg's edition of *The Imitation*, p. 117 (*n.*), and *Hom. I. de Sancto Laurentio* ; also *Lives of the Saints*, August 10.

gravius punietur." This doctrine is clearly taken from the eleventh chapter of the Wisdom of Solomon:[1] "Wherewithal a man sinneth, by the same also shall he be punished" ("per quae peccat quis, per haec et torquetur"). Dante and à Kempis needed no apocalyptic Gospel to teach them the lesson that the unhappy Francesca framed in deathless words, for it lies deep in the humanity of all men—

> "Ed ella a me : Nessun maggior dolore
> Che ricordarsi del tempo felice
> Nella miseria."[2]

Dr Bigg has pointed out the resemblance between a passage in the fourth chapter of the fourth book and one in the *Celestial Hierarchy* (i. 13) of the Pseudo-Dionysius Areopagus. If this was used, as it very probably was, by à Kempis, it was taken from the ninth-century version of Scotus Erigena. Thomas à Kempis writes : " Et si necdum totus coelestis et tam ignitus ut Cherubim et Seraphim esse possum, conabor tamen devotioni insistere, et cor meum praeparare, ut vel modicam divini incendi flammam, ex humili sumptione vivifici Sacramenti conquiram." This idea springs from the conception of Dionysius : " Deinde easdem sanctissimorum Seraphim edoctus est deiformes virtutes, sacra quidem ipsorum cognominatione, quod est ignitum." Dante [3] expresses, drawing his conception rather from Dionysius than Gregory, exactly the idea of à Kempis. The cherubim

---

[1] Ver. 16 (Vulgate, ver. 17). [2] *L'Inferno* (canto v., ll. 120-23).
[3] *Il Paradiso*, canto xxviii., ll. 25-27, 98-102.

and seraphim are an intense " cerchio d'igne " circling immediately round the flaming heart of the universe. So intense is their light, so sublime their vision, that Beatrice likens them to God Himself. To the knowledge of God and the love of God as represented by the Cherubim and the Seraphim the Disciple cannot attain. But by endeavouring to attain a state of true devotion, and by preparation of the heart, he can reach some measure of knowledge and love—a tiny flame of that divine fire which forms the central light of things. À Kempis is as terse as Dante himself, and feels as deeply the mediæval sense of almost physical illumination which the realism of the Pseudo-Dionysius, Gregory, Scotus Erigena, the first father of Scolasticism, and Anselm, its second father, created in their efforts to identify the worlds of reason and revelation.

Anselm himself indeed appears to have contributed one direct idea to the *Imitation*. In chapter thirty-eight of the third book we have the passage : " Qui [Deus] nil inordinatum reliquit in sua creatura." Dr Bigg, with much reason, compares this with the passage from the *Cur Deus Homo* : [1] " Deum vero non decet aliquid in suo regno inordinatum dimittere." The idea is certainly that of Anselm. It is also noticeable that the conception of the natural freedom of the sons of God, " qui stant super praesentia et speculantur aeterna," is a conception used by Dante in the canto (vii.) of the

[1] i. 12.

N

Paradiso where the influence of Anselm is apparent beyond doubt. Can à Kempis have been acquainted with the *Comedy*? It is certainly a temptation to suggest that he had read the *Paradiso*. The famous line in the third canto—

E la sua volontate è nostra pace

is a continual motive in this structure of ecclesiastical music. A notable instance—one instance among many—of an elaborate use of the deep feeling underlying the line, is to be found in the Prayer at the end of the fifteenth chapter of the third book. It is a prayer for the complete fulfilment of God's will which declares that the unity of will must bring unity with God, and that such unity alone is peace. " Tua voluntas mea sit et mea voluntas tuam sequatur semper, et optime ei concordet. Sit mihi unum velle et nolle tecum, nec aliud posse velle et nolle, nisi quod vis, et nolis. . . . Da mihi super omnia desiderata in te quiescere, et cor meum in te pacificare. Tu vera pax cordis, tu sola requies, extra te omnia sunt dura et inquieta. In hac pace, in idipsum, hoc est, in Te uno summo et aeterno Bono, dormiam et requiesciam." If à Kempis did not know the work of Dante, he must at any rate have followed out the same line of contemplative thought, and must have been a child of the same spiritual ancestors. For it is not only in the solitary line quoted, but in the whole of Piccarda's speech that the resemblance is apparent. She says : [1] " Brother, the quality of love

[1] Mr Philip Wicksteed's translation.

¶ A full deuout and gostely treatyse of the Impyta
cion and folowynge the blessed Lyfe of oure moste
mercyfull Sauyoure criste : compyled in Laten by
the right worshypfull Doctor Mayster Iohñ Ger
son: and translate into Englysshe: The yere of oure
lorde. M.D.ii. By mayster wyllyam Atkynson Do
ctor of diuinite: at the specyall request and commaun
dement of the full excellent Pryncesse Margarete
moder to our Souerayne lorde kynge Henry the.
vii.and Countesse of Rychemount and Derby.

I i

WOODCUT--A PIETA—FROM THE FIRST ENGLISH EDITION OF THE
TREATISE "DE IMITATIONE CHRISTI" ISSUED IN LONDON BY
RICHARD PYNSON, 1503.

stilleth our will, and maketh us long only for what we have, and giveth us no other thirst. Did we desire to be more aloft, our longings were discordant from His will who here assorteth us, and for that, thou wilt see, there is no room within these circles, if of necessity we have our being here in love, and if thou think again what is love's nature. Nay, 'tis the essence of this blessed being to hold ourselves within the Divine will, whereby our own wills are themselves made one. So that our being thus, from threshold unto threshold throughout the realm, is a joy to all the realm as to the King, who draweth our wills to what He willeth; and His will is our peace; it is that sea to which all moves that it createth and that nature maketh." Here is set forth the great end of the Contemplative, the physical and spiritual goal at which the Augustinian Platonism aimed, and in the contemplation of which the most modern thinkers find the reconciliation of philosophic contradictions. It was realised as a living fact by Dante in the year 1300, and again by à Kempis a century later. As the struggling spirit comes within sight of the goal, we seem to hear Human Knowledge saying (in the words of the *Moral Play*[1]—

> "Now hath he made ending;
> Methinketh that I hear angels sing
> And make great joy and melody,
> Where Everyman's soul shall received be."

---

[1] *Everyman*, line 890 . . . (F. Sidgwick's edition. H. H. Bullen, London, 1903).

If à Kempis had not studied the works of Dante, the extraordinary resemblance of thought and even of form must be due to the common indebtedness to St Bernard, who profoundly influenced the mind of each of these consummate artists. Mr Philip Wicksteed has pointed out that in Bernard's treatise *On loving God* it is his "consistent doctrine that the blessedness of heaven is found in the complete absorption of the soul in God, self-consciousness being, as it were, replaced not by unconsciousness but by God-consciousness." With St Bernard as with Dante and à Kempis, it is body, soul, and spirit —the entire man—that must yearn for self-recognition in the recognition of God. "Oh how true," says St Bernard, "did he speak who said that all things work together for the good of them that love God! To the soul that loveth God, its body availeth in its infirmity, availeth in its death, availeth in its resurrection; first for the fruit of penitence, second for repose, third for consummation. And rightly doth the soul not will to be made perfect without that which it feeleth hath in every state served it in good things."[1]

In this place it will be convenient to refer to the quotation at the end of chapter fifty of book three from Saint Bonaventura's *Legenda S. Francisci*. It is natural that à Kempis should have been a student of both these personalities, for the fact fits admirably in with the whole tone of the *Imitation*, and particularly

[1] *Il Paradiso*, canto xiv., Mr P. H. Wicksteed's note on lines 64-6, pp. 177-9 (J. M. Dent, London, 1899).

with the precise aspect of the work that I am now considering. St Francis was an unlearned man whose whole gospel was the gospel not of faith, but of love. Mr Wicksteed has finely pointed out that Francis embraced poverty "for pure love of her; that is to say, from a sense that the more we *have*, the less we can *be*, and a passionate joy in coming into naked contact with God and nature."[1] This joy was one that Bernard shared, a joy that seemed to dominate his whole nature, and à Kempis was not far behind Francis and Bernard in their aspiration for personal relationship with God. Bonaventura, a contemplative nearer to Hämmerlein's time, likewise joined in this desire, and set forth the pricelessness of such a relationship in his *Stimulus Amoris*. Bonaventura says of Francis, "He studied, as Christ's disciple, to become vile in his own, and in other men's eyes, remembering how it had been said by our great Master, That which is highly esteemed amongst men is abomination in the sight of God. He was wont, too, to repeat a saying, *What everyone is in God's sight, that is he and no more*."[2] It was this latter phrase that à Kempis incorporated into his work : "nam quantum unusquisque est in oculis tuis, tantum est et non amplius, ait humilis sanctus Franciscus." This sentence lays stress on the necessity of oneness of will between created and Creator, and is full of the spirit of St Bernard. It is curious,

---

[1] *Il Paradiso*, note to canto xii.
[2] Bigg's edition of the *Imitation*, note, p. 300.

therefore, that it was this very passage that dissipated the claims of St Bernard to the authorship of the *Imitation*. That it must do so is of course obvious, for Francis lived and Bonaventura wrote long after Bernard's death. But this fact was not noticed when the claim in favour of the Bernardian authorship was put forward. The manuscripts of the *Musica Ecclesiastica* type — with which I have especially dealt in another chapter—omitted the words " ait sanctus Franciscus " and so possibly confused the issue and enabled the advocates of St Bernard to allege that the words had been improperly introduced. It is certain that the work was attributed in comparatively early manuscripts to St Bernard ; but the fact that the very earliest manuscripts, such as the Burney Codex 314 in the British Museum, contain the words " ait humilis sanctus Franciscus," entirely disposes of his claim.

The reference to St Francis is indeed strong evidence in favour of the authorship of à Kempis, for the Augustinian in his little book entitled *Manuale Monachorum*—a tract containing short sermons or addresses considered suitable for the professed and in structure extremely like many of the shorter chapters of the *Imitation* [1]—deals with the humility of St Francis. This chapter (v.) is entitled "de magna humilitate Sancti Francisci," and runs as follows : " Hic est qui contempsit vitam mundi—quid fecit humilem et sanctum Franciscum tam devotum et deo dilectum

---

[1] *Cf.* also the chapter from *The Garden of Roses*, Appendix ii. hereto.

in hac vita, et tam altum in gloria. Vere profunda humiltas sua, et quia inter omnia beneficia divina et exercitia cotidiana passionem Christi et sacra vulnera doloris ei immensi amoris plena in mente portavit recoluit condoluit gravissime ponderavit amarissime flevit et ardentissime amavit. Nam magna gratia confertur humilibus et passionem Christi cotidie recolentibus. Verus enim humilis non se reputat nec elevat de bonis quae facit sed omnibus viliorem se estimat et cunctis inferiorem veraciter confitetur. Hic propria mala sua inspicit et plangit et aliorum bona videns congaudet pro quibus Deum laudat et benedicit, orans ut sui misereatur et a malis liberet."

In this characteristic passage is to be found both the spiritual and literary note of the *Imitation*. The conclusion of the fiftieth chapter might well be the conclusion of this little sermon. Yet it is not wonderful that the early copyists and printers attributed the work to St Bernard. It is saturated with his thoughts and phrases in combination with those of St Augustine. It will be useful first to consider some of the references to Augustine and then to pass to the influence of Bernard. In the third chapter of the first book, the chapter *de Doctrina Veritatis*, Dr Bigg sees in the opening sentence, "Felix quem veritas per se docet, non per figuras et voces transeuntes, sed sicuti se habet," a direct reference to the memorable and inspired passage in the *Confessions of St Augustine* where the Saint and his mother Monica, as they leaned together one evening against a ledge of a window in the house at Ostia, passed from sweet converse into a vision of the presence of God. The passage must be quoted, as the spirit of it certainly underlies not only the Augustinian's doctrine of truth, but the whole of his mystical revelation of the Way.

" If the tumult of the flesh were hushed ; hushed these shadows of earth, sea, sky ; hushed the heavens and the soul itself, so that it should pass beyond itself and not think of itself ; if all dreams were hushed, and all sensuous revelations, and every tongue and every symbol ; if all that comes and goes were hushed—They all proclaim to him that hath an ear : ' We made not ourselves : He made us who abideth for ever '—But suppose that, having delivered their message, they held their peace, turning their ear to Him who made them, and that He alone spoke, not by them but for Himself, and that we heard His word, not by any fleshly tongue, nor by an Angel's voice, nor in the thunder, nor in any similitude, but His voice whom we love in these His creatures—Suppose we heard him without any intermediary at all—Just now we reached out, and with one flash of thought touched the Eternal Wisdom that abides above all—Suppose this endured, and all other far inferior modes of vision were taken away, and this alone were to ravish the beholder, and absorb him, and plunge him into mystic joy, might not eternal life be like this moment of comprehension for which we sighed ? Is not this the

WOODCUT REPRESENTING THE ADORATION OF
THE MAGI: FROM THE PARIS EDITION OF THE
TREATISE " DE IMITATIONE CHRISTI" ISSUED
IN 1496 BY GEORGIUS MITTELHUS.

meaning of 'Enter thou into the joy of thy Lord'?
Ah, when shall this be? Shall it be when 'we shall
all rise, but shall not all be changed'?"[1]

We may doubt if Bernard, Dante, Francis,
Bonaventura, à Kempis, or any mediæval dreamer
ever rose to this height, ever realised as Augustine
realised the spiritual fact, as opposed to the philosophic dream or the theological conception, of the
"flight of the alone to the Alone." What Plotinus
conceived, Augustine felt, and thus crowned the
philosophy of Alexandria, subtly compounded of
Greek and Hebrew thought, with a personal realisation of its profoundest speculative surmise. It is
true that such experiences were claimed in the
Middle Ages, that Bernard himself was declared to
have conversed in the flesh with God, seeing Him in
His very essence (*per essentiam*) while yet alive.
Dante tells us that Bernard in this world tasted of
the Peace of God by contemplation :—

> " Che in questo mondo,
> Contemplando, gustò di quella pace." (*Par.* Canto xxxi.)

But Bernard's words that follow, though written
by Dante, leave us cold compared with Augustine's
almost inarticulate picture of the vision that eludes
him. It is something more than art. It is
positive experience—a story that Enoch or Elijah
returning might have told. The vision of direct
intercourse with God loses the appearance of reality
in the Middle Ages, and is cold indeed in the mind of

[1] Dr Bigg's translation (Methuen & Co., London).

Anselm, who conceives a colloquy in the presence of God as to the duty of obedience to God! It was only the fourteenth century revival of mysticism in England and the Netherlands that made it possible for à Kempis to conceive even in a measure the intense reality of the Augustinian vision.

The next reference to Augustine—an indirect one—is in chapter three of the third book, where à Kempis uses a quotation from Jeremiah (xxiii. 24) which is, as Dr Bigg has pointed out, a favourite text with St Augustine : " Thou givest all, fillest all." In book one, chapter two, of the *Confessions* we have the same quotation : "Whither can I fly beyond heaven and earth, that my God who hath said I fill heaven and earth [coelum et terram ego impleo] should thence come into me."

It is noticeable that the short passage " Tu solus bonus es, justus et sanctus, Tu omnia potes, omnia praestas, omnia imples," is reminiscent of Luke (xviii. 19, *Nemo bonus nisi solus Deus*), Maccabees (lib. ii. i. 24, *Solus justus*), Kings (lib. i. ii. 2, *Non est sanctus, ut est Dominus*), Job (xlii. 2, *omnia potes*), Timothy (Ep. i. v. 17, *praestat nobis omnia*), and Jeremiah (xxiii. 24, *Coelum et terram ego impleo*). Art and serene patience could no further go. Yet this was the manner and method of the artist in all his work. He built with the patience and success of the coral insect. That dignity of patience which he recommended to others he more than upheld himself.

I turn from this somewhat minor illustration of literary methods to the deep keynote both of the *Imitation* and the *Confessions*. The latter opens with the cry, " Thou hast created us unto Thyself, and our heart finds no rest until it rests in Thee." That is the end of the following of Christ, whether the way be mapped by Augustine or à Kempis. In the twenty-first chapter of the third book there is a passage that is obviously drawn, as Hirsche has pointed out, from this cry of Augustine : " Quoniam quidem non potest cor meum veraciter quiescere, nec totaliter contentari, nisi in te requiescat." These are almost the very words of Augustine : " inquietum est cor nostrum donec requiescat in te." It is no chance selection of phrase. The chapter is built round the idea and is entitled, " That we are to rest in God above all goods and gifts." Up to this point it seems at first sight singularly original. There are two possible references to the Psalms : " Quis dabit mihi pennas sicut columbæ, et volabo, et requiescam ? " (liv. 7), and, " Gustate et videte quoniam suavis est Dominus" (Ps. xxxiii. 9). Otherwise we have no direct Biblical references. On the other hand, the cross references between this chapter and the rest of the first three books are extremely numerous, and prove that it is as artificial as any book in the treatises. At least one other passage is traceable to Augustine : " All beside Thyself is small and unsatisfying whatsoever Thou bestowest on me or revealest of Thyself or promisest, if Thou art not seen nor fully obtained." Hirsche compares this with "satis ostendis, quam magnam creaturam rationalem feceris, cui nullo modo sufficit ad beatam requiem quidquid te minus est."[1]

In the forty-ninth chapter of the third book we have, as Dr Bigg points out, a further reference to Augustine (vii. 17). It is interesting, as it is taken from the Wisdom of Solomon (ix. 15), and is also contained in the *Confession*. The passage in the *Imitation* runs : "Give great thanks to the heavenly goodness : which treats thee with such condescension ; which visits thee with mercy ; arouses thee to fervour ; sustains thee with power : lest through thine own weight thou sink down to earthly things." The passage in the *Confessions* is curiously parallel : "I could not stand still to enjoy my God, but was swept up to Thee by Thy beauty, and again torn away from Thee by my own weight, and fell back with a groan into the world of sense ; and the weight was carnal use and wont." The Latin of the significant phrase in the *Imitation* is "ne proprio pondere ad terrena labaris," while in the *Confessions* it is "moxque diripiebar abs te pondere meo." The idea is of course common enough. It is beautifully used by Dante in the third canto of the *Paradiso* describing the departure of Piccarda :—

> "e cantando vanio
> Come per acqua cupa cosa grave."

---

[1] *Confessions* (xiii. 8).

But both in Augustine and à Kempis the use is somewhat artificial.[1] It obscures the conception of God's universality both of position and influence—"if I go down to hell Thou art there also," Psalm 139—and lacks the logical sequence so passionately developed by Dante—the results that follow from any attempt to fly from the enveloping presence of the Almighty.

It is not, however, by particular passages that we test the influence of the monk of Hippo. The debt of à Kempis to Augustine is in a sense intangible, not to be measured by literary quotations or verbal borrowings. It is, if one may say so, a philosophic rather than a Christian debt. He borrows the cry wrung by the heart from the intelligence of the created being, whether Christian or not, to the Creator. It is the cry of the Greek rather than of the Hebrew, the cry of the man who found the answer to his cry in the Gospel of the disciple whom Jesus loved. Augustine in fact bequeathed to à Kempis the Plotinianism of Victorinus Afer. It is possible to think that it was of Victorinus as revealed by the *Confessions* (viii. 2) that à Kempis wrote in the forty-eighth chapter of the third book : "Blessed is the man who for Thy sake, Lord, gives all created things leave to depart ; who does violence to nature ; and through fervour of the spirit crucifies the lusts of the flesh ; that so with

[2] *Cf.* Eckhardt's sentence : "Deadly sin is also a sickness of the faculties, when a man can never stand up alone for the weight of his sins, nor ever resist following into sin" (*Light, Life, and Love* : W. R. Inge, p. 9).

serene conscience he may offer a pure prayer unto
Thee: and may be worthy to stand among the
choirs angelical, where no earthly thing can find a
place of those that are within or those that are
without." Here is a note not altogether Christian
here, but altogether Plotinian. He is not entirely
a Christian, even in the mind of à Kempis, "qui
naturae vim facit." The non-natural world of
Alexandrian philosophy, the city of God which in
this very chapter à Kempis apostrophises—"O
Supernae Civitatis mansio beatissima!"—has for the
most part been brought into accord with Christian
doctrine as revealed by the New Testament to
the mediæval mystic. But à Kempis is never
primarily a naturalist, he does not instinctively
think, with the greatest of the schoolmen, that the
world of nature and the world of revelation have
the same ultimate contents. The mysticism of the
Alexandrian Greek presents to him at every turn
a God who is aloof and alone, approachable only
along the narrow way of Christ. À Kempis was
an Augustinian in heart as well as in habit—an
Alexandrian born a thousand years too late—yet
because he was too late, he is immortal, for the
spiritual struggle of the millennium that separates
him and Augustine is reflected in every page of the
Imitation. The fact remained, and not even à
Kempis could ignore it, that the passage of a
thousand years had brought men no nearer to the
Plotinian vision of That Which Is; that men had

wandered in the wilderness and found no pathway to God. The morasses of sin and disbelief were still impassable. It was necessary to come down to earth and build a causeway across them that should be broad and clear and well fitted for the Following of Christ. A pathway to reality was needed that the simplest soul could follow. The flight to the Alone had failed. In its place and with the same Plotinian ideal, à Kempis substituted a life-long journey, slow and toilsome, over the marshes of time in the very footsteps of the Man of Nazareth : " qui sequitur me non ambulat in tenebris, dicit Dommus (i. 1) ; nam via tua via nostra, et per sanctam patientiam ambulamus ad te, qui es corona nostra. Nisi tu praecessisses et docuisses, quis sequi curaret ? " (iii. 18).

The great spiritual and literary force that so largely modified the outlook of à Kempis was the influence of St Bernard. In one sense St Bernard may almost be said to be the author of the *Imitation*, for had it not been for his influence the work of the Augustinian Canon must have shared the fate of the rest of the voluminous mystic literature of the late fourteenth and early fifteenth century. It was from a prolonged study of St Bernard's writings that à Kempis acquired his peculiar literary note and his deathless appeal to the human heart. The direct and indirect references to the works of St Bernard in the *Imitation* are numerous, but apart altogether from such references, the

manner of the great Abbot of Clairvaux dominates
the style of the treatises, and his peculiarly direct
human spirituality, as opposed to the vague yearnings of the Alexandrian school, is visible everywhere.
A few quotations from St Bernard[1] which I selected
in the almost certain belief that they occurred in the
Imitation, but which in fact do not occur, will illus-
trate this. They appeared to me so obviously
phrases belonging to the *Imitation*, that I have
been surprised at the failure to find parallel
passages. I believe, however, that many students
of the *Imitation* would attribute them to that work.

1. Fideli homini totus mundus divitiarum est
(in vita Malachi).

2. Sit ergo in corde justicia : et justicia quae
ex fide est. Haec enim sola habet gloriam apud
Deum (in vigilia nativitatis Domini, Sermone 1).

3. Malum voluptas corporis : bonum vero afflictio
est (Sermone 3).

4. Quidni dimmitatur in pace, qui Christum
Dominium habet in pectore : ipse enim est pax
nostra, quae per fidem habitat in cordibus nostris
(in purificatione Mariae, Sermone 1).

5. Licet multos frangat adversitas, tamen multo
plures extollit prosperitas (Dominicae Palmarum,
Sermone 2).

6. Credimus quae minime sufficimus comprae-
hendere (in feste Pentecostes, Sermone 1).

7. Periculosa habitatio eorum qui in meritis suis

---

[1] See *Epistles and Sermons*, 1494 ; *Theologia Divi Bernhardi*, 1581.

sperant : periculosa quia ruinosa (Sermon i. in explanatione de Psalmi *Qui habebat*).

8. Bonum mihi, Domine, tribulari, dummodo ipse sis mecum, quam regnare sine te, sine te gloriari (Sermone 17).

9. Vae nobis si exultaverimus, nisi in Christo et pro Christo (Sermone de verbis libri sapientiae).

10. Quid aliud, quam vita aeterna, tota affectione, divinam in omnibus sequi voluntatem (Sermone de subjectione nostrae voluntatis).

11. Quidam sapiens ait : melior est in malis factis humilis confessio, quam in bonis factis superba gloriatio [Gregory] (cap. 2, Sermone de donis Spiritus Sancti).

12. Quisquis patientior, eo probatur esse prudentior (*ibid.* cap. 7).

13. Scientia secularis, quae quidem inebriat, sed curiositate, non caritate implens, non nutriens : instans, non aedificans : ingurgitans non comfortans (Sermone 9 in Cantica).

14. Si scribas, non sapit mihi, nisi legero ibi Jesum. Si disputes aut conferas, non sapit mihi, nisi sonuerit ibi Jesus. Jesus mel in ore, in aure melos, in corde jubilus. Sed est et medicina (Sermone 15).

15. Grata ignominia . crucis ei, qui crucifixo ingratus non est (Sermone 25).

16. Peccavi peccatum grande, turbatur conscientia, sed non perturbabitur, quoniam vulnerum Domini recordabor (Sermone 61).

o

17. Magnum bonum quaerere Deum (Sermone 84).

18. Ubi amor est, labor non est, sed sapor (Sermone 85).

19. Si te Christus agnoscit in bello recognoscet in coelo (Epistle 3).

20. Dei sunt munera, tam nostra opera, quam ejus praemia (Tractatu de Gratia et libero arbitrio).

21. Felix (ut quidam sanctorum ait) necessitas, quae cogit in melius (Tractatu de praecepto et dispensatione).

22. Voluntas facit usum (in epistola ad fratres de Monte Dei).

23. Cum quo Deus est, nunquam minus solus est, quam cum solus est (*ibid.*).

24. Vere solus est, cum quo Deus non est (in epistola ad fratres de Monte Dei).

25. Quanto amplius vivimus, tanto plus pec-camus, quanto vita est longior, tanto culpa nume-riosior (in Meditionibus, cap. 2).

26. Omne tempus, in quo de Deo non cogitas, hoc te computes perdidisse (*ibid.* cap. 6).

27. Notitia peccati initium est salutis (*ibid.* cap. 11).

28. Non nocet sensus, ubi non est consensus (in tractatu de interiori domo, cap. 19).

29. Multi quaerunt scientiam, pauci vero con-scientiam (cap. 21).

30. Qui sibi displicet, Deo placet (cap. 28).

31. Qui sibi vilis est, Deo carus est (cap. 29).

32. Qualis haberi vis, talis esto (cap. 45).

33. Sit tibi quoque Jesus semper in corde et nunquam imago crucifixi ab animo tuo recedit. Hic tibi sit cibus et potus, dulcedo et consolatio tua, mel tuum et desiderium tuum, lectio tua et meditatio tua, oratio et contemplatio tua, vita mors et resurrectio tua.

34. Ignorantia nox est, fides vero dies (see Clement and *Theologia Divi Bernhardi*).

All the ideas contained in these passages, and in many others which occur throughout the epistles and sermons, are reflected in the *Imitation*, while the alliterative and often almost punning style is so closely akin to that of à Kempis that it is at first sight almost indistinguishable from his. But when we pass to phrases actually adopted from Bernard by à Kempis, we see at once how great is the indebtedness both of idea and style. Dr Bigg has collected in footnotes to his valuable translation some of the more important references, and I shall follow these here. In the second chapter of the first book à Kempis has transferred from his *Little Alphabet of a Monk* the phrase *ama nesciri et pro nihilo reputari* in the passage "si vis utiliter alta scire et discere, ama nesciri, et pro nihilo reputari." The words *ama nesciri* are St Bernard's,[1] and formed, we are told, a favourite phrase among the Brothers of Common Life. In any case it exactly expresses their ideal.

In the fifth chapter of the same book we have the passage "Omnis Scriptura Sacra, eo spiritu debet legi

---

[1] Mabillon's edition (i. 782).

quo facta est." This is identified by Hirsche with
a sentence in an epistle of William, Abbot of St
Theodoric, given by Bernard :[1] "quo enim spiritu
scripturae factae sunt, eo spiritu legi desiderant."
Hirsche again suggests that the passage in the
seventh chapter, "Non nocet ut omnibus te supponas,
nocet autem plurimum si vel uni te praeponas," is in
thought suggested by St Bernard.[2] The whole of
chapter twenty of the first book may be compared
with the Golden Epistle of St Bernard. In the
first chapter of the second book we have a passage
compounded in a most complex fashion from Isaiah,
St John, Micah, and St Bernard. It runs : "Cui
sapiunt omnia prout sunt, non ut dicuntur aut
aestimantur, hic vere sapiens est, et doctus magis
a Deo quam ab hominibus." Hirsche has pointed
out that the beginning of this passage is from a
phrase in a sermon of St Bernard :[3] "est enim sapiens
cui quaeque res sapiunt ut sunt." This origin is of
course perfectly obvious, but the conception of
absolute being independent of opinion or thought
did not originate with St Bernard. He was
only the vehicle of such conceptions to à Kempis.
The rest of the sentence according to Puyol
is compounded from the words *doctos a Domino*
(Isa. liv. 13), *Docibiles Dei* (John vi. 45), and *Docebit
nos de viis suis* (Micah iv. 2).

In chapter twelve of the second book we get a
long passage based on the first sermon by Bernard

---

[1] *Ibid*. ii. 214.   [2] *In cantica sermone*, 37.   [3] *Ad div*. xviii.

on the Annunciation of the Virgin : "Do thou set thyself to endure tribulations and count them the greatest comforts ; for the sufferings of this present time are not worthy to deserve the glory which is to come, even if thou alone couldst endure them all." It is interesting to compare the Latin of this passage with the quotation from Bernard indicated by Hirsche : "Tu vero pone te ad sustinendum tribulationes, et reputa eas maximas consolationes, quia non sunt condignae passiones hujus temporis ad futuram gloriam quae revelabitur in nobis promerendam, etiamsi solus omnes posses sustinere." The passage in the Sermon on the Annunciation runs : "Jam vero de aeterna vita scimus, quia non sunt condignae passiones hujus temporis ad futuram gloriam, nec si unus omnes sustineat." Of course, both passages are based on the Epistle to the Romans (viii. 18) : "For I reckon that the sufferings of this present time are not worthy to be compared with the glory which shall be revealed to usward"; but the rest of the extract from the *Imitation* is clearly from Bernard's sermon. Two other parallel passages will perhaps suffice. They are the last of those indicated by Dr Bigg. One occurs at the opening of the thirty-third chapter of the third book : "Fili noli credere affectui tuo, qui nunc est : cito mutabitur in aliud, "Son, trust not to the feeling which is with thee now : it will quickly be changed into another." Bernard has practically the same sentence : "Noli nimis credere affectui tuo, qui nunc est." Monsignor

Puyol sees in this a reference to the idea contained in the Epistle to the Romans (viii. 20), "Vanitati creatura subjecta est non volens." Whether this is so or not the conception of St Bernard is developed in the thirty-ninth chapter : "Fili mi, saepe homo rem aliquam agitat, quam desiderat, sed quum ad eam pervenerit aliter incipit sentire, quia affectiones circa idem non sunt durabiles, sed magis de uno ad aliud impellunt." The conclusion of the whole matter is tersely stated : "Non ergo minimum est, etiam in minimis se relinquere."

The last parallel I shall note is in the chapter on Divine Love.[1]   "Magnus clamor in auribus Dei est ipse ardens affectus animæ quae dicit : Deus meus! amor meus! tu totus meus, et ego tuus," says à Kempis.   This is certainly an echo from St Bernard's sixteenth sermon on Psalm ninety : "siquidem in Dei auribus desiderium vehemens clamor magnus : e regione autem remissa intentio vox submissa." But the fifth chapter has also much in common with the German mystics who immediately preceded à Kempis. It recalls Eckhardt's declaration that the lover of God is God's prisoner, but the more a prisoner the more free ; love "suffers nought to come near her, that is not God nor God like. Happy is he who is thus imprisoned; the more thou art a prisoner, the more wilt thou be freed."[2] On the other hand à Kempis declares that love

[1] Lib. iii. cap. 5.
[2] *Light, Life, and Love*, by W. R. Inge (Methuen & Co.), p. 14.

"carries a burden which is no burden. . . . The lover flies, runs, and rejoices: he is free and cannot be held. He gives all for all, and has all in all; because he rests in One Highest above all things. . . . My God, my Love: Thou art all mine, and I am all Thine." Both writers at any rate draw from a common source, from the Song of Songs, and it is not perhaps unreasonable to feel that Eckhardt had some direct personal influence upon the rapture of the Augustinian.

Eckhardt too held firmly the doctrines upon which à Kempis based his faith—the doctrine of humility and the doctrine of love, the whole Franciscan creed. Eckhardt, in his familiar style, tells of the colloquy between the great teacher and the faithful beggar in which, answering the question as to what he would do if God threw him into hell, the beggar replied, "Even if He threw me into hell, I should still have two arms wherewith to embrace Him. One arm in true humility, which I should place under Him, and with the arm of love I should embrace Him." [1]

We find again that Eckhardt and à Kempis both derived from Augustine the full idea of rest in God. Eckhardt, writing of sin, declares that "deadly sin . . . is an unrest of the heart. Everything can rest only in its proper place. But the natural place of the soul is God. As St Augustine says, ' Lord, Thou hast made us for

---

[1] *Light, Life, and Love,* by W. R. Inge, p. 11.

Thyself, and our heart is restless till it finds rest in thee.'" It is difficult not to think that this inspired to some extent the twenty-first chapter of the third book : "Above all and in all, O my soul, thou shalt rest in the Lord alway : for He is the eternal Rest of the Saints. . . . For my heart cannot truly rest, nor be entirely contented, unless it rest in Thee, and pass above all gifts and all creatures."

But it was not from Meister Eckhardt, the Plotinus of the thirteenth century, that à Kempis learnt his mysticism, though some influence may perhaps be traced. Eckhardt and à Kempis drew from a common source with different results. Eckhardt evolved a non-Christian philosophy of life, à Kempis compiled a handbook of the *Way*. Eckhardt absorbed the philosophic element of Augustine's writings as they passed through the medium of his mind, while à Kempis absorbed the Christian element. They meet only in those transcendental heights where the dualism between Creator and created is abolished, where religion realises the dogmatism of philosophy.

It is different, when we turn from Eckhardt to Tauler, Suso, and Ruysbroek. It is probable that those writers affected the actual structure of the *Imitation* in a way that cannot be attributed to the Meister, though it might be said with some force that since the mysticism of Eckhardt was ultimately responsible for so spiritual a treatise as the *Theologia Germanica* there would be nothing strange if he

WOODCUT ON THE REVERSE OF THE FLY-
LEAF WHICH HAS THE WOODCUT OF THE
MAGI. PARIS EDITION OF THE TREATISE
"DE IMITATIONE CHRISTI" ISSUED IN 1496
BY GEORGIUS MITTELHUS.

actually inspired the *Imitation*. The debt of à Kempis to Plotinus through Augustine is, however, so clear that it is not necessary to seek his inspiration in a writer who, in the year 1400, was no longer read by or even known to the faithful Catholic.

Tauler strikes the familiar note of the *Imitation* when he tells us that the two mortal sins are pride and inordinate affection, and the two immortal virtues are humility and absolute submission to God, inordinate affection, so to speak, for Him. The sixth chapter of the first book (*De Inordinatis Affectionibus*) strikes this very note: "Resistendo igitur passionibus invenitur pax vera cordis, non autem serviendo eis." The next chapter completes the rule of life: " Jugis pax cum humili, in corde autem superbi zelus et indignatio frequens." It can scarcely be a coincidence that the conception of an earthly battle without which life itself could not reach the highest should be clearly expressed both by à Kempis and Tauler. In chapter eleven of the first book we read: "If we would strive like brave men to stand in the battle, surely we should see the help of the Lord come upon us from Heaven. For He is ready to succour those that strive and trust in His grace: who giveth us occasion to fight in order that we may conquer." The first sentence is very complex in origin. It recalls the passage from the Ephesians (vi. 13), "Wherefore take unto you the whole armour of God, that ye may be able to withstand in the evil day, and having done all to stand;" the opening of the

hundred and twenty-first psalm," "my help cometh
from the Lord"; and the twentieth chapter (17) of
the Second Book of Chronicles : " Stand firm and thou
shalt see the help of the Lord upon you." The Latin
of the text is woven from the Latin of these three
passages ; but the text itself seems to me to be
inspired by Tauler's paradox [1] that "nothing in the
world is so necessary for man as to be constantly
assailed ; for in fighting he learns to know himself,"
and by the picture of the conflict in the seventy-fifth
sermon : " Know of a truth that if thou wouldst truly
overcome the evil spirit, this can only be done by a
complete manful turning away from sin. Say then
with all thy heart : Oh, everlasting God, help me
and give me Thy Divine grace to be my help, for it
is my steadfast desire never again to commit any
deadly sin against Thy Divine will and Thine honour.
So with thy good will and intention thou entirely
overcomest the evil spirit, so that he must fly from
thee ashamed." [2] To what extent Suso influenced the
structural form and general conception of the *Imitation* is not clear. Yet when his Servitor explains to
his spiritual daughter the order of events by which
the spirit should seek to return to God, we seem to
find an order of spiritual development followed by
à Kempis in his autograph edition of the *Imitation*.
" First of all," says Suso, " we should disentangle
ourselves absolutely from the pleasures of the world,
manfully turning our backs upon all vices ; we should

---

[1] Sermon 104.   [2] Inge : *Light, Life, and Love*, p. 20.

turn to God by continual prayers, by seclusion, and holy exercise, that the flesh may thus be subdued to the spirit. Next, we must offer ourselves willingly to endure all the troubles which may come upon us, from God, or from the creatures. Thirdly, we must impress upon ourselves the Passion of Christ crucified ; we must fix upon our minds His sweet teaching, His most gentle conversation, His most pure life, which He gave us for our example, and so we must penetrate deeper and advance further in our Imitation of Him. Fourthly, we must divest ourselves of external occupations, and establish ourselves in a tranquil stillness of soul by an energetic resignation, as if we were dead to self, and thought only of the honour of Christ and His heavenly Father. Lastly, we should be humble towards all men, whether friends or foes."

Here we have what might almost be called a groundplan of the four tracts concerning the *Imitation of Christ*. Suso's first division almost coincides in scheme with the first book—' the admonitions useful for a spiritual life.' The later chapters of this book and the second book cover Suso's second division. His third division coincides with the book *De Sacramento Altaris*—the book which in the earliest manuscripts is placed fourth, but which à Kempis places third in his autograph copy. The long third book—the Book of Internal Consolation —could hardly be better described than in Suso's own words concerning the fourth stage, by which we

return to God. " We must divest ourselves of external occupations, and establish ourselves in a
tranquil stillness of soul by an energetic resignation,
as if we were dead to self, and thought only of the
honour of Christ and His heavenly Father." The
latter chapters of the fourth book, and in particular
chapter fifty, set forth Suso's fifth division—the
doctrine of humility. Personally I feel convinced
that Thomas à Kempis framed his work on the
ground plan devised by Suso. It appears to me
that no coincidence of ideas could account for such
a coincidence of structure. Suso had in his mind
the pathway to spiritual reality, the return to God of
the spirit which he gave. He actually states that
this return can only be secured by " the Imitation "
of Christ, and he traces a " Way " of which the
whole of the *Imitation* is but an elaboration worked
out by the greatest eclectic that the world of literature
has known. The physical shape of the *Imitation*, so
to speak, was determined by Suso, though its detail,
its internal literary form, and its general atmosphere
have little in common with the not entirely healthy
composition of that writer.

Thomas à Kempis is most indebted to Suso, with
respect to the details of construction, in the book that
has attracted the least attention—the *De Sacramento
Altaris*. This is in some considerable measure based
on Suso's *Meditation on the Passion of Christ*. For
Eternal Wisdom à Kempis has substituted *The Voice
of the Beloved*, while the *Servitor* becomes *The Voice*

of the Disciple. But à Kempis has a restraint and a dignity not to be found in Suso, and though apparently adopting from time to time the very phrases of the *Meditation*, yet constructs a work that is quite independent and self-contained. It is perhaps noticeable that in the *Meditation* occurs the phrase "the Imitation of Thee is grievous to a slothful and corruptible body."

If, however, Suso supplied the groundplan of the *Imitation*, as I cannot but believe, it is certain that Ruysbroek, in his *Adornment of the Spiritual Nuptials* and other works, supplied checks, modifications, and fundamental ideas. Ruysbroek's division of life into "the *active* life, which is necessary to all who would be saved," "the inner life, exalted and loving, to which many men arrive by the virtues and by the grace of God," and "the superessential and contemplative life, to which few attain and which few can taste, because of the supreme sublimity of this life," is almost definitely adopted by à Kempis. We see this growth of spiritual virtue specifically inculcated. All are necessary to the full life, the complete life, the life which is an imitation, a following, of the life of Christ. Ruysbroek is the corrective of the non-Christian contemplative ideas adopted from Plotinus and perhaps Eckhardt, and of the super-Christian and unreal physical imitation of Christ put forward by Suso. The direct and healthy influence of Ruysbroek gives the finishing grace and the intellectual directness that lifts the *Imitation* so far above all other works of devotion.

But when all is said and done, when we have traced the direct influences that moulded the shape and structure of the four tracts, when we have analysed the material that goes to the making of the actual chapters, when we have taken into consideration the atmosphere of theology and philosophy, of devotion and opinion that had drifted down the ages into the age of à Kempis and had penetrated into the minds of the simple community that was all his life, we are not really in touch with the literary secret that makes the *Imitation* a living force to-day, and will still make it a living force when this day has been long forgotten. We may dissect the human body, we may analyse its structure and ascertain its component parts with a nicety significant of the age in which we live, but we shall get no nearer to the vital spark nor capably surmise the origin of life. It is not hard to tell the sources of the material that à Kempis used, but it is impossible to discover how he built his material into a work that serenely smiles at the envy of time. The mystery of the *Imitation of Christ* is not its authorship but its existence. It is to-day what Zeiner called it in the year 1487, *Tractatus aureus et perutilis de perfecta Imitatione Christi.*

THE CONTENT OF THE IMITATION

WHEN we turn from the structure to the content—to the theological, philosophical, and social scheme of doctrine—of the *Imitation* we find that, diverse as are the sources from which the writer draws, they have been sought out with definite spiritual and intellectual ends in view. The structure of this beautiful mansion of words is one aspect of the work; the spirits of faith, hope, and charity that built it and inhabit it are another. The content of the *Imitation* is a consistent scheme of doctrine by which holy living and holy dying are to be brought home to the heart of every man.

The first point that we have to note is that Thomas à Kempis will have nothing to do with the scholastic formalism, which was the intellectual armour of the Middle Ages. He himself was not brought up in the traditional school of learning. Such education as he had was the new education, and though echoes of Scholasticism, of Neo-Aristotelianism have crept into his mind, the methods of thought in which Gerson and the other great doctors of that age were brought up had no place in his intellectual training. Thomas à Kempis was in no sense a Nominalist, while he shows distinct traces of the

mystic Realism that followed the reaction from the
extreme scholasticism of Duns Scotus. He was a
child of the Brothers of Common Life, and belonged,
so far as his mental outfit went, to the New Age and
not to the old. If he had comparatively little of the
New Learning, he had none of the Old, and in his
mind the sublety of the Schoolmen received something like its true value. If he did not appreciate
its intellectuality, he at any rate realised its useless-
ness. He looked at it absolutely from without, and
that, indeed, is to my mind a final and conclusive
argument against the Gerson authorship of the
Imitation. Gerson was essentially a Doctor, a lover
of the mental process for its own sake, even though
he realised the need of simple education and simple
faith if the world were ever to be reformed. But
Gerson necessarily looked at Scholasticism from
within, even if he strove to fling aside its cumbrous
armour. Thomas à Kempis had no such armour,
and felt a certain Davidian contempt for it. Its
efficacy was not apparent to him, and he saw that all
who wore it were spiritually hampered at every turn.
Therefore he not only does not attempt to use it but
deprecates its use with all his simple might.

It will be useful to extract from the books
of the *Imitation* instances of this contempt for
the ponderous obsolete weapons of his age and
Church. Consider the first book—the 'admonitions
useful for a spiritual life.' Here we have protest
after protest against mere philosophical thought.

THE FIRST AND SECOND AND PART OF THE THIRD CHAPTERS OF
THE FIRST BOOK OF THE TREATISE "DE IMITATIONE CHRISTI"
FROM THE ADDITIONAL MS. 11,437 (BRITISH MUSEUM)

THE MS. IS UNDATED BUT MAY BE PLACED BETWEEN THE LIMITS 1465 AND 1470
WITH SOME CONFIDENCE. IT CONTAINS ONLY THE FIRST TWO BOOKS.

"Truly profound words do not make a man holy and just: but a virtuous life makes him dear to God."[1] "Every man naturally desires to know; but what avails knowledge without the fear of God? Better surely is a humble peasant that serves God: than a proud philosopher that studies the course of heaven and neglects himself. . . . If I understood all things in the world, and were not in charity, what would it help me, in the sight of God, who will judge me according to my deeds? Cease from an inordinate desire of knowledge: for therein is found great destruction and deceit. Gladly would those who know seem learned and be called wise. There be many things: which to know doth little or nothing profit the soul. . . . Many words do not satisfy the soul. . . . The more and the better thou knowest: the more severely shalt thou be judged unless thy life also be more holy. Be not therefore vain of any art or science; but rather fear for the knowledge that is given thee. Be not overwise; but rather confess thy ignorance. Why wilt thou prefer thyself before any; since there be many more learned than thou, and more skilful in the law? If thou wilt know or learn anything to profit: love to be unknown and to be little esteemed."[2]

The whole of this chapter on "the humble conceit of ourselves" is aimed at vain learning, and the suggestion that it might have been written by Gerson in his still retreat at Lyons, is answered

[1] Cap. 1.　　　　　　Cap. 2.

P

by the fact that the phrase "*ama nesciri et pro nihilo reputari*" is used elsewhere by à Kempis, and was a phrase in common use by the Brothers of Common Life.

The third chapter contains a direct onslaught on Scholasticism, obviously an attack from without and not a revolt from within. "Happy the man whom truth teaches by itself, not by fleeting figures and words : but as it is in itself. Our opinions and our sense often deceive us : and see but little. What profit is there in lengthy quibbling about dark and hidden things ; when we shall not be reproved at the day of judgment because we know them not ? It is great folly to neglect things that are profitable and necessary, and take needless pains for that which is far fetched and hurtful. We have eyes and see not ; and what have we to do with genera and species ? —*et quid nobis de generibus et speciebus ?*"

This passage should be compared with the Voice of the Beloved speaking against vain and secular knowledge in the Book of Internal Consolation.[1] "The time will come when the Master of Masters, Christ the Lord of Angels, shall appear, to hear the lessons of all, that is, to examine the conscience of every one ; and then will He search Jerusalem with candles : and the hidden things of darkness shall be laid open, and the logic of tongues shall be hushed. I am He who in one instant lifts up the humble mind, to understand more reasonings of eternal

[1] Lib. iii. c. 43.

Truth, than if one had studied ten years in the Schools. I teach without noise of words, without confusion of opinions, without pride of emulation, without fence of logic." The further reference in the same chapter is rather obscure : " There was one who by loving me in his inmost soul, learned divine truths : and spoke marvels. He made greater progress by forsaking all things, than by studying subtle niceties." The writer of the *Imitation* doubtless refers to himself, and though the phrasing might appear to have some application to Gerson, it is inconceivable that the humble suppliant of Lyons could have written in so uplifted a manner. Still it must be admitted that this chapter is written by one who had some contact with scholasticism. No doubt Kempis must have become familiar with the mannerisms of the mediæval scholar. That he was a tireless student is a well-known fact of his life, and this is consistent with the references to scholastic learning that so frequently occur. We have further very definite references in the third chapter of the first book. " It wearies me often to read and hear many things : in Thee is all I want and desire. Let all Doctors hold their peace, let all creatures keep silence in Thy sight ; speak thou alone to me . . . no speculation of ours is without some darkness . . . . Truly when the day of judgment comes we shall not be asked what we have read but what we have done ; nor how well we have spoken : but how religiously we have lived. Tell me where now are all those

Doctors and Masters with whom thou wast well acquainted whilst as yet they lived and flourished in learning? Now others possess their livings : and perhaps never think of them. In their lifetime they seemed to be something ; and now they are not spoken of. O how quickly passes the glory of the world. O that their life had been answerable to their learning : then had their study and reading been to good purpose. How many perish through vain learning in this world, who take little care of the service of God."

This is perhaps the most elaborate protest of à Kempis against the vain learning of the Schoolmen, but we have many other references. " We ought as willingly to read devout and simple books, as deep and profound. Let not the authority of the writer move thee, whether he be of small or great learning, but let the love of pure truth draw thee to read. Search not who said this, but mark what is said." [1] " Who is so wise, that he can fully know all things ? Be not therefore too confident in thine own opinion, but be even glad to listen to the thought of others." [2] " Throw aside subtleties ; read thoroughly such books, as rather stir compunction, than furnish occupation." [3] " Then [at the day of judgment] shall a clean and good conscience more rejoice a man, than learned philosophy." [4] " So when we have perused and searched all : be this the final conclusion.

[1] Lib. i. cap. 5. [2] Lib. i. cap. 9.
[3] Lib. i. cap. 20. [4] Lib. i. cap. 24.

That through many tribulations, we must enter into the Kingdom of God." [1]

The author of the *Imitation* turns from the worship of worldly wisdom with an imperative repugnance. It is stale and unprofitable, accomplishing nothing either for the world or for the individual. It is not even a shadow of the pattern laid up in heaven. It has no relationship to the heavenly wisdom. But despite this attitude towards the learning of the schools of à Kempis he offers us nevertheless a definite and precious mystical philosophy. He was, "a profound and blameless mystic" who gathered up into his work the serener elements of ancient and mediæval mysticism. The serene quality of his mind, its perfect balance, and its singularly human outlook has made some very profound students of Christian mysticism name him a "semi-mystic." It is with great respect that I differ from that view, but I am compelled from the evidence of the text to realise that à Kempis had all the elements of mysticism in his nature, if we take that nature to be adequately set forth in the four books of the Following of Christ. This is perhaps best seen by drawing from the text its definite body of doctrine. The whole object of the work is specified in the first chapter. It is to set up "the doctrine of Christ" against "the sayings of all philosophers." What is the doctrine of Christ that we

---

[1] Lib. ii. cap. 12. See also lib. iii. cap. 31 and lib. iii. cap 34. (The wise men of the world . . . are poor in Thy sweet wisdom.)

have to follow, who is this Christ that we have to imitate? Is it the doctrine of Holy Church, the Christ of Holy Scripture? Yes and No.

The doctrine is the doctrine of Holy Church supplemented by that mystical appreciation of eternal and ever-present mysteries which is the very life of the invisible Church. The Christ is the Christ of Holy Scripture viewed through the atmosphere that fourteen centuries of mysticism had woven round the person of Jesus of Nazareth. He is more than the Christ of history. It is not the mere record of an earthly visitation that we have to follow: "The eye is not satisfied with seeing, nor the ear filled with hearing. Study therefore to withdraw thy heart from the love of the visible, and to give thyself over to the invisible."[1] The heart must not only be withdrawn from outward things but the things of the mind also. Love of the visible and love of knowledge are bracketed together. We must turn from the Word of Things and the Word of Thoughts to the Eternal Word—the origin of all Things and Thoughts. The Word is Christ and God, the unifying principle in creation.[2]

This is Christian Neo-Platonism of a type which, as Mr Inge has pointed out,[3] "tended to identify the Logos, as the Second Person of the Trinity, with the Noῦς, 'Mind' or 'Intelligence,' of Plotinus, and rightly." Mr Inge, however, points out that the

---

[1] Lib. i. cap. 1.   [2] Lib. i. cap. 3.
[3] *Christian Mysticism*, p. 94.

WOODCUT IN THE EDITION OF THE TREA-
TISE "DE IMITATIONE CHRISTI" ISSUED
FROM VENICE IN 1488.

Plotinian Logos must be distinguished from the Johannine Logos, which is both immanent and transcendent, in that it represents not so much a personality as a "'Law' regarded as a vital force." The actual words used by à Kempis may be compared with those used by Erigena (quoted by Mr Inge) on the same subject. Erigena says, "Certius cognoscas verbum Naturam omnium esse," while à Kempis states with more completeness and with a fuller expression of the mystic doctrine involved, "ex uno Verbo omnia, et unum loquuntur omnia, et hoc est Principium quod et loquitur nobis," (i. 3). Thomas à Kempis, if we take into account the fact that he was a Christian and Plotinus was not, follows Plotinus up to a certain point with extraordinary closeness. He is not satisfied with the views of Erigena, the great Plotinian of the West. The point that à Kempis as a mystic and also a practical thinker had to consider was the elaboration of a method that should enable the Christian to turn from the things of the flesh and the things of the mind so as to come within the life-giving influence of the Eternal Word. Plotinus had the same difficulty, and up to a point solved it in the way adopted by à Kempis. To Plotinus and à Kempis alike it was false mysticism and false philosophy simply to ignore these things. They must be used, not ignored. Simple absorption in the Word was not the end aimed at. The Asiatic Nirvana has no attraction for the Western mind. We have our earth here, our human nature, which must have a meaning and a use in the scheme of things. Mr Inge has dealt clearly with this position of Plotinus. " The ' lower virtues,' as he calls the duties of the average citizen, are not only purgative, but teach us the principles of *measure* and *rule*, which are divine characteristics. This is immensely important, for it is the point where Platonism and Asiatic mysticism finally part company." Mr Inge goes on to point out that in Plotinus they do not in fact part company. Plotinus passes on to another logical conclusion which renders his philosophy worthless to a workaday world. But the Christian mystics grasped the position at once and left Asia to its dreams. A Kempis declares : " This should be our business, to conquer ourselves " (i. 3), and forsake our own will. In order to do this both outward things and inward thoughts have to be used. Like all the great mystics, à Kempis was essentially practical. The use of worldly wisdom[1] and the love of pure truth[2] are the means first recommended. To live truly and to think truly are the base of the whole matter. The mystic's ladder of perfection, like Jacob's ladder, has its base on earth. The greater part of the first book of the *Imitation*, after the initial doctrine of the All-creating, All-pervading Word has been definitely stated, is occupied in creating a base on which the *Scala Perfectionis* can be set up. But this basis of holy living is merely a means to a consummate

[1] Lib. i. cap. 4.   [2] Lib. i. cap. 5.

end.   Thomas à Kempis held as strongly as any
Syrian monk of the fifth century one aspect of the
doctrine laid down by the so-called " Hierotheus,"
the master of the Pseudo-Dionysius the Areopagite.
" To me," says Hierotheus, " to me it seems right
to speak without words, and understand without
knowledge, that which is above words and knowledge.
This I apprehend to be nothing but the mysterious
silence and mystical quiet which destroys consciousness and dissolves forms.   Seek, therefore, silently
and mystically, that perfect and primitive union with
this Arch-Good."   Thomas à Kempis disclaims this
Asiatic apprehension of what the approach of God
meant.   It did not mean the destruction of consciousness and the dissolution of form.   He felt, indeed, that all knowledge was contained in the Eternal
Word as well as all truth.   But this universal solvent
of ignorance and darkness was to be found not by
losing the Ego in Christ but by moulding the Ego
on the pattern of Christ.   Thus, beginning with a
mystic conception of Christ, the personality is led to
justify the faith in this conception by an approach
to the life of Christ as set forth in Holy Scripture.
The Christ of the mystic is ultimately justified by
the imitation of the Christ of history.   It is the
process of the scientific mind transferred to the
spiritual sphere.   Ages of religious experience
coloured by philosophic inquiry slowly evolved a
hypothesis that seemed to render possible the
intimate approach of the solitary soul of man to the

seemingly solitary but all-pervading and all-loving Soul of Things; that seemed to make "the flight of the alone to the Alone" a fact, and a fact that does not involve the loss of personality or of the sense of responsibility.   Such an hypothesis was one among innumerable hypotheses.   How could its truth be tested?   The *Imitation of Christ* is the answer of the mystic; the imitation or the following of the Christ of history proves, he says, that the hypothesis of mysticism is the only true solution of the mystery of the spiritual life.   Faith begins by an experiment which leads to a hypothesis and concludes with an experience which is a demonstration. It may be said that the demonstration is not complete, inasmuch as the following of Christ is a counsel of perfection to which no man can attain.   The reply to such a criticism is that the perfect following of Christ would in fact be a complete demonstration, since experience shows that the nearer the approximation of the individual to the life of Christ the more nearly is the hypothesis confirmed.   There is nothing in the experience of humanity to show that there is any stage of approximation that denies the hypothesis. It is in very truth never contradicted in spiritual experience any more than the hypothetical law of the inverse square is contradicted in physical experience.   To a reasonable mind the solution of the apparently irreconcilable dualism (the conception of which is almost innate in every human mind) is brought about by an experience which reasonably demonstrates the mystical hypothesis that haunted the minds of the deepest thinkers even in days before there was a Christ to imitate, and made Him, when He came, the inevitable pattern once laid up in heaven, but now brought down to earth for all peoples in all ages to imitate. That the imitation is in nearly all cases desperately remote need not be a cause for despair, since, when all is said and done, every man in the world is impelled,.even against his will or perhaps his knowledge, dimly to feel after Christ. The beginning of the experience which is a demonstration is to be found there as surely as one can foresee in the cave scrawlings of the troglodytes the frescoes of Michael Angelo. Therefore the imitation of Christ throughout the darkness of the Middle Ages was the fundamental idea of the invisible and mystical Church, and therefore Thomas à Kempis, in his four books concerning the imitation of Christ, lays down the rules of human conduct and human thought that made the growth of the experience which is a demonstration, possible.

Having in the first book laid down the doctrine of the Word, he sets forth his admonitions useful for a spiritual life. First, earthly desires, the desires of the flesh great and small, must be resisted, not obeyed.[1] Resistance to desire must be followed by humility. " Unfailing peace is with the humble," [2] and peace is a necessity of the Inner Way. Familiarity with men is inexpedient : "Soli Deo et Angelis eius opta

---

[1] Lib. i. cap. 6.　　　　[2] Lib. i. cap. 7.

familiaris esse (i. 8)." Earthly obedience and subjection is to be desired. Speech must be carefully watched and guarded. Peace must be sought by minding our own affairs and looking rather to eternal than to temporal things. We shall thus have "some experience of heavenly contemplation."[1] Good conduct is the great source of the necessary peace. Earthly crosses are good, for they make man turn rather to God than to man. Temptation must not only be shunned but fought with the weapons of patience and humility. In order to crush out all self-interest in dealing with others one must consciously seek from God the judicial mind. Everything that is done must be done well and done charitably :—" Multum facit, qui multum diligit. Multum facit qui rem bene facit."[2] We must not only be judicial in dealing with others but singularly charitable : " how seldom we weigh our neighbour in the same balance with ourselves."[3]

In the little chapter on the Monastic Life we have, set out in a phrase, the high Christian note : " Thou camest to serve, not to govern." The way to imitate Christ cannot, however, be shown only by precepts. We must see how others followed Him and learn the way from them. " The Saints and friends of Christ served the Lord in hunger and thirst, in cold and nakedness ; in labour and weariness, in watchings and fastings, in prayer and holy meditations, in many persecutions and reproaches. . . . All day

[1] Lib. i. cap. 11.   [2] Lib. i. cap. 15.   [3] Lib. i. cap. 16.

they laboured, and in the night they found time for long prayer, although while they laboured they ceased not from mental prayer. They spent all their time with profit ; every hour seemed short waiting upon God." [1] Concerning those saints and friends of Christ we are told in a singularly beautiful phrase, " Mundo erant alieni, sed Deo proximi et familiares amici." To imitate them is to imitate Christ. But imitation is the result of an inward process : " According to our purpose shall be the course of our growth . . . the purpose of the just depends not upon their own wisdom but upon God's grace." [2] This mystical process is a manifestation of the Eternal Word within the subject. It is a logical as well as a spiritual development from the hypothesis. It is also a beginning of the experience that is to justify the hypothesis. But this purpose must be rendered possible by the behaviour of the whole man. " We must search into and set in order both the outward and the inward : because both are of importance to our progress." The mystic adds significantly : " Never be wholly idle : but either be reading or writing or praying or meditating or endeavouring something for the common good." Here the fundamental distinction between Eastern and Western mysticism stands out in absolute clearness.

A fresh stage is reached with the twentieth chapter of the first book. The golden virtues of

[1] Lib. i. cap. 18.   [2] Lib. i. cap. 19.

solitude and silence are taught, the separation of the
inner self from the world. "In silence and in stillness the religious soul grows and learns the mysteries
of Holy Writ : there she finds rivers of tears, wherein
she may wash and cleanse herself night after night ;
that she may be more familiar with her Creator. . . .
Whoso therefore withdraweth himself from his
acquaintance and friends, God will draw near unto
him with His holy Angels. . . . Shut thy door
behind, and call unto thee Jesus thy Beloved. Stay
with Him in thy cell : for thou shalt not find so
great peace elsewhere." Here is the true mystic
note—the ripening of the actual experience, the
reception of the Eternal Word. But the practical
mind suddenly checks ecstasy. The men of the
Middle Ages knew how dangerous it was. Perfectionism finds no support from the true mystic.
Therefore the rapture of divine intercourse is suddenly checked by a call for compunction of heart.
The spirit of compunction alone can welcome the
Lord of All in the sanctuary of the human heart.
Moreover, in that sacred chamber there must be a
voice declaring that the world is well lost for Christ.
"Woe to them that love this miserable and corrup-
tible life." [1] Christ cannot again come down to us.
We with the Saints of God must spiritually ascend
to him. "Their whole desire was borne up to the
lasting and invisible." In this chapter Thomas à
Kempis, in his renunciation of the world and his

[1] Lib. i. cap. 22.

mystical ascension to the higher life, largely follows St Bernard. In the Golden Epistle the Saint of Clairvaux tells us :[1] " If thou wylt fynde his grace and be trewly solitarye two thynges be necessary to the. The fyrst is that thou so withdrawe thyself fro al transitory thynges that thou care no more for them than if there were none such and that thou sette thyself at so vyle a price in thyne owne syght that thou accompt thyselfe as naught, believing al men to be better than thou arte and more to please God." In the same Epistle he tells us : " Have these three thinges alwayes in the mynde, what thou hast been, what thou art and what thou shalte be." So far as this life is concerned all stages are worthless. As he says elsewhere :[2] " futura non exspectat, praeterita non recogitat, praesentia non experitur." A man must, to use the words of Tauler in his sermon on John the Baptist,[3] " flee and separate himself from all that is temporal and transitory," though Tauler adds with the caution of the true mystic, " God does not grudge man the necessaries of life."

We have not fully prepared the mystic " grund " or basis from which the new life is to be upbuilt, and neither do we see in their true proportions things past, present, and to come until we have meditated upon death. That is the only fact in the human

---

[1] Godfray's English Version (1535 ?).   [2] Sermon 80.
[3] See W. H. Hutton's valuable collection of Tauler's sermons, entitled *The Inner Way*, p. 96.

future that requires consideration, that must be provided against : " Thou oughtest so to order thyself in all thy deeds and thoughts as if to-day thou wert doomed to die. . . . If to die be dreadful, to live long may perhaps prove more dangerous. . . . Study so now to live, that at the hour of death thou mayest rather rejoice than fear. . . . Keep thyself as a pilgrim and a stranger upon the earth." " In omnibus respice finem." Time, Death, and Judgment these three, and the greatest of these is Judgment. For that we must be ready. The love of God which passeth all understanding alone can make us fit to meet the Judge. If we are spiritually one with Him there is nothing to fear. We shall acquiesce in all His works. " For he that loves God with all his heart fears neither Death nor Punishment nor Judgment nor Hell : for perfect love gives fearless access to God."[1] Therefore in the last chapter we have a final practical exhortation for the zealous amendment of our whole life. " Remember always the end and that time lost never returns."

The first book therefore does two things : it states the mystic doctrine or hypothesis and shows how in each soul there can be prepared that mystic " Grund " on which alone the ladder of perfection can be raised. The function of time in the economy of grace is the giving of an opportunity for the preparation of an approach to God. The Christ of history had given a perpetual object-lesson in such

Lib. i. cap. 24.

"O TO WHOM SHALL I MAKE MY MOAN
FOR TO GO WITH ME, IN THAT HEAVY JOURNEY.
. . . . .
O GHOSTLY TREASURE, O RANSOMER AND REDEEMER,
OF ALL THE WORLD, HOPE AND CONDUCTOR."

EVERYMAN, Ll. 463-4, 590-1.

WOODCUT FROM THE ARGENTINE EDITION OF 1489. THIS EDITION
ATTRIBUTES THE WORK TO THOMAS A KEMPIS. THE LINES FROM
"EVERYMAN" ARE NOT GIVEN IN THAT EDITION, BUT ARE CON-
TEMPORARY WORDS.

an use of time. An intuitive or at any rate mystic conception of Christ as the necessary bridge between man and the Supreme Force outside man is necessary in order so to prepare the soul of man that it may be possible for the imitation of Christ to begin. When the soul is so prepared it can make its "Grund" and then raise the ladder that Christ Himself had raised and ascended. That appears to be the position of à Kempis and of many other mediæval mystics.

The second book of the *Imitation* takes the reader into another region. In the first book *The Outer Life*, the life of the world, is the subject of discourse, and the pupil is taught how to use that life as a means, through spiritual admonitions, of apprehending a doctrine and securing a demonstrative experience. With the end of the first book the pupil in the school of Christ is supposed to have secured the machinery of spiritual ascent. The second book deals with the ascent itself. The outer life cannot ascend. It can only assist the inner life, the real being to ascend, and become united to God. The second book sets forth admonitions drawing to the Inner Life. The first chapter describes this life, the· indwelling of the Word. "Christ will come unto thee and show thee His own consolation, if thou prepare for Him a worthy abode within. All His beauty and glory are from within, and there He delights Himself. Frequent are His visits to the inward man . . . make therefore

Q

room for Christ: and deny entrance to all other. When thou hast Christ thou art rich and hast enough; . . . neither shalt thou ever have rest unless thou be inwardly united to Christ. . . . A lover of Jesus and of truth, who truly lives the inner life and is free from inordinate affections, can freely turn himself unto God, and lift himself above himself in spirit, and rest in fruition. He that tastes all things as they are, not as they are said or thought to be, is truly wise and taught of God rather than of men."[1]

This doctrine of reality, of an Inner Life, that is one with the Eternal Word and " tastes all things as they are," is brought home by a new series of admonitions teaching the higher virtues. Absolute humility is enjoined: " Think not that thou hast made any progress unless thou feel thyself inferior to all."[2] Next to humility is the duty of making and keeping peace—the whole duty of altruism. This can only come by endurance. " He that can best tell how to endure, will keep greater peace. That man is conqueror of himself and Lord of the world, the friend of Christ and heir of Heaven."[3] Humility and altruism must be accompanied by simplicity and purity—the wings that lift a man up from earth. This must go side by side with self-criticism and the avoidance of the fault of criticising others. " He that well and rightly considered his own works would find no cause to judge hardly of

[1] Lib. ii. cap. 1.   [2] Lib. ii. cap. 2.   [3] Lib. ii. cap. 3.

another." [1] Beside the virtues must be found that
"glory of a good man," the testimony of a good
conscience accompanied by the love of and familiar
friendship with Christ, and gratitude for the grace
of God.   The few who have these golden virtues of
the Inner Life are fit to tread the King's way of the
Holy Cross. It is an experience without human
sweetness to lighten it. Yet "there is no other
way to life and true inward peace." The ecstasy
of the mystic will be proved along this road—this
desolate desiccate passage from earth to heaven.
"The higher a man hath mounted in the spirit the
heavier crosses he will often find: because the
punishment of his exile increases with love." [2]   Rich
must be the spiritual compensations for a system of
renunciation that not only permits no manner of
earthly comfort, that not only strips humanity of the
humanities, but makes the burden of existence less
tolerable as it increases in holiness. With some
such utilitarian comment even an earthly saint who
was not a mystic might be tempted to receive the
Malleolian doctrine of godliness in this life. Many
attacks levelled at the position developed—the
logical position of Thomas à Kempis—would have
been withheld had it been realised that he was
writing essentially as a mystic and not as a spiritual
economist, that he was describing the evolution of a
subjective experience rather than the manner of the
outward man. It is the Inner Life that he is

[1] Lib. ii. cap. 5.   [2] Lib. ii. cap. 12.

describing, and probably no one will be found to deny that the holier a man is, the more profoundly discontented he must be with the value of that life. The punishment of his exile indeed, one may presume, is never so intense as on that day when the pilgrim and sojourner at last takes ship for the heavenly country which he claims to be his home. If he is troubled by nothing else, he is troubled by the want of that faith which is an intense, an essential, part of an intellectual existence, a necessary part of the machinery of a mysterious world. But à Kempis claims that the growing miseries which belong to the subjective experience of treading the way of the Holy Cross are in fact spiritual fruits, for they demonstrate the growing nearness and dearness of God. He speaks of a man who " would not choose to be without grief and tribulation, because he believes that he shall be dearer unto God " (ii. 12). Such a spiritual experience cannot, no subjective experience can, be translated into words. But the fact that all the mystics, ancient and modern, can unhesitatingly assert this position, proves that the spiritual experience of which à Kempis treats has a real meaning, however difficult, indeed however impossible, it may be for the average everyday professor of Christianity to realise it. An experience is not necessarily absurd because it appears extravagant. Counsels of perfection are sometimes realised by the most unlikely pupils.

À Kempis in fact appreciates the apparent absurdity

of his position. "It is not man's nature," he says, "to carry the Cross, to love the Cross, to chasten the body and bring it into subjection, to flee honours, cheerfully to suffer reproaches, to despise himself, and wish to be despised, to endure misfortune and loss, and to desire no prosperity in the world. If thou look to thyself thou canst of thyself do nothing of the kind " (ii. 12). But the aim of the true mystic is the creation or revelation of a second nature which, without change of the personality, is perfectly attuned to the Eternal Word. The entire process of the imitation of Christ is to attain or bring to light this second nature and therewith " Paradise upon Earth." The Inner Life must come to know itself and the Kingdom of God, of which it forms a part. The second book of the *Imitation* begins with the dogma, " The Kingdom of God is within you," and ends by showing that this kingdom is the Paradise which the Inner Life can attain. The whole experience is subjective, but it is only possible when the outer or objective life is lived according to the highest standard known to the natural man.

Dr Bigg, following the Autograph edition, places the book *De Sacramento Altaris* third in the order of the books. No other early manuscript does this, but it is certainly the right order from the mystical point of view. Dr Bigg says on this question, " The author knew best how to secure the impression which he wished to produce, and there is a special reason for that arrangement which he himself pre-

ferred.   From the time of Dionysius the Areopagite
mystical writers divided the spiritual life into three
stages : Purgation, Illumination, and Consummation.   The first two treatises deal upon the whole
with that moral and spiritual discipline without
which no man can be a true follower of Christ ; the
third, on the Sacrament, points to the Eucharist as
the means of union with Him who is the Light of
the World ; the fourth, of Internal Consolation, tells
of the presence of Christ in the soul, of life in the
spirit, of the mystic vision, as à Kempis understood it."

We may take it therefore that the book concerning
the Sacrament deals with the means by which the
inner self is united to the Eternal Word.   It is part
of the spiritual machinery that lifts the inner life
up to the Inner Kingdom of God.   The Sacrament
is to continue a former metaphor, the ladder—the
Jacob's ladder—of the soul by which the ascent is
made.   It is worth noticing that here, as in the
ladder of Jacob's dream, the action *begins* on the
earth.   Jacob saw the Angels *ascending* and descend-
ing, and in the same way in the case of the Sacrament
the approach to God comes from earth first.   The
idea of union with God indicated in this book and
drawn direct from St John begins with a deliberate
act of ascent in answer to the call of the Word.   But
the whole book deals with the spiritual mechanism
of union with God.   It is not until we reach the
long " Book of Internal Consolation " that we see the
full mystical significance of the *Imitation of Christ*.

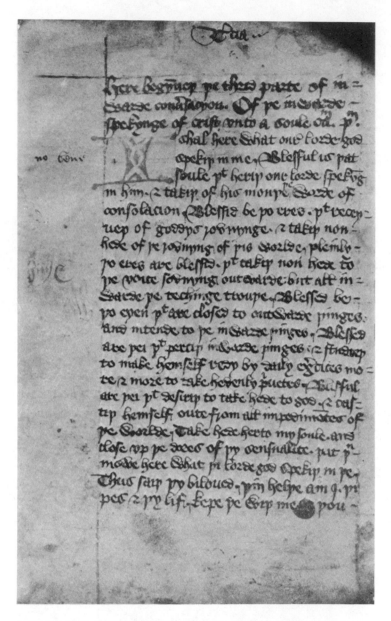

PART OF THE FIRST CHAPTER OF BOOK III (THE BOOK OF INWARD
CONSOLATION) OF THE TREATISE "MUSICA ECCLESIASTICA:" ENGLISH
VERSION. FROM THE MANUSCRIPT IN THE LIBRARY OF TRINITY
COLLEGE, DUBLIN.

THIS MS. CONTAINS THE FIRST THREE BOOKS OF THE TREATISE "DE IMITATIONE CHRISTI"
IN ENGLISH. IT BELONGS TO THE MID-FIFTEENTH CENTURY.

Here we have the Inner Life dwelling in the Inner Kingdom of God. Here in the first chapter we have God speaking, not from without but from within. "Blessed is the soul which hears the Lord speaking within her. . . . Blessed indeed are those ears that listen . . . to the Truth which teaches within. Blessed are the eyes which are shut to the outward, but open to the inward. Blessed are they . . . that prepare themselves more and more by daily exercises for the receipt of heavenly secrets." The second chapter tells us that the truth speaketh inwardly without noise of words. "Speak therefore, Lord, for Thy servant heareth : for Thou hast the words of Eternal Life." The Indwelling Word throughout the book speaks to the Inner Man. "My words are Spirit and Life, not to be weighed by the understanding of man."[1] "Let the Eternal Truth delight thee above all things."[2] The wonderful chapter on Divine Love is a curious echo of the Song of Songs after it had passed through the minds of generations of mystics. "Enlarge me in Love ; that with the inner mouth of my heart I may taste how sweet it is to love, and to be melted and bathed in love" (lib. iv. cap. 5).

The extraordinary ecstasy of this chapter is immediately checked in the manner customary with à Kempis. The lover is told what are the notes of a true lover, and is warned to beware of the wiles of the ancient enemy. Many warnings follow:

[1] Lib. iv. cap. 3 (in autograph MS.).   [2] Lib. iv. cap. 4.

the need of hiding grace under the garb of humility ;
of self-depreciation in the sight of God ; of continual
reference of all things to God ; of renunciation of
the world and self-dedication to God. The Indwelling Word takes up again the admonitions of
the first and second books. The Augustinian has
clearly in his mind the dangers of Perfectionism.
The fear of falling back into worldliness is ceaselessly
before his eyes. The disciple is warned against
desire of every kind, and obedience to the example
of Jesus Christ is almost harshly demanded. "Oh
Dust, learn to obey."[1] He must learn in a harsh
school that comfort is to be found in God alone, and
that "my heart cannot truly rest nor be entirely
contented unless it rest in Thee."[2] In the twenty-
third chapter the Inner Voice speaks once more to
the disciple, telling him of four things that bring
much peace : "Study, son, to do the Will of another
rather than thine own. Choose always to have less
rather than more. Seek always the lowest place
and to be inferior to every one. Wish always and
pray, that the will of God may be wholly fulfilled
in thee. Behold such a man enters the land of
peace and rest."

The mystic position is kept ever before the
reader's mind intermingled with admonitions and
warnings. "A man ought therefore to rise above
all creatures and perfectly to forsake himself and
stand in ecstasy of mind and see that Thou the

[1] Lib. iv. cap. 13.　　　　[2] Lib. iv. cap. 21.

Creator of all things art in nothing like the creature.
. . . Unless a man be lifted up in spirit and freed
from all creatures and united wholly unto God,
whatsoever he knows, whatsoever he possesses is
of no great weight. . . . Nature regards the outward
things of man : grace turns itself to the inward.
The one is often disappointed : the other trusts in
God and is not deceived." [1] " True heavenly
wisdom seems very mean and small, and almost
forgotten among men . . . yet it is the pearl of
price which is hidden from many." [2] " O Everlasting Light, surpassing all created luminaries : dart the
beams of Thy brightness from above and penetrate
all the corners of my heart. Purify, beatify, beautify
and vivify my spirit with all its powers : that I may
cleave unto Thee with transports of jubilation. O
for the coming of that blessed and desirable hour,
when Thou wilt satisfy me with Thy Presence and
be unto me all in all." [3] " Let this be thy aim, this
thy prayer, this thy desire, that thou mayst be
stripped of all that is thine, and naked, follow Jesus
naked ; mayst die to thyself ; and live eternally to
Me." [4] The disciple must seek " the lot and freedom
of the sons of God, who stand above things present
and contemplate things Eternal." [5] " If thou
couldest perfectly annihilate thyself and empty
thyself of all created love, then should I overflow
into thee with great grace." [6] " O home most blessed

[1] Lib. iv. cap 31. [2] Lib. iv. cap 32. [3] Lib. iv. cap 34.
[4] Lib. iv. cap 37. [5] Lib. iv. cap 38. [6] Lib. iv. cap 42.

in the City above. O cloudless day of Eternity which no night obscures, whose never setting sun is the Truth supreme; day ever joyful, ever secure and never changing into its contrary. O that that day had dawned and that all these things of time had come to an end."[1] "There shall thy will be ever one with Mine, shall not desire any outward or personal gain. There . . . all things thou canst desire shall be there together present and refresh thy whole affection and fill it up to the brim."[2] The perfect victory is to triumph over ourselves. "For he that keeps himself in such subjection, that his senses be obedient to reason, and his reason in all things to Me, is truly conqueror of himself and Lord of the World."[3] The fifty-fourth chapter contrasts in great detail Nature and Grace, and shows that Grace is that second nature with which the Inner Life must be clothed. "This Grace is a supernatural light and a special gift of God and the proper seal of the elect and pledge of eternal salvation; it raises up a man from earth to love the things of heaven, and from being carnal makes him spiritual. The more, therefore, Nature is held down and subdued the greater Grace is infused: and every day by new visitations the inward man is reshaped according to the image of God."[4] We slowly move to the conclusion of the whole matter. Man is made unto the image of God and the Inner

[1] Lib. iv. cap. 48. [2] Lib. iv. cap 49.
[3] Lib. iv. cap 53. [4] Lib. iv. cap 54.

Life will re-create the likeness that the Outer Life has obscured. In a curious passage à Kempis speaks of " Natural Reason" being a spark buried in ashes and "encompassed about with great darkness," but yet able to discriminate between the true and the false, between the inner and the outer life. " Hence it is, O my God, that I delight in Thy law after the inward man." [1] But Grace, the second nature, is the only moving force, and it must be used if we are to imitate Christ and thus resume the image of the heavenly : " Grant me grace to imitate Thee." [2] The fulfilment of imitation is seen in the lives of the saints : " For being ravished above self and drawn out of love of self, they plunge wholly into love of Me : in whom also they rest in fruition. Nothing can turn them back or hold them down ; for being full of the eternal Truth, they burn with the fire of unquenchable charity." [3] It is but rarely that à Kempis so vividly, in language so Dantesque, describes the mystic rapture.

But here we are at the culmination of his whole philosophy, which would abolish the dualism of things and give to the illuminated seer the unspeakable fact of personal intercourse with God. If St Bernard saw God face to face as the Middle Ages believed, such a consummation could be attained by the humblest of God's Saints. Yet such a consummation is the dream of a philosophy and not of a religion. It is the goal of a long line of philosophic

[1] Lib. iv. cap 55.   [2] Lib. iv. cap 56.   [3] Lib. iv. cap 58.

thought that threads its way through the minds of the thinkers who through many centuries had turned their eyes from this corruptible world, from this " land of the shadow of death " (as à Kempis calls it in the exquisite *Aurea Oratio* that concludes the *Imitation*), to " the home of everlasting day." It is the mystic's philosophy high and noble, the philosophy that having formulated an hypothesis shows the way to an experience that must confirm the hypothesis. If we imitate the Christ of history we shall find the mystic Christ, the Eternal Word which shall reconcile, without merger, the personality of man to the personality of God. The same conception had illuminated the mystics of all the Christian centuries. It was the need of such a conception that brought Greek philosophy into intimate union with Christian faith. But it was not until à Kempis had finished his immortal work that the conception was stated in such a form that it could appeal to almost every type of mind, and make the simple peasant as well as the great philosopher realise that Christianity is philosophy at its highest exhibited in action.

The *Imitation* within a few years from its completion stood alone. It was the aloe flower that centuries of bitter devotional introspection had produced. The dim yearnings of more than fifteen hundred years for the way of a Messiah, for an imitable reconciler of man and God, for Christ and things Christlike—yearnings that rose bitterly in

the wilderness of time long before the awful
bitterness of the Garden ; yearnings that did not
cease during the hollow splendours of the Empire
or amidst its decadent glories ; that echo in the
darkness of the succeeding centuries and through
the twilight of sacerdotal Rome : these helpless cries
to the far realms of help find their full expression
here. When Christ was raising Lazarus in Bethany,
Philo was proclaiming the Logos in Alexandria, and
declaring that "only he who dies to himself can live
to God." Seventy years after, when John in Patmos
was describing the new heaven and the new earth,
Plutarch was formulating the Logos as he read it,
dæmonic and dynamic, leading man up from himself
to God. Two centuries later, Plotinus enunciated
that "ecstasy of unutterable feeling," that "Flight of
the alone to the Alone," which only could bring
men into union with God and so abolish the dualism
between the old heaven and the old earth. Even
Aurelius had been touched by the same doctrine in
the previous generation : " Live with the gods," he
cries. "And he lives with the gods who continually
displays to them his soul, living in satisfaction with
its lot, and doing the Will of the inward spirit, a
portion of his own divinity which Zeus has given to
every man for a ruler and a guide. This is the
intelligence, the reason that abides in us all." If
Chrysostom the golden-mouthed was glad to scourge
men into reconciliation, his contemporary Augustine
was content for the things of this world and the

knowledge of them and all reasoning about them to vanish out of sight. "Happy is the man who knows Thee, yet not these," for he "possesseth all things by his union with Thee." In the sixth century, when the author of the *City of God* had been dead a hundred years and night had fallen, we find Severinus Boethius attempting the reconciliation of God and man, justifying the ways of God to man in an age when the ways of man in the heart of civilisation were capable of no justification whatsoever. He dreamed, amidst the shows of things, of an eternity possessing "the whole plenitude of an unlimited life at once," and Christianised *ex post facto* by Dante he rests from martyrdom and exile in the charmed circle girt with eternal music where Albert of Cologne and Thomas of Aquino dwell. In the same age the founder of the Benedictines established the cloisters where his disciples

"*Fermar li piedi e tennero il cor saldo*" (*Par.* xxii. 51),

ever contemplating the central light and the sphere where the perfect patterns are laid up.

The cleansing midwinter night of the early Middle Ages has closed round Christendom, and while the midnight bell is sounding the Contemplatives keep watch upon the heaven where they would be. The Venerable Bede, he who shared with Roger Bacon the title of the Admirable Doctor, dictated the learning of Europe while he unfolded the mystical threefold meaning of the Holy Books, made Grammar the divine key of the Word, and was

present at all sacred offices, " lest the angels joining
in the Church's worship should miss his presence
there." His disciple Alcuin, waving aside the cares
and controversies of his toilsome life, put forward in
the *de Fide Sanctae Trinitatis* his ultimate faith. All
of Augustine, much of Plutarch is there. The dualism
between things created and the increate and creative
Spirit was overcome by the dæmonic and moving
agency of angels until the coming of One who is
both God and man, whose footsteps trace the path
of peace to God, who eternally reconciles the finite
and the infinite, and thus satisfies the inborn craving
of man for the Absolute. Alcuin's school, and in
particular his great follower Rabanus Maurus, carried
on his theological tradition, the Augustine tradition
of the relationship of God and man. That tradition,
moreover, received new strength from the support
given to it by a famous contemporary of the Abbot
of Fulda, Johannes Scotus Erigena. The Holy
Sophist enunciated a doctrine of creative ideas
which, proceeding from God, are wholly good, which
as realised in the material universe are tainted with
evil, but become again perfectly good by the
death of self and the ultimate re-union with God.
" Precious," he says, " is the passage of purified souls
into the intimate contemplation of truth which is the
true blessedness and eternity." Plutarch, Augustine,
and Boethius almost entirely inspired his position as
a Contemplative. To them all true philosophy and
true religion were in the end indistinguishable.

The tenth century gives us no speculative name save that of the famous Gerbert, [1] whose physical investigations anticipated the work of Roger Bacon, who declared that the proper study of mankind is man, but who nevertheless seems to place around the apparent universe a speculative world into which man could only see, which he could only enter and enjoy by the aid of faith. Such a thinker, a man profound and pious, who was regarded by his own age (while it awaited, during the four years of his reign, the destruction of the visible world) as a magician, occupies a place in the catenary of the Contemplatives. To him, as to Bacon and even many modern thinkers, the dualism of the universe would disappear if the ultimate mystery of matter could but be solved. That mystery is a fit subject of contemplation, since it may declare the unity about which so many generations had ignorantly philosophised. The ideal and universal whole cannot be realised until the parts themselves have been explored in complete and final detail and correlated with the whole. Idealism even in the mind of Plato fell short of its goal because it could not complete such a relationship. In the case of the mediæval Neo-Platonists, the failure of idealism grew more and more apparent as the religious cry for its success grew more and more urgent. The pathway of Christ needed to be the pathway of reality. In the mind of the theologian it tended to become a

[1] Pope Sylvester II. (999-1003).

grammarian's maze. There were two ways of clearing the thorny ground—there was Abelard's way, and there was Gerbert's way—the doubt that kills and the doubt that makes alive again. Gerbert turned to the investigation of the parts while he recognised the ideal existence of the whole. To have shown the possibility of such an attitude was his contribution to man's conception of the relationship of man and God. He saw things dimly, but he also saw them whole. Abelard doubted that he might enquire not into the facts of nature but into the opinions of men. To him things remained material and God immaterial. His logic could supply no keystone to the arch of nature.

For the moment Gerbert stood alone. To the people he was a magician, and after his death his apparent use lay in the fact that his tomb sweated and his bones rattled as a frequent presage of the death of rapidly succeeding popes. Two centuries and a half were destined to pass before his magic robes were resumed by the Admirable Doctor of Oxford and Paris. Meanwhile the theologians still stood gazing up into heaven. But a new ethical note began to personify the Platonic goodness and to individualise the Christ of the schoolmen. The dispute as to the sanctity of Alfege raised a definite issue. He died for the people, not for the faith. But Anselm justified his canonisation in one striking phrase, "Who dies for justice, dies for Christ." Lanfranc was convinced and the

R

following of Christ acquired for all ages. a wider, a more individualistic meaning. But the philosophic link between the infinite and the finite was not less real to Anselm than to his forerunners. He was, as Maurice has shown, a Platonist at heart. There is a supreme Good which is God. By this Good we are made: "for this Good every man should strive with his whole heart, and whole soul, and whole mind, by loving it and longing for it." But Anselm is more than a Platonist. With St Augustine he calls to God to reveal himself; with Boethius he contrasts the environments of time and eternity; with Alcuin he admits that God can be referred to no species, though it is his property always to have mercy, but claims that that is an argument for the personal existence of the Supreme Good. He seems to say that we may reason from the particular to the general, even if the general be beyond our finite conception. We may think that the unthinkable is the logical goal of a rising scale of things finite. Belief is therefore not unreasonable and, as he declares in his Monologue on *the Essence of the Divinity*, "it is fitting, therefore, for the same human soul to believe this supreme Essence and those things without which it cannot be loved, that by believing it may stretch towards it."

Abelard breaks for a moment the chain of the Contemplatives. One of the greatest of the logicians, he was a follower neither of Plato nor of Aristotle. "By doubting we come to inquiry"

did not exhaust the difference between him
and the holders of the Augustinian tradition. He
was intellectually a nominalist of the most logical
type, more logical than his school. There is no
underlying unity in his conception, no ultimate
reality reconciling Man and God. His cold logic
dispenses with the mystery of the Universe. He
does not stand looking up into heaven, neither does
he peer into the physical mystery of the earth. By
inquiry he never came to doubt the reality of either
God or matter, for he never inquired into the existence of either, though he reasoned about both. His
was a Logic of Assent that, assuming the existence
of one by faith and the other by sight, found no
mystery in either, but merely terms of logical import.
Maurice points out that he acknowledged, as a
thinker (whatever he may have acknowledged as a
man), no " spiritual bond between the Divine Creator
and himself." It seems to the present writer that
Thomas à Kempis deliberately singled out Abelard
(the author of *de Generibus et speciebus*) for attack :
he and his school of arrogant, narrow, pure thought,
stood out as the eternal opponents of the contem-
plativism that was crystallised in the *Imitation*.

St Bernard of Clairvaux (1091-1153) did even
more than St Anselm to bring down the heaven of
mysticism into the heart of man and to make it the
source of a practical faith. He is the direct forerunner of à Kempis. It was a sound literary, a
sound philosophic instinct that made a copyist of the

fifteenth century attribute the *Imitation* to him. We find in his sermons and letters the very spirit, even the very literary note of the *Imitation*. But if the Doctor Mellifluus was the father in literature of à Kempis, pointing the way in which the wisdom of the Fathers and the Doctors could be epigrammatised and crystallised into immortal form, many other forces, as we have already seen, contributed to the thought of the Dutch recluse.

Hugo of St Victor (1097-1141), the German who came to the School of Paris, elaborated a doctrine of spiritual reality that gave a new basis to mysticism. Faith, he taught, is the initial good, since in some measure it makes us realise the actuality of God, the realisation of whom is the highest good. A life of faith is the precursor of an eternity of contemplation. But he recognised the practical side of things. The world must be a better world if any individual life is to fulfil itself. "The integrity of human life requires for its fulfilment science and virtue."

Peter Lombard (1100-1160), the Master of Sentences, completed the didactic formularism of St Bernard and the practical mysticism of Hugo of St Victor. He was an intellectual and spiritual descendant of Augustine. He carried verbal analysis to its extremest limits, but never lost sight of the doctrine that we are what we are by the Grace of God. But his verbosity justified the jest of his contemporary, John of Salisbury, levelled at the mediæval doctors, "there is no getting away from

Genera and Species." A Kempis adopts this very position.

The influence of Joachim the Cistercian (1130-1202) on à Kempis cannot be overlooked. He preached a new dispensation, "the Everlasting Gospel," when man would become spiritually perfect and therefore spiritually free. It was a new but a legitimate step in the cult of mysticism. The spiritual aspiration of Joachim is a marked feature of the *Imitation*. Richard of St Victor (f. 1173), "who was in contemplation more than man," carried forward that intense contemplation of the Trinity that distinguished the mystics and doctors of the twelfth century. The Aristotelian reaction of the thirteenth century, despite the anathemas of the Vatican, brought a new force into mysticism. To Aristotle, God was the Alpha and Omega of a Universe which in its natural structure was sharply divided from him. But this acute dualism was in a measure resolved by a more than Platonic idealism. Aristotle conceived of a *Scala Naturalis* in which each of the finite creatures is "regarded as seeking for the divine, but able to realise it only within the limits of its own form. Aiming at eternity, it is confined within the conditions of an individual existence which is finite and perishable, though it attains to a kind of image of eternity in the continuity of the species. It attains it, however, in a still higher way, in so far as its own limited life is made the basis of a higher life; till in the ascending scale we reach at last the rational life of man, who at least in the pure activity of contemplation, can directly participate in the eternal and divine." But the real difficulty that makes the dualism — the gap between divine intelligence and the material changing world is not explained. To the analyst with human limitations this blur on a scheme of idealism is inevitable. On the other hand, " the general tendency of Plato is to generalise and to unify, to refer each sphere of phenomenal existence to some idea which he regards as the source of all its reality, and the principle through which alone it can be understood ; and, ultimately, to carry back all these ideas to the Good or the divine reason, as the principle of all being and of all thought." With Plato "the universal is the real " ; with Aristotle "the individual is the real." In their higher sense, there is no ultimate antagonism between these propositions, since a universal "means a general principle, viewed as expressing itself in different forms or phases, each of which implies all the others and the whole ; and an individual is just such a whole or totality, viewed as determined in all its forms or phases by one principle." [1]

But the Middle Ages and the schoolmen did not attempt to find idealism in Aristotle himself. They solved the dualism that Aristotle appears to present by the application of Christianity. Hence we find that though for a time purely contemplative creations,

[1] *The Evolution of Theology in the Greek Philosophers*, by Edward Caird, vol. i. pp. 262, 267, 277.

such as the *De Contemplatione* of Innocent III. (1160-
1216), influenced the mystics, we must look for
practical results in the foundation of the great orders
by St Dominic (1170-1221) and St Francis (1182-
1226). The Seraphic Father gave a new missionary,
a speculative and individual, zeal to the Church. We
find that its new thinking force was to be derived
from the work of Albertus Magnus of Cologne
(1193-1280), the Universal Doctor, and his pupil
Thomas of Aquino (1225-1274) the Angelic Doctor.
In that age came two other notable figures : Roger
Bacon (1214-1294) the Admirable Doctor, and
Bonaventura (1221-1274) the Seraphic Doctor.
These men formed a remarkable galaxy of thought,
inspiration, and contemplative power. Albert of
Cologne and Roger Bacon both lay under the same
suspicion that Gerbert suffered. To investigate
nature, to endeavour to proceed from the particular
to the universal was their office and their glory.
Such men were necessarily Aristotelians in the
best sense. The only true method of reconciliation
between God and this world was to find a natural
and a metaphysical as well as a spiritual bond of
union ; to find in the ladders of nature and thought
the union between man and God. The Angelic
Doctor was of another type of mind—the mind
rather of Abelard than Hugo, but of Abelard with
a keener faith. Aquinas deliberately entertained
doubt that he might come to inquiry, and he came
to inquiry that he might approach God by every

intellectual avenue.　He was in no sense an
Augustinian.　He did not believe in patterns laid
up in heaven.　Pure intelligence was the pathway
to reality.　If man is to realise God at all, he seems
to say, he must do it in the mind and not in the
heart.　Such a doctrine must have been repulsive in
the extreme to à Kempis.　He preferred to be on
the side of Seraphs.　But all these influences directly
and indirectly bore upon the content of the *Imitation*.
More often than not the influence was indirect, and
came to à Kempis by way of the German and
Flemish mystics, Eckhardt, Tauler, Suso, Ruysbroek,
who seemed, as we have seen, to offer for his selection
the thoughts of many ages on the ultimate mystery
that underlies the relationship of God and man.

When we turn from the theological and philosophical aspects of the *Imitation* to its doctrines of
social life, we find on examination something quite
different from the superficial view often taken of
this side of its content.　It may readily be admitted
that it is possible to take a series of quotations from
the *Imitation* which would appear to show that its
author knew nothing of the promise of this life and
was merely inspired with an egotism entirely re-
pellant to the modern mind—an egotism that is not
less an egotism from the fact that it substitutes love
of the Creator for the love of the created.　Quotations can, however, like statistics, prove anything.
The tenets of some Christian sects show how the
spirit of the Bible can be obscured or even wholly

hidden by the selective process, and I cannot but think that in the case of the *Imitation* the same mistake has happened. The work falls naturally into two parts : the philosophic part, which preaches the doctrine of a subjective Inner Life based on a philosophic hypothesis and to be approximately realised in an experience that realises the sermon on the Mount and lives the life of Christ ; and the social part, which exhibits a daily Outer Life which all men may, without unreasonable dreams of perfection, live and rejoice in. Before detailing some of the more serious criticisms that have been levelled at the *Imitation*, it will be convenient to draw from the three books which form what is known as the *Ecclesiastical Music*, the doctrines of social life as conceived by Thomas à Kempis. The briefest examination shows that selfishness of any sort was at least as abhorrent to à Kempis as it is to his critics. So far as the Inner Life goes he is, it is true, an individualist of the most unbending type. He knew that all the great decisions of life depend on the individual, and that a profound sense of individual responsibility is the basis of all ethical, all spiritual progress. But in relation to the outer life, the life of common day, he is in fact a socialist rather than an individualist. He preaches from end to end of his work the most practical form of altruism. A series of quotations will show this better than comment can do. "To make no account of ourselves, and to think always well and highly of others is great wisdom and perfection. . . . We all are frail but thou shalt esteem none frailer than thyself."[1] "Be not ashamed to serve others for the love of Jesus Christ . . . think not thyself better than others. . . . If thou hast any good believe better things of others, that thou mayest preserve humility. It hurts not to debase thyself under all men : but it hurts much to prefer thyself even to one."[2] "Keep company with the humble and simple, with the devout and virtuous : and commune with them of those things that may edify."[3] "To refuse to yield to others, when reason or a cause requires it, is a sign of pride and obstinacy."[4] "We so willingly talk because by mutual speech we seek mutual comfort and desire to ease the heart over-wearied by manifold anxieties. . . . Our spiritual progress is not a little helped, by devout communing of spiritual things : especially when men of like mind and spirit be met together in God."[5] "If thou didst but mark how much peace unto thyself and joy *unto others* thou shouldst procure by behaving thyself well, I think thou wouldest be more careful of thy spiritual progress."[6] "Often take counsel in temptation and deal not roughly with him that is tempted, but give him comfort, as thou wouldest wish to be done to thyself."[7]

[1] Lib. i. cap. 2.   [2] Lib. i. cap. 7.   [3] Lib. i. cap. 8.
[4] Lib. i. cap. 9.   [5] Lib. i. cap. 10.   [6] Lib. i. cap. 11.
[7] Lib. i. cap. 13. Dr Bigg points out that John Dygoun, the fifteenth century copyist of Sheen, writes opposite to this tender pastoral, *Nota nota bene.*

"Turn thine eyes upon thyself : and beware thou judge not the actions of others. In judging of others a man labours in vain ; often errs and easily sins."[1] "He does much that loves much. He does much that does a thing well. He does well that serves the community rather than his own will."[2] "We are glad to see others perfect : and yet we mend not our own faults. We will have others severely corrected : and will not be corrected ourselves. . . . We will have others restrained by laws : but will not in any way be checked ourselves. And thus it appears how seldom we weigh our neighbour in the same balance with ourselves. If all men were perfect what should we have to suffer from others for God's sake ? But now God hath so ordered it, that we may learn to bear one another's burdens ; for no man is without fault, no man without his burden : no man sufficient for himself, no man wise enough for himself ; but we ought to bear with one another, comfort one another, help, instruct, and admonish one another."[3] The whole duty of human altruism, the whole doctrine of human solidarity, is contained in these pregnant phrases. Here is no selfish mystic, absorbed in the contemplation of his own soul and his own ultimate perfection. Man must lean upon man if he is to lean upon God, is the specific teaching of the great Augustinian. "Still have an eye to thyself first and admonish thyself especially before all thy beloved friends. . . . A good man finds cause

[1] Lib. i. cap. 14.   [2] Lib. i. cap. 15.   [3] Lib. i. cap. 16.

enough for mourning and weeping. For, whether he consider his own or his neighbour's estate, he knows that none lives here without tribulation." [1] " Man's happiness consists not in abundance of temporal goods but a moderate portion is enough for him." [2] " Whilst thou art in health thou mayest do much good." [3] " A great and wholesome purgatory hath the patient man . . . who prays cheerfully for his gainsayers: and from his heart forgives offences; who delays not to ask forgiveness from others : who is quicker to pity than to wrath. . . . Here we have some pause from toil, and enjoy the comfort of our friends." [4] " Hope in the Lord and do good saith the Prophet, and inhabit the land : and thou shalt be fed in the riches thereof. . . . Be careful also to avoid and conquer those faults especially which often displease thee in others. Gather some profit to thy soul everywhere. . . . Thou wilt always rejoice at eventide if thou spend the day fruitfully." [5]

When we turn to the second book—the book of the Inner Life—we find the same high doctrine of Christian altruism, of devotion to duty and to others. " An inward man . . . finds no hindrance in outward labour, or business necessary for the time; but as things fall out so he accommodates himself to them." [6] " Think not that thou hast made any progress unless thou feel thyself inferior to all." [7] " First, therefore, be severe towards

[1] Lib. i. cap. 21. [2] Lib. i. cap. 22. [3] Lib. i. cap. 23. [4] Lib. i. cap. 24. [5] Lib. i. cap. 25. [6] Lib. ii. cap. 1. [7] Lib. ii. cap. 2.

thyself, and then mayest thou justly be severe also towards thy neighbour. Thou knowest well how to excuse and colour thine own deeds, but thou wilt not admit the excuses of others. It were more just that thou shouldest accuse thyself, and excuse thy brother. If thou wilt be carried, carry also another."[1] Perhaps in no single phrase does à Kempis so adequately set forth his own social views as in the words, "si portari vis, porta et alium." In this phrase is contained the whole statement of the outer life, upon which depends that inner life which is the confessed aim and end of every mystic. This idea is consistently developed: "If thou intend and seek nothing else but the pleasure of God and the good of thy neighbour, thou shalt enjoy perfect internal freedom."[2]

He goes on to declare in a remarkable and mystical sentence that the progress of the world is a positive responsibility of each individual. If the world is evil, it is in fact a reflection of the onlooker's heart. "If *thy* heart were right, then every creature would be a mirror of life, and a book of holy doctrine." If the heart sees evil, it is evil. To the pure in heart all things are pure. If each man will see that his own heart is right, all will soon be very well with the world. "He that well and rightly considered his own works, would find no cause to judge hardly of another."[3]

"Without a friend thou canst not live well; and

[1] Lib. ii. cap. 3.   [2] Lib. ii. cap. 4.   [3] Lib. ii. cap. 5.

if Jesus be not above all a friend to thee, thou wilt
be very sad and desolate . . . love all for Jesus ;
but Jesus for Himself." [1]

Here we have again the conception of human
solidarity with Christ as the uniting link of all
human relationship.   But the friendship of Christ
is the supreme fact : " learn to part even with a
near and dear friend for the love of God." [2]   The
man who wrote that knew what friendship was.
The idea is carried on in the phrase, " If thou wilt
carry the Cross cheerfully, it will carry thee," [3] the
counterpart with respect to Christ of the injunc-
tion with respect to the human friend.   " If thou
wilt be carried, carry also another." [4]   These two
sentences bring out the universality of the doctrine
of vicarious effect, which is another form of the
doctrine of human solidarity.   Every good and
every evil deed done by man is endured or welcomed by every man in the world, is endured or
welcomed even by the risen Christ Himself.   To
charge the author of such a doctrine with selfishness is to misunderstand the meaning of great
ethical principles.   It would be as reasonable to
charge the Founder of Christianity with selfishness.
It will serve no useful purpose to pursue further an
analysis intended to show that à Kempis was an

---

[1] Lib. ii. cap. 8.   [2] Cap. 9.   [3] Lib. ii. cap. 12.
[4] Lib. ii. cap. 3.   Compare "Thy love for thy friend should be
grounded in me " (Lib. iv. cap. 42).   " Come brothers march togeth
Jesus will be with us " (Lib. iv. cap. 56).   ,

altruist and not a spiritual hedonist, [1] but some quotations from the book of Internal Consolation may be given to show something of his outlook on the workaday world. He certainly felt that the things of earth were to be used. " Behold heaven and earth which Thou hast created for the service of man wait upon Thee : and daily perform whatever Thou hast commanded." [2] " Learn to be content with little and find delight in simple things." [3] " Use temporal things : desire eternal." [4] " All that we have in soul and in body, and whatsoever we possess without or within, naturally or supernaturally are Thy benefits and proclaim Thee bountiful, merciful and good, from whom we have received all good things." [5] " Behold, meat, drink, raiment, and other commodities for the sustenance of the body, are a burden to the fervent spirit. Grant me to use such refreshments moderately, not to be entangled with excessive desire. It is not lawful to cast away all things, because nature must be sustained." [6] We are to become one with the Sons of God who " draw the temporal things to serve them well in such ways as are ordained by God and appointed by the Great Work-master, who hath left nothing in His creation without due order." [7] " Thou art flesh, not angel." [8]

---

[1] See also the following references, Lib. iv. cap. 13, cap. 23, cap. 27, cap. 36, cap. 42, cap. 54, cap. 56, cap. 58.

[2] Lib. iv. cap. 10. [3] Lib. iv. cap. 11. [4] Lib. iv. cap. 16.
[5] Lib. iv. cap. 22. [6] Lib. iv. cap. 26. [7] Lib. iv. cap. 38.
[8] Lib. iv. cap. 57.

Thomas à Kempis, in fact, presents, as all true mystics present, a perfectly sane view of the outward life. It is only if we forget this fundamental view and attach to the outward life the mystical conception of the Inner Life as set forth by à Kempis and his school that there is any temptation to accuse the mystic of spiritual hedonism and selfishness. From all we know of à Kempis we have reason to believe that in his quiet way he thoroughly enjoyed his life. He did not in any way spurn the pleasures of the book or of the table, or of companionship, but he took good care that life should not be entirely composed of those things, that they should, in fact, only be admitted in so far as they tended to encourage a high spiritual outlook on the life to be.

One could not, it is quite certain, take this view of à Kempis and of the *De Imitatione Christi* if one accepted the judgment of certain critics. Consider in the light of the foregoing quotations the criticism of Dean Milman. After some interesting and valuable remarks on the merits and influence of the *Imitation*, this distinguished historian proceeds: " But ' the Imitation of Christ,' the last effort of Latin Christianity, is still monastic Christianity. It is absolutely and entirely selfish in its aim, as in its acts. Its sole, single, exclusive object, is the purification, the elevation of the individual soul, of the man absolutely isolated from his kind, of the man dwelling alone in the solitude, in the hermitage of his own thoughts ; with no fears or hopes, no sympathies of our common nature : he has absolutely withdrawn and secluded himself not only from the cares, the sins, the trials, but from the duties, the connexions, the moral and religious fate of the world. Never was misnomer so glaring, if justly considered, as the title of the book, the 'Imitation of Christ.' That which distinguishes Christ, that which distinguishes Christ's Apostles—that which distinguishes Christ's religion—the Love of Man—is entirely and absolutely left out. . . . The 'Imitation of Christ' begins in self—terminates in self. The simple exemplary sentence, 'He went about doing good,' is wanting in the monastic gospel of this pious zealot. Of feeding the hungry, of clothing the naked, of visiting the prisoner, even of preaching, there is profound, total silence. The world is dead to the votary of the Imitation, and he is dead to the world, dead in a sense absolutely repudiated by the first vital principles of the Christian faith. Christianity, to be herself again, must not merely shake off indignantly the barbarism, the vices, but even the virtues of the Mediæval, of Monastic, of Latin, Christianity." [1]

Such a criticism will be read with absolute amazement by anyone who has considered fairly and with an unbiassed mind the quotations from the *Imitation* set out above. There is a temptation to feel that the late Dean of St Paul's had never really considered

[1] *The History of Latin Christianity*, by Henry Hart Milman, D.D., Dean of St Paul's, Book xiv. cap. 3 (3rd ed., 1872, vol. ix. pp. 163-5).

S

the precepts of the *De Imitatione Christi*, but had assumed that it was the last effort of Latin Christianity, whatever that may mean, and had adopted a theory of its contents that fitted in with the theory of a decadent Church. The answer to Dean Milman's criticism is the text of the *Imitation*, and such phrases as *si portari vis, porta et alium*. No critic who had realised the meaning of that sentence could say that " the Love of Man is entirely and absolutely left out " from the work in which it occurs. Moreover, the historian of Latin Christianity shows how entirely he misapprehended the place of the *Imitation* in the history of religion when he declared that it was " the last effort of Latin Christianity." Even from Dean Milman's point of view it would have seemed reasonable to suppose that that last effort was the educational activity of the Jesuits in the Far East and the Near West. But the *Imitation*, even if we are so destitute of the literary faculty as to suppose that it was written by Jean le Charlier de Gerson, had no relation to Latin Christianity, if by that term we mean the Christianity of Avignon and Rome. It was the product of Germanic Christianity —by which I mean the Invisible Church that was preparing the Reformation in England and West Central and Northern Europe. Absolutely the only reason for calling the work an effort of Latin Christianity is that it was written—as were the great treatises of Luther—in Latin. But England, Holland and France had vernacular versions early in the fifteenth century, and for long ages it was in England actually believed by the best critics that the work was written by an Englishman in English. The mystic element in the work, and the fact that it was written by a monk, no doubt give colour at first sight to the idea that the *Imitation* was a product of the Latin Church, but the idea vanishes when it is realised that the Latin Church was at the best a step-mother to true mysticism, and that monasticism provided the chief elements of revolt from and reformation in that Church.

However, Dean Milman's views have been widely accepted. Moreover, his statement "that this book supplies some imperious want in the Christianity of mankind, that it supplied it with a fullness and felicity, which left nothing, at this period of Christianity, to be desired, its boundless popularity is the one unanswerable testimony," shows that he recognised some of the intrinsic merits of the work. The same cannot be said of another distinguished writer of the same generation. W. M. Thackeray, in a letter dated Christmas Day 1849, summed up his view of the book in his incomparable manner. " The scheme of that book," he wrote, " carried out would make the world the most wretched, useless, dreary, doting place of sojourn. There would be no manhood, no love, no tender ties of mother and child, no use of intellect, no trade or science—a set of selfish beings, crawling about, avoiding one another, and howling a perpetual

Miserere." [1] The mid-nineteenth century, against
the materialism of which Thackeray tilted with all
his noble might, stood out in extraordinary contrast
to the ideal world painted by à Kempis. Social
conditions in England were at that time at their
very worst. Eighty per cent. of the people were
without education, were ill-fed, ill-clothed, ill-housed.
That world might with some justice have been
described as containing "a set of selfish beings,
crawling about, avoiding one another, and howling
a perpetual *Miserere.*" Extremes meet, a curious
meeting, especially when we realise that the mystic
ideals of à Kempis were, in fact, a path of spiritual
escape from the soul-destroying and awful social
conditions of the Middle Ages.

The views held by Milman and Thackeray about
the *Imitation* were, however, most unusual among
distinguished thinkers. It is true that Dr Johnson,
if we may believe his early biographer, Sir John
Hawkins,[2] "was for some time pleased with Kempis'
tract *De Imitatione Christi*, but at length laid it
aside, saying that the main design of it was to
promote monastic piety and inculcate ecclesiastical
obedience"; but in fact Johnson's views about the
Imitation were very different. He may have
objected to certain chapters, but the work was a
very real fact in his life. In the year 1778,
when he was sixty-nine, he observed to Boswell,

[1] *Letters of W. M. Thackeray* (London, 1887), p. 96.
[2] *Life of Johnson* (1789), p. 544.

" Thomas à Kempis must be a good book, as the world has opened its arms to receive it. It is said to have been printed in one language or others, as many times as there have been months since it first came out. I always was struck with this sentence in it, ' Be not angry that you cannot make others as you wish them to be, since you cannot make yourself as you wish to be.' " [1] He seems to have been a constant reader of the *Imitation*, and according to *Croker's Boswell* (p. 884), he told on his deathbed a curious story of himself in relation to the *Imitation*. He said to Mr Hoole, " About two years since I feared that I had neglected God, and that then I had not a *mind* to give Him ; on which I set about to read Thomas à Kempis in Low Dutch, which I accomplished, and thence I judged that my mind was not impaired, Low Dutch having no affinity with any of the languages that I knew." [2] In another version he stated that he only read a part of this translation. He was in the habit of speaking on the subject of various editions, it seems, for on Monday, May 17th 1784, Boswell dined with him and raised the question : " When I mentioned that I had seen in the king's library sixty-three editions of my favourite *Thomas à Kempis*, amongst which it was in eight languages, Latin, German, French, Italian, Spanish, English, Arabic, and

[1] Boswell's *Life of Johnson* (Hill edition, vol. iii. p. 226). The passage is from lib. i. cap. 16, " Si non potes te talem facere qualem vis, quomodo poteris alium habere ad bene placitum tuum ? "
[2] *Miscellanies* (Hill), vol. ii. p. 153.

Armenian, he said he thought it unnecessary to collect many editions, which were all the same, except as to paper and print; he would have the original, and all the editions which had any variation in the text." The *Imitation* was in fact very popular in the eighteenth century. In Fielding's novel *Joseph Andrews*, we find in chapter iii. the passage: " He [Joseph Andrews] told him [Parson Adams] likewise that ever since he was in Sir Thomas' country he had employed all his leisure in reading good books; that he had read the Bible, the *Whole Duty of Man*, and *Thomas à Kempis*, and that he had also studied a great book "—Baker's *Chronicle*. It would be a lengthy task to set up against the views of Dean Milman and Thackeray those of the many great thinkers who used and loved the *Imitation* and saw nothing either absurd, impossible or selfish in its attitude. The famous Leibnitz, in one of his letters, sums up the whole position: " The *Imitation of Christ* is one of the most excellent treatises that have been composed. Happy is he who puts its contents into practice and is not satisfied with merely reading them." Bernard le Bovier de Fontenelle (1657-1757), the famous essayist, a nephew of Corneille, has a curious and felicitous passage about the book—" le plus beau qui soit parti de la main des hommes, puisque l'Évangile n'en vient pas." There is a striking and characteristic passage in J. F. de la Harpe (1739-

---

[1] *Letters*, p. 77.

1803), describing the emotions that arose from casually reading the *Imitation* as he lay in prison. An excitable and impressionable essayist—he was under sentence for libel—it is perhaps not surprising that the work should have had certain emotional effects on him. The interest in the passage is that it shows one of the many different types of mind that are affected by the book. "J'avois sur une table l'Imitation ; et l'on m'avoit dit que dans cet excellent livre je trouverois souvent la réponse à mes pensées. Je l'ouvre au hasard, et je tombe, en l'ouvrant, sur ces paroles : *me voici, mon fils ! je viens à vous parce que vous m'avez invoqué.* Je n'en lus pas davantage : l'impression subite que j'éprouvai est au-dessus de toute expression, et il ne m'est pas plus possible de la rendre que de l'oublier. Je tombai la face contre terre, baigné de larmes, etouffé de sanglot, jetant des cris et des paroles entrecoupées. Je sentois mon cœur soulagé et dilaté, mais en même temps comme prêt à se fendre. Assailli d'une foule d'idées et de sentiments, je pleurai assez long-temps, sans qu'il me reste d'ailleurs d'autre souvenir de cette situation, si ce n'est que c'est, sans aucune comparaison, ce que mon cœur a jamais senti de plus violent et de plus délicieux ; et que ces mots : *me voici, mon fils !* ne cessoient de retenir dans mon ame, et d'en ébranler puissamment toutes les facultés." F. R. de Lamennais (1782-1854), quoting this passage, says : "Que de grâces cachées renferme un livre dont un seul passage, aussi court que simple, a pu toucher de la sorte une ame longtemps endurcie par l'orgueil philosophique!"[1] But he adds significantly : " Qu'on ne s'y trompe pas, cependant : pour produire ces vives et soudaines impressions, et même un effet vraiment salutaire, l'Imitation demande un cœur préparé." It is interesting to turn from these French writers to English critics of even higher rank. Thomas Carlyle felt the extraordinary charm of the book, though he shows a characteristic scorn for one of its commentators. In 1833 he sent to his mother from Edinburgh a copy of the *Imitation*, with an introduction by Chalmers. The latter he declared was "wholly or in great part a *dud*." Of the book itself he says, " None, I believe, except the Bible, has been so universally read and loved by Christians of all tongues and sects. It gives me pleasure to think that the Christian heart of my good mother may also derive nourishment and strengthening from what has already nourished and strengthened so many."[2] On the farther side of Milman and Thackeray in point of time, we have this striking testimony. On the hither side of these writers we have an even more distinguished man writing in subdued tones of the *Imitation*. Mr Gladstone, in a letter dated March 5th 1861, wrote, " I always think *Thomas à Kempis* a golden book for all times, but most for times like these ; for

[1] *L'Imitation de Jésus Christ*, traduction nouvelle par M. l'Abbé F. de Lamennais (Paris, 1844, 12th Ed.), p. 5.
[2] *Froude's Life*, vol. ii. p. 337.

though it does not treat professedly of sorrow, it is such a wonderful exhibition of the Man of Sorrows." A year later (April 4th 1862), he writes : "I must at some time try to explain a little more my reference to *Thomas à Kempis*. I have given that book to men of uncultivated minds, who were *also* Presbyterians, but all relish it. I do not believe it is possible for any one to read that book earnestly from its beginning, and think of Popish or non-Popish, or of anything but the man whom it presents and brings to us."[1] On the whole I think the world will be prepared to accept the tribute of Carlyle and Mr Gladstone rather than the criticism of Thackeray and Dean Milman. Mr Gladstone's reference to the acceptableness of the book to uncultivated minds may well be balanced by its equal acceptableness to minds of the subtlest modern type —to Frenchmen such as Comte and Renan, to Englishmen such as De Quincey and Matthew Arnold. We are fortunately in a position to know exactly what the *Imitation* meant to the latter thinker. His Note-Books, as edited by Mrs Wodehouse, show that over this great and subtle mind the work of à Kempis cast a spell that was as lasting as it was all-embracing. I shall conclude this volume by setting forth in detail the references to the *Imitation* entered year by year in the workaday note-book of the great poet-critic.

Matthew Arnold's Note-Books contain in brief his

[1] Morley's *Life of Gladstone*, vol. ii. p. 186.

philosophy of life as set forth in the aphorisms of favourite writers. The author from whom he quotes most frequently and most continuously is Thomas à Kempis, whose thoughts are frequently supplemented by quotations from the New and Old Testaments and the Apocrypha. In Mrs Wodehouse's little volume there are extracts from the first, second, or third books of the *Imitation* under the years 1857, 1859, 1863, 1868, 1873, 1878, 1883, and 1888. The fourth book, the tract *De Sacramento Altaris*—a work very definitely separated from the other tracts, and omitted altogether from many manuscripts of the fifteenth century and from all the curious class of manuscripts, mostly English, entitled *Musica Ecclesiastica*—is not represented in the Note-Books. Its formal theology and attitude differing from that of the other tracts excluded it from Arnold's lists of books to be read. He was in search of the philosophy and not the theology of life, and one may perhaps believe in view of its exclusion from the Note-Books that his critical gift recognised, as many transcribers of the fifteenth century recognised, a different hand in a work in which, according to the first printed edition, "specialiter tractatur de venerabili sacramento altaris." The quotations from the other books cover a period of over thirty years and are numerous. There are in all about a hundred extracts. It is difficult to tell the exact number, as none of the *Imitation* quotations are referred to their source, but I have verified nearly ninety and there

are others that could probably be traced without
much difficulty.   It is a matter of considerable
critical interest to notice the passages that seemed
to carry special weight in Arnold's mind.   The
Imitation has appealed to various types of literary
thinkers.   To Leibnitz it was a work of the first
magnitude.   He considered it "one of the most
excellent treatises that have been composed.   Happy
is he who puts its contents into practice and is not
satisfied with merely reading them."   To Dr
Johnson it appealed with peculiar force and
illuminated his dying hours.   Renan felt its power
and praised its anonymity.   To George Eliot it was
a mirror of the soul.   Arnold did not write about
it, but he used it as persistently as the humblest
devotee.   Here, he seems to say over and over
again in his Note-Books, is the philosophy of life
that conquers all things—even death.

The key of this philosophy he found in the phrase
semper aliquid certi proponendum est (lib. i. cap. 19).
Life must always have a definite purpose.   He
writes it first in his Note-Book for 1857 the year
of his election as the professor of poetry at Oxford
—that and the further phrase from this chapter
*secundum propositum nostrum est cursus profectus
nostri.*   The *aliquid certi* to him was a necessity, find
it where he could.   It alone could shape the course of
life.   The phrase is repeated over and over again in
the Note-Books.   We find it in 1857, 1859, 1863,
twice in 1868 and in 1883.   In 1873 it is omitted,

but we have in its place the phrase *Homo remissus et suum propositum deserens varie tentatur* (i. 13). Matthew Arnold at this date had perhaps lost the *aliquid certi* of earlier years. He had formally abandoned much that had once seemed essential. An enthusiasm for humanity, for work, for the perfect personal life definitely replaced certainties that had become uncertain.

The year 1868 is the year in which the *Following of Christ* (to use the early English title) is most voluminously quoted in the Note-Books. In that year we find set out some twenty-two quotations from the first book, eight from the second, and seventeen from the third—say some fifty in all. The year was one of great intellectual activity and great personal sorrows. It opened with the death of his little son Basil and closed with the death of his eldest son. In it appeared his Report on Continental Universities and Schools. He also seems to have been closely engaged in thinking out the theological position that he began to develop in 1870. The various books actually read in that year point to this conclusion. They included, besides the three books of the *Imitation, Romans, The Synoptic Gospels, Aristotle's Ethics, George Herbert's Poems, Wordsworth, Smith's Discourses, Robinson's Sermons, Herken's Ideen, Reimer's Goethe, Légende Dorée, Renan on St Paul, Proverbs,* and *The Psalms after Ewald.*

The quotations from the *Imitation* for this year

form a continuous and complete philosophy of life.
They begin with the fundamental aphorism *semper
aliquid certi proponendum est.* Then follow two
quotations from the chapter *De Doctrina Veritatis*
(i. 3), that carry on the doctrine of the *aliquid certi.*
*Bonus et devotus homo opera sua prius intus disponit
quae foris agere debet.* But inward determination is
useless without inward conquest. Therefore it is
asked and declared, "Who strives more sternly than
he who strives to conquer himself? This is our
main affair: to overcome ourselves and daily to
become stronger than ourselves and move forward
toward better things" (i. 3). But a goal and a determination to gain it, even if coupled with the conquest
of self, is useless without work. Idleness is the great
enemy. *Nunquam sis ex toto otiosus, sed aut legens,
aut scribens, aut orans, aut meditans, aut aliquid
utilitatis pro communi laborans* (i. 19). But there
are other sides of life beside that of accomplishment.
The conquest of passion, the overcoming of temptation, the leading of a good life may be perhaps
included in that conquest of self which is essential
to the accomplishment of anything. But life includes
goodness for its own sake, inward peace that has no
utilitarian purpose, and faith in God which transcends,
in the hour of bitter grief, all human consolations.
We find on these themes a remarkable list of
passages from the *Imitation.* "By resisting passions,
not by obeying them is found true peace of heart"
(i. 6). "He who is unjust and unpurposeful has

many temptations" (i. 13). The soul must fling itself beyond the need of human consolations : "A man should so rest in God that it would be needless for him to seek many human consolations" (i. 12). "If we were but more dead to ourselves and less involved in earthly things, we should then be able to taste divine things" (i. 11). Personal goodness will give us this power. *Resiste in principio inclinationi tuae, et malam dedisce consuetudinem* (i. 11). "If in each year we were to root out one vice, quickly we should become perfect men" (i. 11). And then follows the passionate cry, "O, if thou didst but realise how much peace for thyself, how much joy for others, thou wouldst gain by the nobler life" (i. 11). This personal goodness is related both to the perfect life, whose pattern is in heaven, and to the active life that looks to the *aliquid certi* of this world. But it is only by continual watchfulness that any noble standard can be attained. "In the morning make thy plans, in the evening examine thy conduct how thou hast done this day in word, deed, and thought" (i. 19). But if attained, it abolishes selfishness : "The good man envies no man since he loves no private joy" (i. 15). The soul needs must seek the highest : *Tu intende illis, quae tibi praecipit Deus* (i. 20), but must seek in secret : *Nemo secure apparet, nisi qui libenter latet* (i. 20). The spiritual life does not consist in outward manifestation and power. It must grow, like the cared-for seed, in secret. *Melius est latere*

et sui curam agere, quam se neglecto signa facere
(lib. i. 20).

Arnold then turns again to the necessity of a fixed
and definite purpose in life.   It is true that the man
with a purpose may fail, but the man without a
purpose must fail : *Si fortiter proponens saepe deficit,
quid ille, qui raro aut minus fixe aliquid proponit ?*
(i. 19).   Watchfulness, he repeats, is ever necessary ;
we must never slumber.   How can there be peace
or rest till the heart is holy?   " Woe to us if we
yearn for rest, as if peace and safety were with us,
when as yet no sign of true holiness appears in our
lives " (i. 22).   We must watch and pray : *vigilandum
est et orandum, ne tempus otiose transeat* (i. 10).   We
must yearn for the nobler life and cry *utinam per
unum diem bene essemus conversati in hoc mundo* (i. 23).
We must die to ourselves in order that we may live
unto God : *quanto quisque plus sibi moritur, tanto
magis Deo vivere incipit* (ii. 12).   When at last we
have found peace, we can bestow it upon others :
Pone te primus in pace, et tunc poteris alios pacificare
(ii. 3).   But peace is not found in the world, except
by helping others.   Talk will not do it : *vellem me
pluries tacuisse, et inter homines non fuisse.*   To
help others is the way to spread the truce of God :
*Si portari vis, porta et alium . . . sunt, qui seipos in
pace tenent, et cum aliis etiam pacem habent* (ii. 3).
Arnold did not take Milman's view as to the pure
selfishness of Haemmerlein's philosophy.   Altruism
was at least one aspect of it : *si portari vis, porta et*

alium. Arnold quotes this more than once. He might have supplemented it by a passage from the same book : *Diligantur homines propter Jesum* (ii. 8).

Arnold's quotations go on to declare that there is only one way that the peace-seeker can tread—the thorny way of the Cross : " The only way that leads to life and a quiet conscience is the way of Holy Cross where we die daily" (ii. 12). The one thing needful for a man is to cast away all self-love and to leave himself out of all count : *quid illud summe necessarium ? ut homo omnibus relictis se relinquat et a se totaliter exeat, nihilque de privato amore retineat.* The further we tread the thorny way the harder it becomes. To rise grows harder and harder, for the standard of abnegation rises too : *et quanto altius quis in spiritu profecerit, tanto graviores cruces semper inveniet; quia exilii sui poena magis ex amore crescit* (ii. 12). From these transcendental regions of Christian mysticism described in the famous chapter *De Regia Via Sanctae Crucis*—a chapter that brings into focus the whole mysticism of the early Middle Ages—the great critic turns, with an instinctive grasp of the frailties of human nature, to expose the dangers that so often threaten those who attempt to tread the path of mystic religious revivalism, and thereby become, in the sinister eighteenth-century meaning of the phrase, enthusiasts. He sets forth the warning that à Kempis takes from Ecclesiasticus, " Beware of reaction and the desires of the flesh " : *post concupiscentias tuas ne eas et a*

WOODCUT FROM THE PARIS EDITION OF THE TREATISE "DE IMITA-
TIONE CHRISTI." ISSUED IN 1498.

voluntate tua avertere (iii. cap 12). Return to the
aliquid certi, to the definite purpose with which you
set out : *Forte serva propositum et intentionem rectam
ad Deum* (iii. 6). The inward consciousness of
doing right, Arnold seems to feel with Martineau,
is the ultimate test of earthly and spiritual effort :
suaviter requiesces si cor tuum te non reprehenderet
(ii. 6). He adds : " Possess a good conscience and
ever joyful shalt thou be " (ii. 6). Truth dwells
within us, and from Truth we can draw perfect consolation : *Beatum et verum solatium, quod intus a
veritate percipitur* (iii. 16). The internal Will must
come into accord with the external Will : " Thy will
may it be mine and may mine follow Thine always
as in perfect harmony " (iii. 15). This doctrine of
the Inner Will and the Inner Fountain of Truth is
almost exactly that developed along other lines of
spiritual thought by Martineau. It is perhaps
singular that the *Following of Christ* should possess
a successive power of revelation that could meet the
spirituality of Martineau without breaking with the
Roman tradition. It is, however, just this power
that insures the book's immortality. It has a
message of consolation for the noblest of each
successive age.

The result of the union between the internal and
external will is the ennobling of the personal life.
" In the tearing away of all the lowest delights
appears thy blessing " (iii. 12). We shall rise above
the praise and glory of the world in this union of the

T

inward will, drawing its strength for union from the inward Truth, with the Creator : *Non totus mundus eriget, quem veritas sibi subjecit; nec omnium laudantium ore movebitur, qui totam spem suam in Deo firmavit* (iii. 14). The words of the world fall unheeded : "if thy pathway is directed from within thou wilt not greatly heed words that fly past thee from without" (iii. 28). Spiritually armed you can overcome all opposition. "Manfully you must pass through all things and use a strong hand to clear the way" (iii. 35). "To him that conquers is given the heavenly manna, but to the slothful there remain many miseries" (iii. 35). So we come back again to the insistence on work. But the doctrine of the *aliquid certi*, and of tireless toil, is now supplemented by the union between the inward and the outward realities. A sacred Tabernacle where all doubts can be solved has been discovered, therefore *in quâlibet causâ intra cum Moyse in tabernaculum ad consulendum Dominum* (iii. 38). That being certain, we can return to the motive underlying all spiritual philosophy. Arnold therefore again gives us the aphorism : *semper aliquid certi proponendum est.* This certainty will be reached by work, it will be the reward of work : *Age, quod agis; fideliter labora in vinea. meâ; ego ero merces tua* (iii. 47). But, it is again pointed out, outward show and the seeking after praise are hinderers of inward peace : "how sure a plan is it for the preserving of heavenly grace to fly from the phantasm of earthly things, to avoid those outward shows that seem to be a source of wonder" (iii. 45). Instead lay hold on God, being downcast by no burden : *Fili, sta firmiter et spera in me* (iii. 46) ; "break not, my child, under the burdens that thou hast, for my sake, taken upon thee" (iii. 47). Bear all, cheerfully, manfully : eternal life is worthy of all things : *Scribe, lege, canta, geme, tace, ora, sustine viriliter contraria ; digna est his omnibus et majoribus proeliis vita aeterna* (iii. 47). Then death itself is swallowed in victory—even in this life : *leva igitur faciem tuam in coelo !* (iii. 47) —and the soul, triumphant in the dust, cries out : "Thou, Lord, Thou alone amongst all are perfect in faithfulness and beside Thee there is none other such" (iii. 45). With these last words from the *Following of Christ* did Arnold complete his year of quotations and that philosophy of life which he phrased in the rhythmic Latin of à Kempis. Without peering with rude eyes into the inner life that stands partly revealed by these note-books, we may say that his philosophy gave him power to withstand the slings and arrows of untimely death. His eldest son had been taken away and yet he wrote with the Augustinian, *Tu, Domine, tu solus es fidelissimus in omnibus, et praeter te non est alter talis* ; and with Baruch (iv. 23), "for I sent you out with mourning and weeping ; but God will give you to me again with joy and gladness for ever."

The year 1868 was clearly one of stress and storm, of sorrow, disappointment, accomplishment, and increasing purpose. Perhaps its most important, if its least salient, result was the formation, or rather the completion, of a philosophy of life that enabled the poet-critic henceforth to move through the world with a certain unimpairable serenity. As the years go by, we see the old maxims repeated with assured conviction of their truth. " If thou desirest to be carried, carry another "; " According as a man dies to himself, so shall he begin to live unto God"; " He who is ungirt and unpurposeful suffers many temptations"; " True inward peace is found not by obeying but by resisting the passions"; " In the wrenching away of every base delight will appear thy blessing." But there are also new maxims : " Thou wilt rejoice at eventide if fruitfully thou spendest the daylight " (i. 25). " Strive like a man ; let good root out evil" (*certa viriliter ; consuetudo consuetudine vincitur*, i. 21). The note of detachment from the world is perhaps deepened. There is a sad quotation from the chapter *de Meditatione Mortis :* " Sooner than thou thinkest men will forget thee " (i. 23) ; and one hardly less sad from the third book : " In the deep of thy judgments on me all vain glory is vanished" (iii. 14).

When we reach the year 1878 we find a cheerier mood and a mind less in revolt than was the case ten years before. *Ecce labora et noli contristari* he cries and adds, *Gaudebis vespere si diem expendas fructuose* (i. 25). The doctrine of charity and self revelation is largely set forth. " In the same spirit that

thou lookest upon others shall they look upon thee"
(i. 25). In words that recall the famous saying of
St Francis he cries : " Thou art but what thou art ;
words cannot make thee better than thou art by
the witness of God" (ii. 6). " None but the
servants of the Cross find the way of blessedness
and perfect light" (iii. 56). " He indeed is great
who hath great love " (i. 3). These three passages,
one from each of the books, come together. They
certainly are strong evidence of the unity of conception that binds the three books. The passage
from the third is a parallel to the passage from the
second quoted in 1868 : " Non est alia via ad vitam
et ad veram internam pacem, nisi via sanctae crucis
et quotidianae mortificationis " (ii. 12). The passage
from the second book is very closely paralleled by
the quotation from St Francis at the end of
the fifteenth chapter of the third : "for what
every one is in Thy sight, that he is and no more,
saith humble St Francis." The passage from the
first, *verè magnus est, qui magnam habet caritatem,*
is paralleled over and over again in all three.
Matthew Arnold next turns to the Doctrine of the
Way, giving two remarkable quotations from the
third book : " If thou continuest in My Way thou
shalt grasp the Truth, and the Truth shall set thee
free and thou shalt lay hold on the life eternal " (iii.
56). " I am the way, the truth, the life " : *sine viâ non
itur, sine veritate non cognoscitur, sine vitâ non vivitur*
(iii. 56). The essential music of the *Ecclesiastica*

Musica sounds through these phrases and draws the mind to the subtle truths that they convey.

The critic turns from the ideal to the workaday world again with the familiar aphorism twice before repeated : " Never be altogether idle, but either be reading or writing or praying or meditating or performing some act of usefulness for the community " (i. 19). Then again he turns to the doctrine of the Way and repeats the quotation given above (*Non est alia via ad vitam . . .*) from the second book, and this is followed by a repetition of the cry quoted in 1868 : " O, if thou didst but realise how much peace for thyself, how much joy for others thou wouldst gain by the nobler life ! " (i. 11). Then we have four quotations from the last chapter of the first book that have not been given before : " Without anxiousness and carefulness thou shalt not acquire excellence " ; " If thou givest thyself over unto zeal thou shalt find great peace and feel the lightening of thy labour. The eager and careful man is ready for all things." " Keep watch upon thyself, awaken thyself, admonish thyself ; and whatever be the attitude of others, neglect not thine own life " ; " The more thou restrainest thyself, the farther shalt thou go." This is followed by three quotations from the eighth chapter of the second book : " Without a friend thou canst not live well, and if Jesus be not to thee a friend above all friends, sad wilt thou be indeed and desolate " ; " Be humble and peace-making and Jesus will be with thee " ; " Be devout and calm and

Jesus will abide with thee." But these aspirations are hard to attain : "We reprove small things in others, while greater acts in ourselves we pass over" (ii. 5). The old conclusion is arrived at : "In the wrenching away of all base delights will appear thy blessing" (iii. 12). When we reach the year 1883 the quotations have grown sparser, but the old note is still predominant : *Pone te primo in pace et tunc poteris alios pacificare* (ii. 3). "All is vanity save the loving of God and the serving of Him alone" (i. 1) ; "Thou Lord, Thou alone amongst all art perfect in faithfulness, and beside Thee there is none other such" (iii. 45). The old certainty seems to be returning, for the Critic turns again to the old fundamental proposition, *Semper aliquid certi proponendum est*, and adds the sentence, *scias pro certo, quia morientem te oportet ducere vitam* (ii. 12)—the sentence that introduces the oft quoted aphorism, "According as a man dies to himself, so shall he begin to live unto God." And later in the same year we find two quotations from the attack towards the end of the third book on the natural man : "Nature is full of greed, loves what is personal and her own, receives freely rather than gives freely ; Grace is gentle and loves others, lives an unseeking life, judging it better to give than to receive" (iii. 54). "Nature is speedily overcome by want and trouble" (iii. 54).

When we come to the few quotations in the last year of Arnold's life we find the old themes still predominant : *Resiste in principio inclinationi tuae, et*

malam dedisce consuetudinem (i. 11). "Begin perfectly
to conquer thyself and to walk sturdily in the Way of
God. Then thou wilt think less of those things that
before seemed to thee weighty" (ii. 4). "He truly
is wise that discerns things as they really are" (ii.
1). "The spiritually minded man can speedily take
courage, for his whole being is not devoted to outward things" (ii. 1). Arnold's last quotation is from
the same chapter : We must die unto ourselves if we
would not be displeased and troubled : *Ideo multa
tibi displicent et saepe conturbant, quia adhuc non es
perfecte tibi ipsi mortuus.*

The philosophy of life that Thomas à Kempis
taught is maintained to the last. It is in fact
summed up in a paradox—the paradox that has
meant everything to the Christian mystic in all
ages—he that would lay hold on personal immortality must lay aside self. Matthew Arnold
realised and makes us realise that so far from the
philosophy of Thomas Haemmerlein being a selfish
philosophy, it is in fact the cult of selflessness and of
the highest altruism. "Put on the new man : and
be changed into another man." So spake the
mysterious Hermit in the market-place of Cologne
to Gerard Groote ; and so speaks Groote's disciple
to all who care to listen in the thronged market-place
of this "corruptible" world.

APPENDIX I

THE

DE MEDITATIONE CORDIS

OF

JEAN LE CHARLIER DE GERSON

CHANCELLOR OF PARIS

[The present text of this tract is based upon the Leipsic (?) edition printed by Thanner (?), undated, the Milan edition of 1488, an edition of 1492, without named place of origin, and the text contained in the Nuremberg edition of the works of Thomas à Kempis, issued in 1494. The *De Meditatione Cordis* appears to have been first printed at Cologne by Ulrich Zel between 1467 and 1472 (British Museum, I. A. 2802). The text of this *Editio princeps* differs in many small particulars, and in the last chapter differs entirely from the text here printed. The *Editio princeps* includes other works by Gerson (on the Seventh Psalm, etc). The work was printed again at Louvain (?) in 1480 (?) in a volume (British Museum, I. A. 43906) containing other tracts of Gerson, such as the *De Simplificatione Cordis*. It was subsequently issued with numerous editions of the *De Imitatione Christi* between 1485 and 1526, and 1570 and 1575. There appears to be no modern edition. As an internal test of the authorship of the *Imitation* the reader should contrast the style of this work with the passage in Appendix II. from the pen of Thomas à Kempis, and should compare both with the *De Imitatione Christi*.]

INCIPIT TRACTATUS VENERABILIS MAGISTRI JOHANNIS GERSON CANCELLARII PARISIENSIS DE MEDITATIONE CORDIS

CAP. I.

Meditatio cordis mei in conspectu tuo semper. Felix certe qui cum propheta potest ex sententia dicere verbum istud deo. Sed videamus in primis quid sit meditatio cordis, non pro carnali solo sed spirituali corde. Est autem meditatio vehemens cordis applicatio ad aliquod investigandum et inveniendum. Et haec applicatio fortis habet difficultatem quae quandocunque major est quandocunque minor. Quod ut intelligatur presupponatur ex creditis et ab experientia, cor nostrum conditum esse et tres habere species oculorum mentales oculos rationales oculos sensuales. Et ex illis est utrobique unus oculus in cognitionem alius in affectionem. Fundatur haec distinctio in altera quod dicimus hominem habere portionem seu faciem rationis duplicem, quorum superior vertitur ad leges eternas, altera ad temporales, neutra tamen in actu suo dependet ab organo corporeo. Sub istis est ratio demersa corpori quae sensualitas appellatur. Primus oculorum vocatur ab aliis oculus mentis, alter oculus rationis, tertius oculus carnis.

Cap. II.

Fuerat ab initio bene conditae rationalis naturae talis ordo ordinisque tranquillitas, quod ad nutum et merum imperium sensualitas rationi inferiori et inferior ratio superiori serviebat, et erat ab inferioribus ad superna pronus et facilis ascensus, faciente hoc levitate originalis justitiae sublevantis sursum corda quemadmodum naturaliter ignis sua levitate sursus fertur. At vero postquam adversus dominum supremum ingrata proditio demeruit auferri justitiam hanc originalem subintroiit pondus gravissimum concomitans peccatum, quod miseram et captivatam animam trahere non cessat ad infima, tanquam circumligatad sit funibus, catenis et compedibus vincta, in mendicitate et ferro. Sic quidem mirabili immo miserabili confusione facta est ordinis prioris perversio, quod in homine sic merso tenebris et carcere caeco conturbatus est in ira triplex utrimque oculus per imperfectionem in sensualitate per obnubilationem in inferiori rationis perfectione et per quamdam excaecationem in superiori rationis portione.

Cap. III.

Habemus ecce causam primam difficultatis quam in meditatione sentimus, quam in habendis semper ad dominum oculis experimur. Facit hoc penalis illa gravedo deorsum jugiter impellens quemadmodum videre est sensibiliter in aqueductu qui tota facilitate

defluit in(f)ima.[1] Continetur aut vel sursus levatur non nisi cum
violentia, non aliter cor ad infima pronum leviter effluit hac illacque
veluti sine retinaculo vel labore quum "facilis descensus Averni,"
ait poeta, "sed revocare gradus superasque evadere ad auras, hoc
opus, hoc labor est."

CAP. IV.

Perscrutemur consequenter ex praedictis naturam seu proprie-
tatem meditationis, quoniam ex hoc ipso quam necessaria nobis
ad deum tendentibus existat videbimus.   Diximus autem et
repetimus quod meditatio est fortis et vehemens applicatio vel
attentio animi ad aliquod investigandum vel inveniendum fructuose.
Addimus fructuose ne meditatio vergat aut in·suspicionem aut in
curiositatem aut in melancolicam stoliditatem.   Dicamus ergo
complectentes quod meditacio est vehemens et salubris animi
applicacio ad aliquid investigandum vel experimentaliter cogno-
scendum.   Ponimus hoc ultimum propter naturam ipsius affectionis quae diversa sortitur nomina proportionaliter ad condicionem
cognitionis.   Non enim potest aliter affectio cognosci quam experimentaliter ab eo qui per eam afficitur.   Quam experimentalem
affectionis cognicionem non potest eam habens in alterum verbis
quibuslibet infundere nisi similiter affectus sit alter ille.   Quoniam
solus novit (sicut in Apocalypsi scribitur) qui accipit.   Propterea
vocatur manna absconditum.   Exemplum est perspicuum in illo
qui novit dulcedinem mellis solum per doctrinam.   Sic medicus
sanus noscit infirmitatis dolorem.   Haec autem dulcedo a gustante,
hic dolor ab aegrotante aliter longe cognoscuntur.

CAP. V.

Perpendamus ex his quam profunde senserit propheta naturam
meditacionis dum ait "in meditatione mea exardescet ignis,"
utrumque enim complexus est, et lumen in intellectu et ardorem
in affectu.   Quam vero sit difficile quod ignis devotionis spiritu-
alis exardescat flatu meditacionis fiet notum considerantibus
ignem materialem cum quaeritur a lignis aquosis viridibus luto
respersis elici.   Suffla quantum potes, iterum atque iterum multo
conatu resuffla, emerget plurimus ab initio fumus conturbans
oculos, vix emicabit scintilla quae mox evanescet.   Disperges

---

[1] In the *Editio princeps* this reads "in yma."   The correct MS. reading
was probably "in infima."

forsitan iratus congesta prius ligna, si non in longanimitate praestiteris : Quam longanimitatem appellamus hic meditationem aut meditationi conjungendam.

CAP. VI.

Meminimus aliquas nos scripsisse doctrinas vel industrias nedum latino sed Gallico sermone super habenda meditacione tali. Licet fortassis uteremur aliis terminis in tractatulo de mistica theologia, parte ea quae praxim ejus docet, et in altero de monte contemplacionis edito, in altero rursum de mendicitate spirituali compilato. Denique tanta reperitur difficultas, tanta per diversitatem hominum varietas, in practicando doctrinam verae sanctaeque meditacionis, quod an silere vel aliquid scribere consultius sit videor egomet mihi ipsi quandoque sub dubio fluctuans.

CAP. VII.

Dum enim recogito quod absque meditacionis exercitio nullus, secluso dei miraculo speciali, ad perfectionem contemplacionis dirigitur aut pervenit, nullus ad rectissimam Christianae religionis normam vir se componit, audeo zelans ardeoque studium sanctae meditacionis suadere. At vero, dum totiens expertus pericula sedulus recogito difficultatem et arduam raritatem perveniendi quo trahere meditatio nititur, ego quasi torpens et stupidus efficior. Quaesierit aliquis quo pacto sic venit quod nimium frequenter expertum est studium meditationis converti dilabique in morbum melancolicae passionis propter immoderacionem, vel propter superbiam dari in reprobum sensum diabolycae illusionis.

CAP. VIII.

Manducamus exemplis id quod dicimus : scimus vinum in jocunditatem et hominis salutem conditum esse. Sic enim scriptura, sic ratio loquitur. Videmus tamen ex abusu potantium, praesertim dum febrium discrasia laborant, quod potus vini, alioquin salubris, causat vel aegritudinis augmentum vel maniam et furorem aut quandoque mortem. Nos autem filios omnes Adam quis aegrotos quis febricitantes esse pessimis animae febribus negaverit ? Quibus utuntur in nauseam et amaritudinem optima divinorum eloquiorum verba, quibus in fel convertitur suavissimus divini verbi panis. Heu miseros heu quam ex intima

consideracione talis miseriae conclamavit apostolus "Infelix,
ego, quis me liberabit de corpore mortis hujus?" Subjungit,
"Grâtia Dei per Jesum Christum."

CAP. IX.

Quid agimus ergo? Quid abimus precipites per abrupta
viciorum? Ibimusne post desideria cordis nostri et in adinven-
tionibus nostris pessimis, desperati, sine lege, sine freno, sine
ordine? Num quidem sufficient nobis cogitationes instabiles,
sordidae, fluxae, somniorumque simillimae, quae non consolationes vel edificationes allaturae sunt, sed desolacionem, mesticiam,
et ruinam, oblectantibus se in eisdem? Respondebimus ne-
quaquam id fieri debere, sed adsit discretio moderatrix in omnibus, quam non securius habere post divinam gratiam poterimus,
quam per sedulum et securum alterius experti, nosque diligentis
et agnoscentis, consilium.

CAP. X.

Clamat Aristoteles, vocem experientiae loquens, quod ars et
vita sunt circa difficilia, ut ars pingendi, ars scribendi, ars
cytharizandi; virtus caritatis, virtus fortitudinis, virtus sobrietatis;
hoc verum sic intelligendum est, quod ab initio virtus et ars
multas in acquisitione sua patiuntur difficultates, dum vero fuerint
conquisitae facilia sunt eis. Omnia pingit faciliter pictor exerci-
tatus in arte; sic de scriptore, sic de cytharizante, videmus, ita ut
dixerit idem Aristoteles quod ars perfecta non deliberat, tam
sibi facilis est actus suus.[1]

CAP. XI.

Utamur ista comparatione dum de meditatione loquimur;
attendamus quod in trahendo passim lineas picturae vel scripturae difficultas nulla est, sicut nec in discussione digitorum
per cytharae chordas. Invenimus similiter in cogitatione; non
enim difficulter aut laboriose nunc hoc nunc illud prout occur-
rerit cogitatur. Sed quod nullus inde resultet effectus vides in
sic pingente sic scribente et sic cytharizante, ita neque prorsus in

---

[1] In the *Editio princeps* (Cologne, 1467-72) the "Nona Consideratio"
comprises chapters ix. and x. as given in the above text. The edition is
divided into seventeen "Considerationes," each of which has its own title.

sic cogitante : immo cum se talibus cogitationibus vagis oblectaverit, ut dicit Seneca, tristis remanebit. Porro laboriose, studiose, et attentissime, cum mira tarditate pingendo, scribendo, et cytharizando, fit quandoque ut bene et celeriter ista fiant.

Cap. XII.

Quorsum ista? Nimirum ut ostendamus queumadmodum de cogitatione nullus unquam proficiet aut emerget in meditationem ; quanto minus in contemplationem. Ex meditatione vero quae summam habet difficultatem, si bona fide, simplici, et discreta, diligenter exerceater, perveniemus ad hanc perfectionem, quod absque ulla difficultate fiet apud nos fructuose quod summo meditationis studio conquirere voluimus. Ita denique transibit meditatio in contemplationem ; non enim differt meditatio a contemplatione nisi penes facile et difficile, quum utrobique est fructus aliter quam in cogitatione.

Cap. XIII.

Describitur autem contemplatio quod est liber et expeditus mentis intuitus in res perspiciendas usquequaque, et hoc quoad contemplationem quae respicit intellectum ; porro quoad contemplationem quae constitit in affectu et in praxi, describit eam Hugo quod est per sublevantem mentis jubilum mors quaedam carnalium desideriorum. Hoc est gustare quam suavis est Dominus ; quem gustum sequitur alia longe cognitio : quoniam fuerit intellectualis solum visio vel quaedam auditio per fidem aut per scripturam.

Cap. XIV.

Meditabitur ecce aliquis, gemens et suspirans ut columba, dicet cum propheta, " meditatus sum nocte cum corde meo, exercitabar et scopebam spiritum meum." Facit hoc anxie difficulter et laboriose recogitando, nunc omnes annos suos in amaritudine animae suae, nunc judicia Dei quae sunt abyssus multa in coelo sursum et in abyssis deorsum, et ita de reliquiis circa quae versatur meditantis attentio vehemens, ut ea quae meditatur vel cogitat limpidius vel firmius in affectum suum trahat, efficiet tandem ut haec omnia tanta felicitate recogitet et sapiat. Quam

facilis est ipsa cogitatio docent nos exempla praedicta si dubi-
tamus, non enim plus laboris habent scriptor, pictor, cytharista,
bene agendo quod optime didicerint, quam vagus et vanus aliquis
ab initio discurrens sine arte et ordine per lineas picturae vel
scripturae aut per cytharae chordas.

Cap. XV.

Addendum est ad praemissa nihilominus quod vir est aliquis
ita perfectus in arte sua quin assidue possit ad aliqua vel
cognoscenda vel agenda proficere qualia necesse est ut non
habeat cum labore. Multo magis hoc verum est in ipsa de qua
loquimur meditatione quae novos veritatis aut devotionis fetus
jugiter parere student. Sed non deest parturitionis dolor
propter illud maledictum, spiritualiter intellectum, "in dolore
paries filios tuos": non meminit tamen passurae propter
gaudium quod natus est sibi novus cognitionis et affectionis
sanctae fetus in animi sui mundum.

Cap. XVI.

Venit autem ab initio frequentius ut dum aliquis nondum
purgatus a viciis satagit meditari ut columba, meditatur quasi
vetus simia dolos [et] odia, meditatur sicut canis rabiosa
"silentia rodens," juxta verbum satirici, meditatur quasi sordida
sus, dum foedissimas in animo versat reversatque cogitationes.
Quid porro de blasphemii spiritu, quam abominabilis, quam
horridus non nunquam resurgit, territans meditantem, loquens
adversus Deum sanctos sanctasque ingentia quae nec fari licet?
Jaciuntur infidelitatis jaculae, baratrum desperationis aperietur.
Experimentum quoque manifestat quam recte jusserit sapiens
"fili, accedens ad servitutem Dei, praepara animam tuam ad
tentationem"—Sequitur praesidium certissimum "sta in timore:
beatus enim vir qui semper est pavidus."

Cap. XVII.

Pavidus vero semper quo modo beatus quaeret aliquis dum timor
additur timori scrupulus scrupulis pusillanimitas pusillanimitati,
praesertim cum non adest assidue conciliator dux et permon-
strator itineris arti et recti: si vero talis qui rarus est inventus

forte fuerit cum otio novum meditantem instruendi quantum libuerit, felix quidem erit ipse novus tiro. Si tamen protinus absque ulla trepidatione paratus est credere concilio, sed O quoties bone Jesu, quoties hesitabit et idem repetet iterum iterumque, quasi falli reformidans, quaeret idem, denique non utetur erga dantem sibi concilium doctrina Jacobi, quae est ut postulet in fide nihil haesitans. Scripsi quaedam super hujusmodi scrupulis tractatulo de praeparatione ad missam; aliquid similiter de cautelis contra spiritum blasphemiae durissimum: adversus quae remedium optimum est contemnere nec curare quin potius irridere. Neque super his solicite confiteri, nisi forsitan in principio pro cautela ad habendum concilium. De scrupulis vero teneatur haec regula, quod adversus eos agendum est, si ita prudens aliquis et expertus conciliator dictaverit, mandaverit, aut jusserit, nec aget in hoc contra consciam suam demeritorie, dum illam ad concilium sapientiorum per rationis libertatem ab animo suo mutat et disponit, quamvis assidue sensualitatis remurmuratio forte sentiatur; alioquin nunquam fiet in pace Deo locus cordis. Rursus advertendum quod, sic dicente Aristotele, omnis nostra cognitio venit a sensu, iterum necesse est omnem intelligentem phantasmata speculari. Sic originatur meditatio nostri cordis a sensibilibus quae figurata sunt et colorata et caeteris accidentibus temporis et loci circumvoluta. Hinc sunt meditationes conscriptae hinc imagines pictae vel sculptae hinc generaliter fit istud psalmistae, "meditatus sum in omnibus operibus tuis et in factis manuum tuarum meditabar," quae utique facta vel opera sunt corporalia. Nihilominus debet assurgere meditans et ultra progredi, veluti per scalam aliquam, ex visibilibus ad invisibilia: sicut dicit Apostolus, "quoniam invisibilia Dei, ex his quae facta sunt intellecta, conspiciuntur, sempiterna quoque virtus ejus et divinitas." Propterea, docens nos a corporalibus ad spiritualia migrare, dicebat, "et si Christum secundum carnem cognovimus, nunc tamen secundum carnem non cognoscimus."

Cap. XVIII.

Advertendum vero quod meditaturis duplices inter caeteras tenduntur insidiae, una dum petunt concilium super occurrentibus scrupulis in meditatione sua, praesertim mulier a viro; altera

dum sunt in actu meditationis. Fit in primo casu crebrius et levius
quam a multis credi potest aglutinatio quaedam animorum velata
pallio sanctae devotaeque dilectionis. Quae primo confabula-
tionibus sub tipo quaerendi concilii quaeritur ; de hinc anima
veluti confricata calescit et sensim igne caeco carnalis amoris
carpitur et uritur, nec intelligitur primo donec tandem ad risus
leves ad facetos blandosque gestus perventum est— Avertat Deus
a servis suis quod reliquum silemus. "Timeo" inquit apostolus
"ne dum spiritum coeperitis carne consumamini." Scripsi jam
pluries talia consequenter ad Augustinum, nominatim in tractatulo de probatione spirituum. Incurrunt aliud periculum meditationes dum in solis phantasiis, dum solis imaginibus corporeis
se tradunt, et toto corde vehementer incumbunt; fit perinde
quod meditans dum transire satagit in contemplationem collabatur
ad melancolicam seu phantasticam lesionem, ita tandem ut imagines
iterum versatas in imaginativa virtute pro rebus ipsis exterioribus
accipiat ; et sic evenit in somniantibus dum dormiunt. Non
aliter istis in vigilia contingit, quorum verba et opera nulla inter
se conectione nullum ordinem servant ubi neque est principium
neque finis ubi, sicut vulgo dicitur, neque est caput neque cauda,
sed de gallo fit saltus ad cygnum, ita ut vigilantes somniare
videantur, de quolibet dicunt vulgares, "ilz resuent on font en
resuerie." Porro timent non timenda sperant non speranda, nunc
gaudio dissolvuntur nunc subito maerore tabescunt ; quales
egent amplius fomento Socratis quam monitione sapientis.
    Explicit Johannis Gerson Cancellarii Parisiensis de Meditatione
Cordis.[1]

APPENDIX II

Liber Ortuli Rosarum Thomae Kempis Capitulum XVI. de amore
Christi et odio mundi.

Manete in dilectione mea. Vox Christi vox dulcis ad audiendum,
salubris omnibus ad obediendum. Amor Christi jocunditas mentis,
paradisus animae; excludit mundum, vincit diabolum, claudit infernum, aperit coelum. Amor Christi et mundi contrarii sunt et nihil

---

[1] The 17th *Consideratio* of the *Editio princeps* is entirely different.

U

commune habent, nec simul commorari possunt. Amor Christi currus helye [helii?] ascendens in coelum; amor mundi quadriga dyaboli trahens ad infernum. Amor sui lesio sui: oblivio mundi inventio celi. Plus nocet blanda locutio ficti amici: quam dura correptio hominis justi. Cogitatio dolosi fingit mendatia; mens justi recte procedit in causis. Non evadet scandalum, qui alteri infert scandalum. Rector et cognitor omnium Deus non diu patitur oviculam suam errare et balare, sed aut baculo timoris feriens revocat, aut amoris oculo intuens ad consciam reducit. Ubi pax et concordia: ibi Deus et omnia bona. Ubi lis et dissensio: ibi diabolus et omnia mala. Ubi humilitas: ibi sapientia. Ubi superbia: ibi radix maliciae. Vince superbiam: et invenies pacem magnam. Ubi dura verba: ibi laeduntur charitatis viscera. Ubi solitudo et silentium: ibi quies monachorum. Ubi labor et disciplina: ibi perfectus religiosorum. Ubi risus et dissolutio: ibi fugit devotio. Ociosus et verbosus raro compunctus, raro a delicto purus. Ubi prompta obedientia: ibi laeta conscientia. Ubi fabulatio longa: ibi operis negligentia. Ubi propria exquisitio: ibi caritatis defectus. Ubi doctrina Christi viget: ibi salus animae crescit. Ubi fratrum concordia: ibi dulcis melodia. Ubi mediocritas servatur: ibi virtus concordiae diutius perseverat. Ubi discretio in corripiendo culpas aliorum custoditur: ibi nemo juste conqueri debet nec facile praelato indignari. Inquit quidam "omnibus adde modum: modus est pulcherrima virtus." Ubi patientia: ibi magna hostis victoria. Ubi turbatio intrat: ibi pax cito de domo recedit. Claude oris ostium et pondera verba tua antequam loquaris. Ubi fides et veritas ibi pacis securitas. Ubi dolus et nequitia: ibi stulta cogitatio et caeca prudentia. Ubi caritas: ibi spiritus sanctus. Ubi levis suspitio: ibi frequens indignatio. Ubi veritatis cognitio: ibi recta cordis laetitia. Ubi ficta narratio: ibi saepe amici deceptio latet. Ubi humilis confessio: ibi facilis veniae impetratio. Ubi terrena sapientia deficit: ibi divina protectio amplius est invocanda. Quicunque malitiose injusta praetendit, ipse malum finem consequetur. Pax multa bene agenti et ad patientiam se preparanti. Vae impio in malo et ficto in bono, quoniam nemini plus nocet iniquitas sua quam ipsa sibi. Ubi duplicitas: ibi inconstantia et multa nequitia. Bene simplici et justo sine dolo, quoniam Deus cum eo dirigens omnia opera ejus itinere recto. Qui verbum suum male servat quis facile ei

credet? qui autem verbum suum in melius mutat, verbum veritatis
non infringit.   Delectabile est bona audire, sed laudabile magis
opere exercere.   Optima collatio vitae emendatio ; fructus bonae
collationis abstinere a peccatis et proficere in virtutibus.   Fructus
devotae orationis unire cor suum cum Deo in fervore sancti spiritus.
Ille devote orat qui omnia vana a se excludit.   Qui imaginem
crucifixi sibi praeponit, Diabolica phantasmata cito repellit. Pulchra
animae imaginatio passionis Christi jugis recordatio. Qui sacra Jesu
vulnera quotidie pensat mentis suae vulnera mitigat purgat et
curat.   Qui omnia terrena tanquam lutum vilipendit nec honores
desiderat, cordis mundiciam acquirit et ideo libere vacare potest.
Ille Deum summe laudat et honorat qui se ipsum profunde
humiliat et defectus suos caute considerat gemit et plorat.
Magnus clamor in auribus Dei [1] vera contritio cordis ex ore
humilis pectoris.   Quidquid boni facis ad laudem Dei facias.
Qui virtutes suas et aliorum quaelibet opera bona simpliciter et
integre pure et libere ad laudem et honorem Dei refert, totum
Deo ascribendo, nil meritis suis nec viribus attribuendo, sed ab
omnibus se spoliat et denudat, superbiam invidiam et vanam
gloriam funditus calcat et necat.   Eterna namque gloria et honore
se privat qui in se et non in Deo solo summo bono gaudet.
Ideoque beata virgo Maria pro maximis donis sibi collatis in suo
devotissimo cantico jubilans dicit "exultavit spiritus meus in Deo
salutari meo."   "Qui se aliquid esse putat cum nihil sit se ipsum
seducit" ait apostolus Paulus, qui in tertium caelum raptus [2] non
est ex hoc elatus, sed quidquid boni fecit, docuit, et dictavit, hoc
totum fideliter Deo attribuit, dicens "Gratia Dei sum id quod
sum." [3]

[1] Compare *de Imitatione Christi*, lib. iii. cap. 5: "*Magnus clamor in
auribus Dei* est ipse ardens affectus animae quae dicit: Deus meus! amor
meus! Tu totus meus, et ego tuus!" This identity of phrase (hitherto unnoticed) is remarkable (see p. 214 above).

[2] Compare *de Imitatione Christi*, lib. ii. cap. 12: "Etiamsi raptus fueris
in tertium coelum cum Paulo."

[3] Nuremberg Edition, 1494, of the works of Thomas à Kempis, fol. 157*b*.

INDEX